The Nuclear Revolution
International Politics before and after Hiroshima

The Nuclear Revolution: International Politics before and after Hiroshima

MICHAEL MANDELBAUM

Harvard University

CAMBRIDGE UNIVERSITY PRESS

CAMBRIDGE

LONDON   NEW YORK   NEW ROCHELLE

MELBOURNE   SYDNEY

Published by the Press Syndicate of the University of Cambridge
The Pitt Building, Trumpington Street, Cambridge CB2 1RP
32 East 57th Street, New York, NY 10022, USA
296 Beaconsfield Parade, Middle Park, Melbourne 3206, Australia

© Cambridge University Press 1981

First published 1981

Printed in the United States of America
Typeset by David E. Seham, Inc., Metuchen, New Jersey
Printed and bound by Halliday Lithograph Corp., West Hanover, Massachusetts

Library of Congress Cataloging in Publication Data
Mandelbaum, Michael.
The nuclear revolution.
Includes bibliographical references and index.
1. World politics—1945— 2. Atomic
weapons. 3. Military policy. I. Title.
D843.M244   327'.09045   80-24194
ISBN 0 521 23819 6 hard covers
ISBN 0 521 28239 X paperback

Written under the auspices of the Center for Science and
International Affairs, Harvard University.

To my parents, Ruth and David Mandelbaum

Contents

vii

Preface

This book addresses a single question: How have nuclear weapons affected international politics? It consists of an introduction, which sets out the framework for considering the question, and seven essays, each of which investigates the impact of these weapons of mass destruction on a particular aspect of relations among sovereign states. Because they revolve around the same question the essays have a common theme. They do not, however, form a single argument; the question does not have a single answer. Each of the essays can stand independently of the others, although all draw upon the general considerations outlined in the introductory chapter.

Each essay begins with a reference to Thucydides's account of the Peloponnesian War, to emphasize the fact that whatever else has changed since 1945 one thing remains the same: There is still a system of independent yet interdependent states of the sort that has existed since antiquity, a point that is elaborated in Chapter 1.

The book's approach is historical and comparative. I seek to answer its central question by discovering differences and similarities between the nuclear age and previous periods of international history. The last three and a half decades are not matched against the same period of prenuclear history in each chapter. Two of them, in fact, Chapters 2 and 5, do not involve comparisons across time at all, but between nuclear weapons and other kinds of armaments in the first case, and between nuclear weapons and a different form of international competition in the second. Nor are all other factors held constant so that such differences as appear, between alliances before and after 1945, for example, can be laid with certainty to the presence and absence of nuclear weapons. These essays are exercises in historical interpretation, not scientific proof. The last chapter, in particular, is intended to be suggestive rather than conclusive.

The Nuclear Revolution is the third of a three-part study of nuclear weapons. The first part, *The Nuclear Question: The United States and Nuclear Weapons, 1946–1976* (Cambridge University Press, 1979), is a history of American nuclear weapons policy, with the emphasis on the years 1961–3, when the main lines of American policy were established. It tells, from the American perspective, how the world's nuclear arrangements came about. The second part, an extended essay entitled "International Stability and Nuclear Order: The First Nuclear Regime," which appears in David C. Gompert, editor, *Nuclear Weapons and World Politics* (McGraw-Hill, 1977), describes these arrangements in some detail. The present volume is about the differences that these arrangements have made – that is, about how these arrangements have and have not altered relations among sovereign states.

The Nuclear Revolution does not explicitly address issues that confront the American or other governments. Nonetheless, it does have some relevance for matters of public policy. Chapter 3, for example, explores the circumstances in which nuclear war might begin. Chapters 4 and 5 are pertinent to the prospects for restraining the competition in accumulating nuclear armaments between the United States and the Soviet Union. Chapter 5 also bears on the debate over the value of a strategic nuclear "counterforce" capacity, and Chapter 6 touches on the question of what kinds of nuclear armaments are needed to protect Western Europe from the Soviet Union.

While writing this book, I have been a research fellow of the Center for Science and International Affairs at Harvard University. I am grateful to the Center, and to its Director, Paul Doty, for supporting the enterprise. I spent part of a year sponsored by a fellowship from the Institute for the Study of World Politics completing the book.

All but the first and last chapters were originally presented to the Center for Science and International Affairs Working

Group on Domestic Politics and Security Policy. I owe thanks, for their comments and suggestions, to those who have participated in this group over several years: Stephen Flanagan, Thomas Garwin, Thane Gustafson, Derek Leebaert, Thomas McNaugher, Steven Miller, Jonathan Pollack, Jane M. O. Sharp, Anthony Smith, John Steinbruner, and Paul Walker. I am indebted as well to others who read, and commented on, parts of the book: Daniel M. Begel, M. D. Feld, Tony Judt, Charles Lipson, Peter Malone, Joseph S. Nye, Jr., Judith N. Shklar, and Barry H. Steiner.

The idea for the book was suggested by an essay on future research in international politics by Stanley Hoffmann,* and I have profited as well from many conversations with him on these subjects.

Nicholas X. Rizopoulos, Vice President and Executive Director of the Lehrman Institute of New York City, brought his formidable combination of historical sophistication and editorial acumen to bear on these chapters.

I received able research assistance from Raymond McGuire, Steven Gold, Eugene Mathews, and Krister Sairsingh, and was fortunate to have Mary Ann Spano-Wells and Barbara Talhouni type the manuscript.

My greatest debt is to my wife, Anne Hebald Mandelbaum, who edited the entire manuscript.

January, 1981   Michael Mandelbaum

---

* Stanley Hoffmann, editor, *Contemporary Theory in International Relations* (Englewood Cliffs, N.J.: Prentice-Hall, 1960), pp. 174–84.

1

The Nuclear Revolution

Two revolutions

How have nuclear weapons affected international politics? At the dawn of the nuclear age, after the first atomic bomb had shattered the Japanese city of Hiroshima and the second had crushed Nagasaki, the general lines of the answer seemed plain. All had changed, changed utterly. August 1945 seemed one of those rare moments when a new world could be seen being born, when a great transformation seemed to occur palpably and almost instantaneously. The word "revolution" was popular in describing what had happened. The day after the attack on Hiroshima a *New York Times* editorial warned that "civilization and humanity can now survive only if there is a revolution in mankind's political thinking."[1] Two months later President Truman proclaimed that "in international relations as in domestic affairs the release of atomic energy constitutes a new force too revolutionary to consider in the framework of old ideas."[2]

Those who pondered the consequences of human control of atomic energy generally expected two revolutions. The first was technical, the result of the enormous destructive power of controlled atomic energy. The second was political. The familiar international institutions and practices, the old ways of doing business among nations, seemed suddenly and completely obsolete. This expectation recalled the principal theme of the most influential of the nineteenth-century writers on revolution, Karl Marx, who envisioned that technological change would produce political upheaval. "At a certain stage of their development," he had written, "the material forces of production in society come into conflict with the existing rela-

1

tions of production, or – what is but a legal expression for the same thing – with the property relations within which they had been at work before. From forms of development of the forces of production these relations turn into their fetters. Then comes the period of social revolution.''[3] The material forces of production were technical, the existing relations of production political. The industrial revolution, Marx believed, would transform politics *within* states. At the dawn of the nuclear age it was similarly believed that nuclear weapons would transform politics *among* states.

In the immediate aftermath of Hiroshima the expected political revolution lay in the future, the unfinished business of the nations of the world. Even with Hiroshima and Nagasaki, however, the technical revolution had not yet fully occurred. Neither bomb did as much damage as had the air raids that the United States had conducted, with nonnuclear explosives, against Tokyo, Yokohama, and Dresden. In the earlier attacks, hundreds of airplanes had dropped thousands of bombs. Hiroshima and Nagasaki were each destroyed by a single bomb. But those were the only two nuclear weapons in existence in August 1945.

Thirty-five years later both the United States and the Soviet Union had thousands of atomic weapons. The first bombs were like the pyramids of Egypt and the Great Wall of China: visible, dramatic, singular public works projects, the fruit of an enormous, centrally directed concentration of resources. Three years and $2 billion had been required to make them. Now the explosives, if not the vehicles for delivering them, are more like automobiles: mass-produced, with periodic minor improvements.

Even as the first two bombs were vastly more powerful than all previous man-made explosives, so the present models are far more devastating than those that destroyed Hiroshima and Nagasaki. The first two drew their power from the process of splitting atoms apart, which is known as nuclear fission; they were equal in explosive force to about fifteen to twenty thousand tons of the explosive TNT. Their successors are based on the fusing of atoms together. The explosive force of fusion, or hydrogen bombs is measured in the millions of tons of TNT equivalent. These bombs are thus a thousand times more powerful than fission, or atomic, explosives. For all practical purposes the yields of fusion explosives are limitless.[4] "There is an immense gulf between the atomic and hydrogen bomb," Churchill once observed. "The atomic bomb, with all its terror, did not carry us outside the scope of human control or manageable events in thought or action, in peace or war. But ... [with] the hydrogen bomb, the entire foundation of human affairs was revolutionized."[5]

In thirty-five years not only did there come to be many more bombs that were many times more powerful than the first two, but the means of sending them to their targets grew swifter and surer. After the first successful detonation of a fusion bomb in 1953, the principal developments in nuclear technology involved not the explosives themselves but their delivery systems. Airplanes carried the Hiroshima and Nagasaki bombs, and they had certain shortcomings as attack vehicles. They had to reach their targets by maneuvering uncertainly against interceptor aircraft and through curtains of antiaircraft fire.[6] Thirty-five years later fusion warheads mounted on rockets and traveling outside the earth's atmosphere could cross continents in a matter of minutes. The warheads that these missiles carried represented an enormous advance in destructive power over the explosives of World War II bombers; comparable progress in defending against attacks did not, however, take place. There was virtually no chance of deflecting or repulsing all nuclear explosives, and thus avoiding untold destruction, in a large-scale nuclear attack, a point that the United States and the Soviet Union conceded formally in 1972 with the signing of a treaty that made effectively illegal the deployment of systems of defense against ballistic missiles. The most plausible defense against a nuclear attack – as with artillery assaults between 1914 and 1918 – was to burrow underground, but the extraordinary explosive power of nuclear artillery made survival a far more dubious prospect in a putative third world war than it had been in the first one.

Did this expansion of force amount to a technical revolution? There can be no doubt that the difference between the military force available before and after 1945 is immense. That difference altered the character of military operations: "To compress a catastrophic war within the span of time that a man can stay awake drastically changes the politics of war, the process of decision, the possibility of central control and restraint, the motivations of the people in charge, and the capacity to think and reflect while war is in progress."[7]

Nuclear weapons are revolutionary because familiar moral categories, ideas of right and wrong in warfare, do not fit all-out nuclear war.[8] They are revolutionary because cultural mechanisms for coping with death do not work for the scale of death and destruction that nuclear weapons make possible.[9] They are revolutionary because whereas all battles of the past have been conflicts of will between soldiers, a large-scale exchange of nuclear force would be a contest in the endurance of annihilation by civilian populations. Indeed, in the sense that the term "war" connotes some proportion between damage done and political goals sought, an all-out nuclear conflict would not be a war at all.[10]

Two wars

How has the extraordinary revolutionary expansion of destructive force that nuclear weapons represent affect relations among nation–states? In important ways international relations have *not* changed. Consider the following account. Two states join forces to defeat a menacing barbarian power. After their victory the two find themselves considerably more powerful than any of their neighbors. Former allies of the two victors who had counted themselves their equals must now defer to them. The wartime partnership dissolves, and the two giants become rivals. Each blames the other for their falling-out. Each feels aggrieved. Each feels threatened. The leaders on each side conduct a war of words, a propaganda campaign to persuade their own people and citizens of third countries that the other is to blame for the quarrel.

Domestic dissimilarities contribute to the friction between

them. One city–state is democratic, the other autocratic. The people of one live throughout the known world. The citizens of the other stay largely within their own borders.

The two city–states have different strategic strengths, as well. The democracy is a formidable sea power. The authoritarian state enjoys a reputation for prowess on land. Each surrounds itself with allies. Here, too, their styles differ. The autocracy prefers to install similar regimes in the states allied to it. The democracy insists simply that its allies share their resources. As the two principal powers jockey for advantage they try to avoid being dragged into open conflict with each other by their allies. Several times, however, they come to the brink of war.

This is, of course, a description of the rivalry between the United States and the Soviet Union since 1945. It is also a description, and an equally accurate one, of the conflict between the two leading city–states of Greece in the fifth century B.C. – Democratic Athens and autocratic Sparta – which combined to repel the Persian invasion and almost immediately thereafter found themselves at odds with each other.[11]

The correspondences between the two pairs of domestic regimes are coincidental,[12] but the common patterns of rivalry are not. They are due to something that fifth-century B.C. Greece and the world of the second half of the twentieth century have in common: a system of sovereign, independent political units in regular contact with each other, that is, an "anarchical" system. In neither has a supreme authority existed to enforce rules of behavior. In both, the individual sovereign states have had to rely upon themselves for protection.

Politics in the anarchical international system differs from politics in the domestic arena, where there is hierarchy, not anarchy, because a supreme authority, the state, does hold sway. National politics, in Kenneth Waltz's phrase, "is the realm of authority, of administration, and of law. International politics is the realm of power, of struggle, and of accommodation."[13] This has been true wherever political communities have become interlinked in anarchical fashion. It was true in Thucydides's day, as it was in Renaissance Italy. It has been true in Europe since at least the seventeenth century, and it is true of the entire world today.

Anarchy invariably produces insecurity, because there is no international equivalent of the state to guarantee safety. All members of anarchical systems have had to cope with insecurity. They have faced a common set of problems. For example, anarchy presents states with a particular kind of choice, which arises from the fact that a state's security depends on both its own actions and its neighbors' intentions, and these are related in unpredictable ways.

This is a theme in Thucydides's account. Corcyra, a neutral state, asks to join the Athenian alliance system. By agreeing, Athens may arouse the displeasure of Sparta, the ally of Corcyra's enemy, Corinth. Athens must decide whether to accept or reject Corcyra. There are risks to both courses. It is plain that relations between the two principal city–states will worsen if the Athenians accept. The likelihood of war will increase. In putting their case before the Athenians, the Corcyreans counter that war with Sparta is inevitable whatever the response to their request. By welcoming them, Athens will be strengthening itself for the coming war; by turning them away, it will simply forego a valuable ally.[14]

Accepting Corcyra may make Athens strong enough to intimidate the Spartans and prevent war or put the Athenians in a favorable military position when the war begins. On the other hand, the same policy may provoke Spartan animosity, which would not have arisen had the Athenian–Corcyrean alliance not occurred. In that case the Athenians would be worse off than without the Corcyreans. An aggressive policy, therefore, can lead to deterrence or provocation; there is no way to be certain in advance which will be the consequence.

Alternatively, the Athenians can deny the Corcyrean request, which will please Sparta. This, too, can have one of two radically different consequences. The Spartans may be mollified, relations with them improved, the chances of war diminished. Or Sparta simply may be encouraged to attack Athens, which has voluntarily denied itself a military asset. The outcome depends on Spartan decisions, and these, too, cannot be foretold (perhaps by Sparta as well as Athens) in advance of the need to make them.

The problem of whether to be aggressive or conciliatory has been no less acute for states in the twentieth century than it was for Athens twenty-five centuries before. Wilhelmine Germany feared being left behind in the struggle of European states for power and place, and so embarked on an aggressive foreign policy at the outset of the century. The effect was not deterrence, however, but provocation. Britain, France, and Russia joined together, despite differences of interest and outlook among them, in an anti-German coalition that might not have been formed but for Germany's clumsy bellicosity. In the 1930s Britain tried to conciliate Hitler's Germany by permitting German expansion in central Europe. Far from winning Hitler to the cause of peace and international responsibility, of course, this policy merely whetted his appetite for further expansion. Ultimately Britain had to fight him, and from a weaker position than if the policy of appeasement had not been carried out.[15] After 1967 the overriding issue in Israel's foreign policy posed the same kind of choice that the security dilemma had obliged the Athenians to make: Would returning territories captured from the Arabs eliminate Arab grievances against the Jewish state and thus, at last, bring peace? Or would it simply allow them to launch their next war closer to the Israeli heartland than if Israel had kept control of the territories?

The foundations of international relations have not changed. The Athenians and the Spartans would find the choices that modern leaders must make, even leaders in the nuclear age, entirely familiar. Anarchy connects the world of twenty-five centuries ago with our own.

In the sense that anarchy has persisted, nuclear weapons have not changed the world. The political revolution that was so widely expected in 1945 would have made international politics more like domestic politics by abolishing anarchy, and so, by placing supreme power in the hands of a single authority, would have abolished war. This revolution has not taken place.

Three levels of analysis

How have nuclear weapons affected international politics? They have not produced a revolutionary change in the international system. Relations among sovereign states are still governed by the principle of anarchy. War is still possible. This is not to say, however, that the technical revolution in weaponry has had no political effect at all. There is a cardinal difference between the Soviet–American rivalry and the conflict between Athens and Sparta. The Greek city–states went to war, and fought intermittently for thirty years. The United States and the Soviet Union have, so far, kept their quarrels from turning into open warfare. Theirs has been a "Cold War," a divisive and often bitter conflict in which, nonetheless (with a few scattered exceptions), neither side has fired a shot in anger at the other. There has been no direct military engagement of any kind between the two principal nuclear powers, let alone a nuclear exchange.

It cannot be said with certainty, of course, that the United States and the Soviet Union have kept their rivalry short of war because, and only because, of the existence of nuclear weapons. (Nor, of course, can it be said with certainty that there will never be a war between two states with nuclear weapons, or a war between the United States and the Soviet Union, whether nuclear or not.) The world may owe the relative peace that it has enjoyed since 1945 to the "bipolar" distribution of power. The United States and the Soviet Union have towered over all other countries in military terms. Their margin of superiority, although making it difficult for them to avoid becoming military rivals, has at the same time made it easier for them to manage their rivalry so as to avoid war. Neither has had to take the policies of third parties seriously into account in dealing with the other. This has simplified matters.[16]

Still, it is plain that nuclear weapons have had *something* to do with the peace that has prevailed at the heart of the international system since the end of World War II. This is logical to assume; it was scarcely possible to be oblivious to the threat that they pose. There is evidence for it also. National leaders have said that they exert a restraining influence.[17] In crises, when the United States and the Soviet Union have seemed on the verge of war, the record shows that their fear of nuclear devastation has influenced the calculations that they have made.[18]

Nuclear weapons have not produced a political revolution comparable to the technical revolution that they represent. Yet they have had political consequences, of the sort for which there is a parallel in the history of the industrial revolution.

In Marx's day Britain was the country where it had gone furthest, and thus where political revolution seemed to Marx most imminent. There has been no British revolution. A century later Britain remains a constitutional monarchy, with authority vested in a Parliament that is chosen by regular elections pitting two competing political parties against each other. During that century the British political system has, however, changed considerably. Her Majesty's government has the same legal powers as before, but has taken on many new tasks. Effective power within Parliament has shifted – from Parliament as a whole to the cabinet to the Prime Minister. Although their legal status is what is was in the nineteenth century, the social composition, political role, and electoral tactics of the two principal parties have all changed enormously. Political institutions are the same; political behavior has changed. So it is with the international system in the nuclear age. The system remains anarchical. War is still possible. The possibility of nuclear war, however, has encouraged the two principal rival powers to behave cautiously, carefully, and prudently where the interests of the other are concerned. They have behaved like fencers on a tightrope, ever alert but never striking, for fear that both would topple into the abyss.[19]

The caution with which the United States and the Soviet Union have treated each other is the clearest effect of nuclear weapons on international politics. Are there others? An analogy is suggestive. War is to international politics as a strike is to industrial relations.[20] It is an extreme, because dangerous and disruptive, tactic in relations between natural adversaries (labor and management find themselves in a position analogous to that of sovereign states) that harms both sides and that each would therefore prefer to avoid. A strike does not actually have to be staged to influence negotiations between labor and management. The threat of a strike ordinarily hangs over their deliberations, just as the threat of war hangs over politics among nations and encourages compromise, because the loss that a concession in bargaining represents will usually be smaller than the loss that a suspension of production will inflict. Actual strikes are not, however, irrelevant to negotiations. The influence of the threat of a strike depends on its credibility; actual strikes bolster the credibility of subsequent strike threats.

Relations between the United States and the Soviet Union in the nuclear age have resembled the labor relations of a firm on the verge of bankruptcy, where both sides realize that a strike would spell disaster for labor and management alike. Both will therefore proceed with extreme caution. Both may realize that a work stoppage will benefit neither, and none may have taken place for a very long time; still, the possibility of a strike persists. The potency of the threat of a strike is high in these circumstances, as it is for nuclear war, not because strikes or nuclear wars are frequent but because they are possible and their consequences are potentially so grave.

Neither the workers nor the managers of a troubled firm will be content to rely solely on cautious negotiating tactics to keep the enterprise from collapsing. The danger will always exist that a reckless labor leader or management representative will push too far. There will be a possibility of miscalculation on both sides. So there will be, as well, the temptation to change the system of industrial relations so as to make certain that a strike cannot occur. The surest way to do so is for labor to abjure the right to strike and for management to give up the prerogative of setting wages, turning this over to an outside authority with supreme power over the firm. This, however, would mark the end of the system of free collective bargaining. It would be a revolutionary change in labor relations. It is not likely to appeal to management or unions, which will be reluctant to put themselves out of business. More modest changes in the system will have greater appeal. The two sides might reach an understanding – tacit or explicit – that neither will press the other too far. Each could extend to the other formal or informal assurances of limited cooperation even though they remain adversaries.

There is a parallel here with relations between the United States and the Soviet Union since 1945. Hiroshima and Nagasaki gave rise to the impulse to remake the international system so as to prevent the nightmare of nuclear war. Historically there have been two approaches to altering the international system, which correspond to the two logical ways of reshaping a system of collective bargaining. Nuclear weapons inspired the revival of both.

The first is the radical approach. A logical way to do away with war among nation–states is to abolish national armaments altogether. This, in turn, requires abolishing the incentives for states to have armaments. They have them because of the insecurity that arises from the anarchical structure of the international system. So the requirement for disarmament is the disappearance of anarchy, in favor of an international system organized along the lines of the state in domestic politics. States must give up sovereignty. This is the political revolution that some anticipated in 1945 but that has not come to pass. The United States and the Soviet Union have devoted time and effort to nuclear disarmament, which implies the end of national sovereignty, or at least to talking about nuclear disarmament. Their efforts constitute one of the effects of nuclear weapons on international politics.

The second way of changing the international system to prevent war is more modest. It is less certain to stifle international conflict than is disarmament, but it has proven easier to carry out. It accepts anarchy. It accepts the idea that political differences among sovereign states will arise and that these will give grounds for conflict. It tries to keep conflict within bounds in two ways: by promoting rules of conduct to govern relations among the most important states, and by arranging the distribution of military might in the system so that no single state can hope to gain preponderance. This approach has historically been known as the "balance of power," and the advent of nuclear weapons fostered it.

In the case of a firm on the edge of bankruptcy neither labor nor management can be certain that no strike will ever occur. Each will therefore feel obliged to prepare for one. Preparations for strikes can contribute to preventing them; when one side appears able to weather a hiatus in work, the other may refrain from provoking it. To prepare for a strike each side may strengthen itself – the union by building up a strike fund from which to pay its workers when they are idle, management by stockpiling inventory. Either or both may also reach out for assistance elsewhere – labor from other unions, management from other firms.

Similarly, although every nation would like to have a guarantee of perpetual peace, in an anarchical international system, few ever feel secure enough not to prepare for war. Since 1945 neither the United States nor the Soviet Union has felt able not to do so. Just as managers and workers take two different tacks in preparing for a strike, so the great nuclear powers have prepared for war in two ways, which are the ways that states have sought to increase their military strength since the time of Thucydides. (The United States and the Soviet Union in the nuclear age have been more concerned with strengthening themselves in order *not* to have to fight, like the workers and the managers of a firm near bankruptcy, than has been the case in the past.) The two nuclear giants have joined with others. After 1945, as before, like-minded states gathered together in common cause. The nuclear age has seen the formation of alliances. The other way of increasing national strength involves self-reliance. Each great nuclear power has increased its own stockpile of nuclear armaments. As in the past, this has become a competitive exercise, with each accumulating weaponry with an eye on the acquisitions of the other. One of the most conspicuous effects of nuclear weapons on international politics has been the nuclear arms race between the United States and the Soviet Union.

The danger of a strike in an ailing firm must affect the people whose livelihoods are at risk, although the effects may not be as visible as the efforts to change the system of collective bargaining and the methods of preparing for a strike that the situation will inspire. The pressures will differ for labor and management. The manager directs the business. He has some control over its fate and hence a measure of personal responsibility for it. Whereas he must worry about the whole enterprise, the worker worries about his job. Although he has less control over the firm's fate, the worker, because he may have difficulty finding other employment, may have more to lose from its collapse.

So it is with the impact of nuclear weapons, which is felt by those whose lives the armaments threaten. The burden is unequally distributed. The experience of war is different for commanders than for ordinary soldiers. Historians see the larger patterns of war, the strategy and the tactics, through the eyes of the commanders. What happens to the men who do the fighting is more often recorded in fiction, or not recorded at all.[21] In the nuclear era, Soviet and American national leaders, charged with custody of the thousands of fusion warheads that each side possesses, have special, unprecedented, awesome responsibilities. They must decide how, when, indeed whether nuclear weapons will be used. These leaders bear a particular psychological and political burden, which others, who have almost no say in these fateful questions, do not share. Others will, however, feel the consequences. These might be horrible beyond all precedent, and this possibility is bound to influence, at some level, the way people think and feel about their lives, their world, and themselves.

The influence of nuclear weapons is thus apparent at three levels: the level of the system as a whole, where these weapons have prompted efforts at reconstruction in order to make war impossible, or at least unlikely; the level of the state, where both the United States and the Soviet Union have attempted to strengthen themselves; and the level of the individual, at which Americans (as well as Soviet citizens and others) must bear the psychological and political burden of the threat of annihilation.[22]

Three military revolutions

How have the traditional features of politics in an anarchical international system – and these include not only war but the impulse for disarmament and for a balance of power, alliances and arms races, and the politics of leadership and the psychology of those they lead – changed since 1945 as a result of the nuclear revolution?

A further consideration is relevant in addressing the question. The influence of nuclear weapons is not simply the result of the increase in destructive power over what was previously available to the national leaders who wield them. Since the slingshot that David used to slay Goliath, the power of weapons has grown. For the most part, however, that growth has been slow and steady. The curve of military potency over time has risen gradually for most of recorded history. Nuclear weapons caused the curve to turn suddenly and sharply upward.

It was the magnitude and speed of the change in human destructive capacity embodied in nuclear weapons that made them revolutionary. In this sense, however, the nuclear revolution in warfare is not the only one of modern times. There have been two others since the eighteenth century. Twice before, a dramatic increase in the potential for organized violence, based not simply on a new weapon but on a new source of military power, emerged in the midst of a major war. Each made the war far bloodier than had been anticipated. At the war's end the world had, in each case, to come to terms with the political implications of the new source of military might. The quantum leap forward in destructive potential that distinguishes nuclear weapons from other military innovations makes the nuclear revolution similar to the Napoleonic and the mechanical revolutions in warfare. This raises the question of how much the changes that nuclear weapons have produced in international politics owe to their status as a military revolution, and how much to the revolution's nuclear character.

In eighteenth-century Europe, standing professional armies under the control of hereditary absolute monarchs fought for goals limited by the material resources at hand,[23] using weapons and tactics that were familiar to all. Well-drilled troops were considered the crucial element of military success. In campaigns, the emphasis was on holding an advantageous position rather than on seizing territory. The spirit of eighteenth-century warfare was distinctly reticent: "Circumspection and defense prevailed over audacity and offense. Preservation of a force was the first object, the results of its action secondary."[24]

Then came the French Revolution. The revolution called into being an army more powerful than any that Europe had seen before. The unprecedented military proficiency of France's fighting force had its roots in social and political changes in French society that the revolution nourished. Clausewitz, the Prussian soldier who wrote the military classic On War and who fought against the French – first for his native state and then, when the Hohenzollerns briefly allied with France, for Russia – grasped the basis of France's victories: "Clearly the tremendous effects of the French Revolution abroad were caused not so much by new military methods and concepts as by radical changes in policies and administration, by the new character of government, altered conditions in the French people, and the like."[25]

Several crucial features of the "Napoleonic revolution" (a term that is misleading in the sense that the armies Napoleon commanded brought to fruition changes that predated his rise to power) are commonly combined in the phrase "the nation in arms." The grande armée filled its ranks through conscription. This practice, combined with the growth in the population of France in the eighteenth century, made Napoleon's army the largest in Europe since the Roman legions. Even Frenchmen who did not fight assisted the army, and this, too, broke with precedent. The Napoleonic army is sometimes credited with being the first to enlist the talents of scientists.[26]

It was not, strictly speaking, scientists, pushing back the frontiers of theoretical knowledge using the experimental method, who took part in the war effort. It was rather technicians – tinkerers, inventors, and craftsmen. They contrived to produce weapons quickly on a large scale. The revolutionary armies were, however, eager, as eighteenth-century armies had not been, to employ scientific developments for military purposes.[27]

Everyone contributed to the war effort, which was no longer, as it had been previously, the affair of a small group of professional soldiers. The Committee of Public Safety's decree of *levée en masse* of August 23, 1793, captures the spirit of public participation that marked the Napoleonic revolution:

From this moment until that in which every enemy has been driven from the territory of the Republic, every Frenchman is permanently requisitioned for service with the armies. The young men shall fight; married men will manufacture weapons and transport stores; women shall make tents and nurse in the hospitals; children shall turn old linen into lint; the old men shall repair to the public squares to raise the courage of the warriors and preach the unity of the Republic and hatred against the kings.[28]

"The nation in arms" meant that Napoleon's army was a fighting force of the people. Before the revolution, only the nobility could aspire to high military rank; afterward, the army, like other occupations, became a career open to talent. This meant that the army was for the people as well. Before the revolution, the French army served as the personal arm of the monarch. It fought for his purposes and his glory. The *grande armée* fought for liberty, equality, and fraternity, and for France – not for Louis Bourbon. Ultimately it fought harder than had the monarchical armies.

The French fighting force was organized differently than its eighteenth-century predecessors, and this also contributed to the Napoleonic revolution in warfare. Each division became an army in miniature, with its own infantry, cavalry, and artillery.[29] Functionally integrated divisions made for greater mobility than had been possible before. France gained in mobility as well from the practice, which Napoleon revived, of sustaining the troops by what is sometimes euphemistically called "living off the land" and is also more bluntly termed "plunder." Whatever the name, the practice decreased the dependence of the army on supply lines, and in general reduced the logistical problems that had tethered eighteenth-century armies close to home.[30]

The nation in arms and the new organization of the French army made possible the third main feature of the Napoleonic revolution in warfare – a dramatic shift in tactics. Eighteenth-century war was an exercise in posturing. Bluffs and feints were the rule. The siege was the commonest operation. Commanders were happy to avoid battle. Marshal Saxe, perhaps the most respected authority on warfare of the eighteenth century, wrote: "I do not favor pitched battles, especially at the beginning of a war, and I am convinced that a skillful general could make war all his life without being forced into one."[31] Napoleon's strategic convictions and policies ran directly counter to the spirit of the age of classical warfare. He sought, relished, and profited from battle. He put the highest premium on the offensive. He made his goal the destruction of the enemy's main force. Attack, pursue, annihilate – these were his military watchwords, and from 1790 to 1820 battles were three times as frequent in Europe as they had been during the previous three centuries.[32]

The French army's superiority of maneuver permitted the concentration of forces at decisive points and brought victory over more numerous forces. Mass, mobility, enthusiasm, and attack yielded sweeping victories. Napoleon became the greatest European conquerer since the Roman emperors. When a coalition of the other European powers finally brought him down, they had, in trying to reconstruct the international system over which he had run roughshod, to take into account the military force that he had unleashed, just as the nuclear revolution helped to shape international politics after 1945.

A century after the downfall of Napoleon, another military revolution burst upon Europe. The mechanical revolution in warfare was partly the continuation of the developments of the Napoleonic. Conscription reached deeper into national societies. More civilians worked to support the war effort. Real scientists, not just inspired tinkerers and artisans, lent their talents to the cause of victory on the battlefield. What distinguished World War I from its predecessors, however, what caused a quantum leap forward in destructive power, making it a military revolution, was the large-scale use of machines.

One important machine was the railroad, which could transport hundreds of thousands of troops over long distances more rapidly than ever before and then keep them supplied in the field. The railroad made possible the modern mass army because it enabled one nation to put its entire military strength into the territory of another.[33]

Once in place, the troops operated highly efficient machines for killing each other. The level of battlefield violence between 1914 and 1918 soared far beyond anything soldiers had known in the past. The Germans, for example, used more explosives in a single battle than their entire army had used in the Franco–Prussian War of 1870–1.[34] Supplies of explosives were plentiful on both sides, and more efficient means of delivering them were at hand, the most prominent of which could fire dozens of rounds of ammunition per minute – the machine gun.

World War I marked the introduction of mobile machines, not just for bringing troops to the battlefield but for maneuvering on and over it as well. The tank and the airplane were too primitive, and arrived too late, to be decisive in 1918, but as Churchill predicted, they came to dominate land combat thereafter.

The industrial revolution in economic production, of which the mechanical revolution in warfare was a result, was in full swing a century before the First World War. Industrial innovations were adapted only gradually to military purposes. Navies incorporated industrial innovations – steam propulsion, big guns, and ever-stronger armor – well before armies did. Even so, there were foreshadowings of mechanical warfare before 1914. In the American Civil War, the larger industrial base of the North gave it a telling advantage over the South. The Franco–Prussian War of 1870–1 underscored the importance of rapid rail-bound mobilization.[35]

Still, World War I came as a "technical surprise." [36] No one expected the level of violence, the scale of destruction, the toll of casualties that it brought. In the wars of the French Revolution only one side had the revolutionary source of military might at its disposal, at least until nearly the end. The result was France's conquests. In World War I both sides, the Triple Alliance and the Triple Entente, waged mechanical war. The result was a bloody, horrible stalemate. The combination of industrial technology with the Napoleonic penchant for the offensive proved disastrous. Commanders on both sides, imbued with the spirit of attack, pursuit, and annihilation, sent waves of troops charging across battlefields in northern France. Their opponents, sunk into fortified trenches, mowed the attackers down with their machine guns. The result was casualties numbering in the millions. In 1919, as in 1815, the international system had to be reconstructed. After World War I, as after the Napoleonic wars, and as, of course, after World War II, that reconstruction took place in the shadow of a military revolution.

There are marked similarities among the three military revolutions. Each had its basis in a long-term social trend. The increase in the population of Europe in the eighteenth century made possible the Napoleonic revolution; the industrial revolution of the nineteenth century in economic production the mechanical; the great discoveries of twentieth-century science, especially physics, the nuclear. Each pushed the decisions on which victory and defeat depended further, in time and space, from the battlefield. In the Napoleonic campaigns, the skill of field commanders still influenced the outcome of battles. In World War I, the various general staffs generally drew up plans in advance, which the troops executed. Victory in a nuclear war between the United States and the Soviet Union will be decided, insofar as the concepts of winning and losing still make sense, by the ingenuity of the scientists and engineers who have designed the weapons.

There are differences among the three revolutions as well. One difference is in the basis for them. The first was social and political in character; the second and third were technical. If war is a product, the dramatic expansion in output that the Napoleonic wars represented came from changes in labor; in the mechanical and nuclear revolutions "improvements" in capital were responsible. The crucial mechanical change involved the means of delivering destructive force; with the nuclear revolution the explosive itself grew dramatically in power.

The revolutions differ, as well, in that the first two stemmed from, and formed part of, broad historical forces that reshaped Western societies and are now at work the world over. The force in the first case was political; the Napoleonic revolution stemmed from the French Revolution, which in turn began what may be called the process of "democratization," by which ordinary men and women have come to have a say in how they are governed. In the second revolution, the broad historical force was economic – the dominion of the machine in production and the dramatic changes in the material conditions of social life that this brought. The nuclear revolution was more isolated and specialized. It was the result of a specifically military innovation, which has proved, so far at least, to have comparatively limited application to civilian pursuits.

The three revolutions had differing effects on the age-old military contest between the offense and the defense as well; together they form a dialectical pattern. The Napoleonic revolution favored the offensive. The French campaigns were not skirmishes, with the emphasis on maneuver, as in the eighteenth century, but wars of conquest. The mechanical revolution in warfare tilted the balance back to the defense between 1914 and 1918, although not thereafter.[37] World War I produced not a quick victory for either side but a bloody war of attrition. The nuclear revolution represents a synthesis. It has restored, indeed perhaps established definitively, the supremacy of the offense. The third world war would likely be a war of annihilation. This would, however, because of the distribution of nuclear weapons, be mutual, and the mutual possession of the capacity for annihilation on the part of the United States and the Soviet Union has had the same effect as the superiority of the defense – a stalemate.

All three revolutions, however, commonly made war suddenly and dramatically far more costly than it had been before, although leaving intact the anarchical international system, thus preserving the possibility that a terrible war *could* break out. So to the extent that since 1945 international politics has been influenced by the rise in the costs of war, this may not be due solely to the advent of nuclear armaments. The terrible example of industrial war between 1914 and 1918 did not, it is true, suffice to prevent World War II. The added experience of 1939 to 1945, however, might have been enough to forestall World War III even without Hiroshima and Nagasaki. The tanks and the artillery of the Second World War, and especially the aircraft that reduced Dresden and Tokyo to rubble might have been terrifying enough by themselves to keep the peace between the United States and the Soviet Union.[38] Moreover, nuclear weapons may have had the same effects as previous revolutions. Their impact may be evident not only in the differences between relations among sovereign states before and after Hiroshima but in the similarities as well.

How have nuclear weapons affected international politics? The original question needs a final rephrasing: How has the dramatic expansion in destructive potential that nuclear weapons represent affected disarmament, the balance of power, alliances, arms races, the politics of leadership, and the psychology of vulnerability, and how are these effects different from, and similar to, those of the Napoleonic and mechanical revolutions in warfare? The seven chapters that follow examine the nuclear impact on each of these aspects of international politics.

2

Nuclear Weapons and Chemical and Biological Weapons

The disarmament impulse

Thucydides tells us that between the victory of the Greek coalition over the Persians and the outbreak of war among the members of that coalition, the Spartans proposed that the Athenians refrain from fortifying their city. They further suggested that all fortifications outside the Peloponnese, where Sparta was situated, be dismantled. This is the first recorded plan for disarmament. It is far from the last. History, especially contemporary history, is rich in proposals to abolish the instruments of war. In the nuclear age they have been especially numerous. Hiroshima and Nagasaki inspired a series of schemes for abolishing national armaments in general and national nuclear arsenals in particular.

The United States offered the first one in 1946. It became known as the Baruch Plan, after Bernard Baruch, the financier whom President Harry Truman chose to present it to the newly organized United Nations. Under its terms every stage of the nuclear weapon-making process, from the mining of uranium ore to the fabrication of explosives, was to come under the control of a supranational body, whose monopoly would prevent any individual state from equipping itself with the bomb.

Like the Spartans' proposal for dismantling fortifications, the Baruch Plan was not adopted. The immediate cause of rejection was the same in each case: Both would have had unequal effects; each plan would have given an advantage to its

proposer. The Athenians were unwilling to leave their city un-
fortified and thus open to attack while the Spartan fortifications stood. Similarly, the Baruch Plan, if carried out, would
have left the United States with the experience of having made
a bomb, whereas the Soviet Union would have remained cut
off from this nuclear know-how.[1]

In response to the Spartan proposal the Athenians dissem-
bled. They sent an envoy to Sparta for discussions. Mean-
while, they put up fortifications as quickly as they could. They
used disarmament talks as camouflage for a rapid arms
buildup. When the city walls had been completed, the Athenian emissary, Themistocles, told the Spartans what Athens
had done and asserted that the fortifications enabled them to
deal with Sparta on an equal footing. Similarly, while Soviet
representatives sparred with the Americans at the United Nations over the merits of the Baruch Plan, the Soviet nuclear
weapons program proceeded secretly until, in 1949, it produced a nuclear explosion. The Soviets, too, had the bomb.

Another more deeply rooted cause of the failure of the
Baruch Plan became apparent in the ensuing decade as the
United States and the Soviet Union put forward other blue-
prints for disarmament. A supranational body with authority
superseding that of any individual nation, of the kind that the
Baruch Plan had envisioned, turned out to be the necessary
condition of any disarmament program. Doing away with
weapons meant abolishing, or at least severely curtailing, the
autonomy of the political units that used them. Disarmament
required doing away with what has been the fundamental condition of politics among sovereign political communities from
fifth-century B.C. Greece to the nuclear age – anarchy.

There is a logical connection between the fragmentation of
the international system into separate sovereign units and the
existence of weapons, especially nuclear weapons. States arm
themselves for the purpose of self-protection in a milieu in
which the absence of an overarching authority makes the use
of force perpetually possible, and thus preparations to use it
perpetually prudent. Where the possibility of being attacked
exists, preparation is the better part of valor. This logic has a

powerful appeal. It proved persuasive to Athens, to the Soviet Union, and to most other members of the anarchical international system in the intervening two millennia. To void it would require a fundamental change in the system itself. Over the course of those two millennia sovereign states have resisted such a change. They have not voluntarily surrendered their sovereign prerogatives, especially the ultimate prerogative of self-defense. Sovereignty has stood, from the time of Thucydides to the present, as the unbudgeable obstacle to disarmament.

In the nuclear age, even more modest proposals aimed at controlling these weapons of mass destruction than wholesale disarmament have foundered on the question of sovereignty. In the 1950s the United States and the Soviet Union began negotiations to stop the testing of nuclear weapons that both were carrying out. The Americans insisted on the right to inspect Soviet territory to check on shocks of uncertain provenance – to make sure they were caused by earthquakes, not clandestine nuclear tests. The Soviets refused; such inspection violated their sovereign prerogative to control the entry of foreigners into their country.[2]

The impulse for disarmament, to which nuclear weapons gave particular urgency, is therefore ultimately an impulse to remake the international system itself. The hope of restructuring the system is not new. Proposals for doing away with sovereignty appeared in Europe as long ago as the thirteenth century, and by the seventeenth century these proposals were explicitly designed to prevent war.[3] This should not be surprising. War is a recurrent problem among sovereign communities. The logical solution to the problem is therefore to deprive these communities of their independence.

Schemes for disarmament are also familiar. They became especially prominent after the first of the three modern military revolutions. At the end of the Napoleonic wars, Czar Alexander I of Russia suggested that the armies of all the major European powers be reduced in number. The response of the other European leaders echoed that of the Athenians to the Spartan proposal for refraining from building fortifications and that of the Soviet Union to the Baruch Plan. They regarded it at best as impractical, at worst as a ploy to secure a strategic advantage for Russia.[4]

Alexander's scheme faded away, but the impulse for disarmament that the Napoleonic wars had inspired grew in strength. Peace societies began to be organized in Britain and the United States, which agitated for the abolition of armaments.[5] By the end of the nineteenth century, the idea of abolishing armaments had gained sufficient popularity and legitimacy for disarmament conferences to attract representatives of all the world's great powers. None, however, was willing to take the step necessary to bring it about: relinquishing sovereignty.

The mechanical revolution in warfare that took place during World War I gave even greater force to the disarmament impulse. The carnage in the trenches made the task of abolishing weapons (as well as the related task of abolishing war) seem more pressing than ever. Disarmament was one of the preoccupations of the League of Nations and was the subject of extensive discussion in the interwar period. A few nations, notably Britain, did actually scale down their armaments, but well before September 1939 the failure of this second revolution in warfare to lead to disarmament was plain.

It has been the achievement of the three modern military revolutions to elevate disarmament to a place of ever-increasing importance on the agenda of international politics. The pattern has been the same in each case. The revolution has occurred in wartime. After the war, attempts have been launched to prevent a repetition of the unexpected and wholly unwelcome slaughter by abolishing all weapons. Disarmament has invariably been linked, sometimes explicitly and always at least tacitly, to the abolition of sovereign states.

The pattern shows some change over time. During a century and a half the disarmament impulse has become stronger. The cries for the abolition of weapons have grown louder, the proposals more numerous. They have received increasingly respectful attention from national leaders. At the outset of the nineteenth century the dream of disarmament was the property of a few eccentric visionaries (a category that, as his sub-sequent personal history confirms, included Alexander I, Czar of all the Russians). By the middle of the twentieth century, powerful national leaders had become its proponents.

For 150 years, however, one thing remained constant – fail-ure. The dream remained just that. The increasingly destruc-tive potential of the weapons at the disposal of nation–states has never persuaded these states to give up their sovereign prerogatives to make certain that the weapons are not used.

This, then, is one way that nuclear weapons have affected the international system: They have rekindled the impulse for disarmament that the two preceding military revolutions in-spired. This impulse has led to proposals that foundered on the same rock as their predecessors: To be carried out they required a revolution in the structure of the international sys-tem, an alteration in the basic condition of international poli-tics that has never taken place. In the wake of this failure after 1945 the United States and the Soviet Union have each equipped themselves with thousands of nuclear explosives.

This is not to say, however, that where total disarmament is impossible full-scale deployment is inevitable. There is a status for weaponry that falls between the two. It is the status of a class of armaments that resemble nuclear weapons in im-portant ways. These are weapons that have direct toxic effects on humans, animals, and plants, and are commonly known as "chemical weapons."

Both nuclear weapons and chemical weapons are the fruits of scientific revolutions – quantum leaps forward in the hu-man understanding of the material world. Nuclear weapons arose from the revolution in physics that took place in the first decades of the twentieth century; chemical weapons arose from earlier scientific discoveries that gave birth to the mod-ern field of chemistry. Both emerged from special programs of research and development undertaken by scientists in war-time – chemical weapons during World War I, nuclear weapons during World War II. The first model in each case was a dramatic but not a truly revolutionary development in warfare. Just as the first two fission bombs have been suc-

ceeded by thousands of much more powerful fusion explosives, so the V-agents, or "nerve gases," of the present are on
the order of a thousand times more effective than the chlorine
and mustard gases of World War I.[6]

Chemical weapons of the most deadly type, like nuclear
weapons, are "potentially unconfined in their effects." Thus,
like nuclear weapons, they are in the special category of
"weapons of mass destruction."[7] As with nuclear weapons,
there have been efforts to abolish chemical armaments. They
have bumped up against a familiar obstacle: the unwillingness
of the Soviet Union to agree to provisions for inspection satisfactory to the United States.[8]

Yet there are significant differences between nuclear and
chemical weapons. The world has a considerable supply of
both, but it is closer to being rid of chemical than of nuclear
weapons. The point is certainly arguable, but on a hypothetical (and difficult-to-construct) scale with disarmament at one
end and full-fledged assimilation at the other, a case can be
made that chemical weapons stand closer to disarmament
than do nuclear weapons.[9]

It is true that chemical weapons have been used more often
than nuclear armaments. But nuclear weapons are in other
ways more central to international politics. There are, after all,
elaborate, expensive, and publicly announced and justified
nuclear weapons programs. Both the United States and the Soviet Union base the defense of their borders and of their interests abroad on, and have contrived their strategic doctrines in
accordance with, nuclear weapons. Chemical weapons are
very much on the periphery of their foreign policies. According to American defense officials, Soviet chemical weapons
are deployed in forward areas in Europe and along the Chinese border, but the NATO chemical stockpiles are located
mainly in the continental United States and would be difficult
to transport to Europe for use during wartime.[10] Moreover, a
few countries, notably Britain, have actually destroyed their
stockpiles of chemical munitions. Nothing of the sort has happened with nuclear armaments. Fewer states are now
equipped with chemical weapons than in the past.[11] Although

the world worries that membership in the "nuclear weapons club" will expand, the "chemical club" is losing members. It is, of course, impossible to estimate with any precision, but it is fair to suppose that a nuclear war between the United States and the Soviet Union is likelier than a conflict in which large-scale casualties are caused by the use of chemical weapons.

The principal impact of nuclear weapons on the international system was the rekindling of the impulse for disarmament. This failed. The reasons for its failure are familiar and plain. A modest measure of disarmament without the abolition of sovereignty – that is to say, greater restrictions on weapons than presently apply to nuclear armaments – is, however, possible, as the case of chemical weapons attests. What accounts for the difference between these two weapons of mass destruction? Why is there less nuclear disarmament than, given the example of chemical weapons, there might be?

The difference has two principal causes. Two kinds of restraints, with deep historical roots, which make possible a measure of disarmament along with the persistence of sovereignty, apply more firmly to chemical than to nuclear weapons. These restraints differ according to social origins. They emanate from different social locations. Cultural restraints arise from sentiments, held in society at large, that are expressed in laws, customs, theology, and secular moral arguments. They have to do with ideas of right and wrong and with notions of what is forbidden and what is permitted. Institutional restraints stem from groups that do the society's fighting and have to do with considerations of usefulness on the field of battle. In both cultural and institutional terms chemical weapons have been more restrained than nuclear armaments.

Cultural restraints

Limits on war arising from considerations of right and wrong are a perennial feature of human society. Thucydides records the debate between the Athenians and the citizens of the island of Melos about the rights and responsibilities of large and small nations. The Athenians contend that moral standards are irrelevant; or, rather that might makes right: "The strong do what they have the power to do, the weak accept what they have to accept."[12] Then they proceed to do what they have the power to do: They conquer Melos, kill its male citizens, and send its women and children into slavery. But they feel obliged to justify their policy as obedience to the universal law of international politics. Earlier in Thucydides's chronicle they decide to reverse an order to visit the same punishment on the citizens of Mytilene, on the grounds that it is a "great and cruel decree."[13]

In medieval Europe the Roman Catholic Church posited elaborate rules of warfare, which it called upon Christian states to follow. Often they did.[14] In modern times, international organizations and conferences have produced a vast body of international law. No agency with the power to enforce these laws has come into being. They are not, however, entirely irrelevant to international practice, because they often reflect public sentiment, which in the modern era has some influence on what governments do.

Cultural restraints on war are of two basic types: those that bear on the question of when to fight, and those that govern how to fight. There are restraints, that is, on the ends and on the means of war.[15] The choice of weapons falls into the second category. This second kind of restraint has proved to be firmer for chemical than for nuclear weapons.

A special kind of moral opprobrium is reserved for chemical armaments. They are said to be the subject of "deep-rooted and widespread inhibitions" and to arouse a "deep psychological aversion among the majority of people, including the military."[16] Leaks of nerve gas stored on the island of Okinawa touched off anti-American riots in Japan.[17] A plan to ship similar weapons across the United States by rail caused a public outcry.[18] The use of CS or tear gas in Vietnam was so controversial that whether or not it should be permitted became, in the public debate, a separate issue from the rightness of the war itself.[19] Allegations that the invading Soviet army was using lethal and nonlethal chemicals in Afghanistan caused an international uproar.[20]

Nuclear weapons inspire distaste, even revulsion, but not to the same extent as chemical weapons. The transportation of nuclear weapons across the continental United States, for example, has not provoked the kind of public opposition that the movement of chemical munitions created. The European members of NATO have protested the American deployment of both nuclear and chemical weapons in their countries. They have, however, registered opposite protests in the two cases, demanding that a full complement of nuclear weapons remain and lobbying for the removal of chemical armaments.[21]

Agreements regulating the possession of nuclear weapons have been negotiated, which tacitly concede that these armaments are a permanent feature of international politics. The Strategic Arms Limitation Talks (SALT) have left the United States and the Soviet Union with huge nuclear stockpiles, and although both sides have paid lip service to the goal of reducing their arsenals, reductions have not taken place. The Nonproliferation Treaty of 1970 affords even more explicit recognition of the role of nuclear armaments in international politics. It officially designates two categories of states: those with, and those without nuclear weapons at the time of ratification. The second class implicitly brands the possession of nuclear weapons legitimate, although the treaty does pay rhetorical homage to disarmament as an ultimate goal. There is nothing comparable for chemical weapons. Partial restrictions, of the sort that have been imposed on national nuclear arsenals, as distinct from total disarmament, have not received serious consideration.

The 1925 Geneva Protocol prohibits the use of chemical armaments. Virtually every major country has signed it. Almost all have coupled adherence with the condition that they will observe its terms only as long as others do so as well. They have thereby made, in effect, a "no first use" pledge for chemical weapons, promising not to launch a chemical attack except in response to one.

On the other hand, the United States has insisted on retaining the right to initiate nuclear combat.[22] During the 1963 congressional debate over the Limited Test Ban Treaty, State Department legal officials gave assurances that although the accord prohibited atmospheric nuclear explosions for experimental purposes, it did not make such explosions in wartime illegal.[23] This judgment stands in sharp contrast to the fact that, since World War I, "no state has ever expressed the opinion that it could legally initiate the use of CBW [Chemical and Biological Weapons], and the opposite conviction has often been stated, even by states which were not parties to the Geneva Protocol."[24]

Norms governing how, as distinct from when, to fight can themselves be divided into two separate categories that further illustrate the differences between the cultural restraints on chemical and nuclear weapons. The first category consists of generally accepted rules or customs regarding how it is permissible to kill in warfare; the second involves norms, both tacit and explicit, concerning whom it is proper to kill.[25] The first category consists primarily of simple prohibitions against particular kinds of weapons. The second is more complicated. Historically it has included the principle of utility, which holds that force should not be used for purposes other than winning the war, and the principle of proportionality, according to which the harm done by the use of force should not grossly outweigh the benefits gained. Norms governing whom soldiers may kill have also, in the Western tradition, generally included a prohibition against killing noncombatants, modified by the "double effects" rule, whereby civilian casualties cannot be avoided. Together these three rules, which have appeared as customs or international laws since medieval times, constitute what Michael Walzer has called the "war convention."[26]

The cultural restraints on chemical weapons fall, as noted, into the first category. They have a history, which predates the 1925 Geneva Convention, of being considered flatly illegal to use.[27] For a time, during the Vietnam War, the American government asserted that chemical weapons belonged in the second category. The American use of tear gas in Vietnam was justified by the United States on the grounds that because it was not lethal and was employed only to control riots and not, properly speaking, in combat, the Geneva Protocol (which the United States had not yet signed) did not apply. In 1975 the United States abandoned this position, conceding a broad understanding of the terms of the Geneva Protocol and finally signing it.[28]

Nuclear weapons belong in the second category of rules concerning how to fight. The general attitude has not been that it would always be wrong to use them, as has been the case with chemical armaments, but rather that it would be wrong to use them if this use violated the precepts of the war convention. Those who have examined the matter have, on the whole, concluded that in practice *any* use of nuclear weapons would inevitably violate these precepts. A nuclear attack could probably not discriminate between soldiers and civilians because the radius of destruction of even a modest nuclear explosive would be so great. Nor could there be any guarantee that the destruction inflicted would be confined to a level that any set of political goals could justify; the danger of escalation into an armageddon would always be present. But if both were possible, if the limitation of nuclear destruction could be achieved, the use of nuclear weapons would be acceptable – to judge by prevailing attitudes toward them so far – in a way that the use of chemical weapons would not.

Attempts have been made to fit nuclear armaments into the terms of the war convention, especially in the second decade of the nuclear age. The American government designed and produced "tactical" nuclear weapons, intended to be suitable for battlefield use, and posited a "counterforce" targeting doctrine expressly designed to avoid civilian deaths as far as possible in a nuclear war.[29] Theologians and philosophers tried to square the reigning strategic doctrine of deterrence – by which the United States threatened to kill millions of Soviet citizens – with the war convention, no reading of which would justify carrying out such a threat.[30] The results of their efforts are not altogether impressive, but they were made. No comparable efforts were made for chemical armaments.

The second category of norms governing how to fight, which stipulates whom soldiers may kill, may be more enduring than the first, the prohibitions on how they may kill. The first are perishable, particular to time and place. They are often overridden. The prohibitions against the use of chemical weapons have been overridden, and more than once. Even when observed, they may make no difference in the conduct of war; the victim of a grenade is as dead as if a forbidden dumdum bullet had killed him. In this sense, the second class of restraints is more formidable than the first.[31]

But while they stand, restraints of the first category are more restrictive than those of the second. They are certainly more restrictive of the use of particular weapons, if not of the general conduct of war. Restraints in the first category are taboos; they may fall, but while they last they brook no exceptions. Those in the second category are guidelines. There are circumstances in which it would not be wrong to use nuclear weapons. These circumstances, in which nuclear usage meets the requirements the guidelines establish, are imaginable if not plausible. In this sense, the cultural restraints on chemical weapons are stronger than those on nuclear weapons.

Perhaps the best evidence that this is so comes from two occasions on which nuclear weapons were the subject of broad public concern. On the whole, there has been little public response to the competitive accumulation of nuclear weaponry in which the United States and the Soviet Union have engaged since World War II. Protests have regularly come from a handful of people and a few organizations, as well as from the rostrum of the United Nations. The American and Soviet governments have, however, been able to do more or less as they pleased where nuclear weapons were concerned, with two exceptions.

In the 1950s there was public disquiet over the radioactive fallout from nuclear weapons tests that the United States and the Soviet Union were conducting. Scientists warned that the tests produced cancer-causing strontium 90, which seeped into milk through the grass eaten by cows. The American government insisted that testing posed no serious health hazard. The scientists disagreed. The controversy became front-page news. Petitions were circulated and protest marches staged.

The campaign against nuclear testing was international in scope; radioactivity, after all, did not respect national boundaries.

The issue played a part in the 1956 presidential election. Dwight Eisenhower, who favored the continuation of testing, won. But by 1959, polls showed that a majority of Americans wanted the tests stopped,[32] and this forced a change in government policy. The United States ceased testing, and with the 1963 accord with the Soviet Union the ban on experimental nuclear explosions everywhere except underground became permanent.

The second occasion on which public sentiment shaped nuclear policy was the controversy, in 1977, over the "neutron bomb." Nuclear weapons cause damage by three means; blast, heat, and radiation. The first two leveled Hiroshima and Nagasaki. The third produced cancer in thousands who survived. (The danger from nuclear tests, which were simply bomb blasts in uninhabited regions, was from radioactivity.) The United States proposed to deploy a nuclear explosive in Europe that would have minimal blast and thermal effects but was capable of generating considerable radiation. It was called the "enhanced radiation warhead" and became known commonly as the "neutron bomb," after the radioactive particles that it would emit. The prospect of neutron bombs stationed throughout Western Europe provoked indignation from public officials, editorial writers, and members of the scientific community on both sides of the Atlantic, as the placement of several thousand nuclear weapons of different design had not. The American President, Jimmy Carter, felt compelled to hedge his original plan to deploy them.

The two episodes have a common theme. In both cases, the nuclear weapons that aroused broad public opposition were, in effect, chemical weapons. Radiation causes damage in the same way as the substances that chemical munitions release – entering through the respiratory system or the skin and causing toxic effects that are sometimes immediate and sometimes delayed. Both are Trojan horses of the human body: They slip inside and then attack. Nuclear testing and the neutron bomb posed the danger not of being blown up but of being poisoned.[33] Nuclear weapons have proved most objectionable, and most subject to cultural restraints, when they have been chemical weapons.[34]

The controversy about nuclear-generated electric power reinforces the point. Again, nuclear power is more unpopular than nuclear weapons have ever been.[35] The danger from a nuclear power plant is the leakage of radiation; it is physically impossible for light-water reactors to explode. Bombs are, of course, designed to explode. Yet nuclear power has stirred more controversy.

To some scientists, at least, this opposition has seemed anomalous, because "the chance of mass destruction by an atomic war is several orders of magnitude larger than that of imagined accidents which might occur with nuclear plants." The nuclear power controversy therefore "seems to be a diversion from the more acute problems."[36]

In this sense, the existence of firmer cultural restraints on chemical than on nuclear weapons is also anomalous. For just as the fallout from testing or from a reactor accident is less dangerous than the blast of a bomb,[37] so chemical weapons are potentially far less destructive than nuclear armaments. Fission and fusion explosives seem inevitably to be weapons of mass destruction, despite efforts to produce less catastrophically devastating varieties. It is, by contrast, entirely possible to make chemical weapons of far more modest power; indeed, they have been made. It is possible to produce chemical munitions that are, arguably, humane in their effects, weapons that hold out the possibility of "war without death." Such weapons have had enthusiastic proponents.[38]

There is another reason for expecting cultural restraints to be more binding for nuclear than for chemical weapons. Chemical weapons have been used. Nuclear weapons have, of course, been used as well. But chemical weapons have been used more often – over a longer period of time during the war in which they were introduced and subsequently in other conflicts as well. If chemical weapons are more restrained than nuclear weapons, their use is also more familiar.

This seems a contradiction. In fact, the second may be the cause of the first. Familiarity may breed restraint. There is evidence for this hypothesis. The experience of World War I did create inhibitions that operated during World War II. Ironically, the World War II leader with the most direct experience of chemical weapons, and for whom the inhibitions were most firmly grounded in personal revulsion, was Adolf Hitler, who had been gassed during his tour of duty as a corporal in the Austrian army. The memory of this episode apparently affected his thinking, at least in the early years of the war.[39] Of course Hitler had no scruples about asphyxiating millions of defenseless civilians.

On this theory, the cultural restraints on nuclear weapons should be strongest where these weapons have actually been used, in Japan. There is evidence that this, too, is the case. Relative distaste for nuclear armaments among different countries is not easy to measure, but it is clearly powerful among the Japanese. A Japanese nuclear arsenal would offer certain strategic advantages (as well as disadvantages). A deeply rooted phobia against acquiring one has so far ruled out even the serious discussion of such a policy. The Japanese government has proclaimed three nonnuclear principles: Japan will not manufacture nuclear weapons, will not possess nuclear weapons, and will not allow such weapons into the country.[40] Public opinion polls show overwhelming support for these principles.[41]

If chemical weapons are more familiar than nuclear weapons, it is still true that only a small number of people in this century have known them at first hand. Approximations of the effects of chemical armaments, however, are part of everyday life in a way that is not true for nuclear weapons. Men undergoing basic training in the U.S. Army are exposed to noxious fumes. Those caught up, by accident or by design, in civil disturbances sometimes have had the opportunity to inhale tear gas. Virtually all city dwellers come in contact with monoxide from automobiles, pesticides sprayed in gardens and parks, and pollution from factories. We all have some personal basis for an aversion to harmful chemicals.

"We" here means citizens of industrial countries. But even nonindustrial societies have deep-seated and often formally recognized aversions to toxic substances. The poison taboo recurs through time and across cultures.[42] "Poison and disease can unnerve people to an extent which other dangers cannot; and the outbreaks of mass hysteria and the superstitions which they have provoked in the past are well recorded."[43]

This suggests that restraints on chemical weapons may be deeply and broadly based in human culture. They may be related to taboos that serve the basic human need of ordering the universe, of drawing boundaries for human activity.[44]

Chemical weapons may offend this deep-rooted sensibility by transgressing two boundaries. One separates sickness from health or, to put it in slightly different terms, the soldier from the doctor. The warrior injures by assault. The doctor, or the cultural equivalent, the shaman or priest, heals by providing medicine that is ingested. Chemical weapons fuse the two. They seek the results of the warrior by the methods of the doctor. Because this process is disruptive of normal social boundaries, it seems particularly pernicious. It is certainly true that in a wide variety of literature, from Shakespeare to Indian myths, the poisoner is a particularly foul villain, whereas the warrior is often a hero.

The second fundamental distinction that chemical weapons may violate is that between war and peace. Battle is ordinarily bounded in time and place. Its accompanying signs are clear: the din and clatter of combat and missiles of varying sizes and deadliness flying through the air. With silence, with the sheathing of swords and the dying away of gunfire – usually, historically, at nightfall – comes peace. Chemical weapons permit no such clear division. The poisons they release linger on the battlefield, drift beyond it, and do their work long after the firing has stopped. Radioactivity, the chemical product of nuclear weapons, causes cancers that appear years after it has been released. Its effects can even show up generations later.

The aversion to chemical weapons may be even more deeply rooted in human nature itself. The discipline of sociobiology holds that much of human behavior has a genetic basis.[45] The mind, according to this view, has undergone the same evolutionary process as the rest of the body. Behavior, like physical characteristics, evolved through natural selection: Traits useful for reproductive success were more likely than others to persist, and thus came ultimately, over generations, to predominate.

An inbred aversion to toxic substances would certainly improve its possessors' chances to survive and reproduce. The species *Homo sapiens* and its forerunners have always been prey to poisons. Some internal alarm system may have evolved, which chemical weapons trigger. Poison is an old enough danger, in evolutionary terms, for a genetic defense mechanism against it to develop. Explosions are of much more recent provenance. Dating them to the first Chinese experiments with gunpowder makes them no more than two thousand years old. In biological time this is a split second; it seems unlikely that any significant evolutionary development in human beings has taken place in the last ten thousand years.[46] The supposition that an aversion to chemical weapons has a genetic basis, whereas distaste for nuclear armaments is not so ingrained, is in keeping with the biologist Edward O. Wilson's observation that phobias "are most often evoked by snakes, spiders, rats, heights, close spaces, and other elements that were potentially dangerous in our ancient environment, but only rarely by modern artifacts such as knives, guns, and electrical outlets."[47]

Cultural restraints on chemical weapons may be deeply rooted, perhaps in human chromosomes themselves. They are not, however, so formidable as to be impossible to override. They have been overridden, in World War I and afterward. Other weapon taboos, against the long bow, for instance, have also been overridden. The heat of battle melts resistance to armaments that had seemed too hideous to use in peacetime. The enemy seems uglier and less human, the laws of war less worthy of respect than before.

Cultural restraints are effective when restraints of other sorts buttress them. These other restraints may originate in the institution that comes to the fore whenever war breaks out. In wartime, warmakers tend to prevail over lawgivers when they clash. "When the crunch comes," one observer of the American government noted, "the Pentagon sets the requirements and [the Department of] State finds the reason why it's legal."[48] During fighting and in planning for war, however, chemical weapons have seemed to the Pentagon and its equivalent institutions in other countries less appealing, less useful, less urgently required than nuclear weapons.

Institutional restraints

Institutional restraints on weapons – when soldiers or armies choose for one reason or another not to use particular armaments – are as old as cultural ones. They were especially prominent in Europe in medieval times, when the knightly class, which carried on warfare, shunned certain weapons as unsuited to what was for them a vocation. French nobles in the fourteenth century, for example, deliberately fought dismounted "out of considerations of pure gallantry; a dismounted knight could not flee to save himself but had to stand and fight."[49] It was often more important to be faithful to the code of chivalry than to prevail in battle. Honor and style reigned supreme. Perhaps the most striking triumph of courtly values was the reversion of the Japanese samurai from firearms to the sword between the sixteenth and nineteenth centuries. The sword regained favor because it more readily distinguished the noble from the peasant than did the gun and was more graceful to use.[50]

Inventors of new weapons have been known to have reservations about what they have wrought, and to try to hold back or even destroy their creations. The Englishman Roger Bacon concealed his thirteenth-century formula for gunpowder. Niccolo Tartaglia, the father of modern ballistics, at first kept secret some of his work – until the Turks invaded his native Italy. John Napier, a sixteenth-century Scottish mathematician, was another who made military discoveries and then attempted to conceal them.[51] Of course, the inventors of new weapons have also been their enthusiastic champions. The young Leonardo da Vinci offered his services as a designer of cannons, siege works, and fire throwers.[52] Scientists conceived, developed, and promoted both nuclear and chemical weapons, neither of which initially had strong military sponsorship.

In neither case is there a clear line of demarcation between institutional and cultural restraints. The resistance of warriors and the reluctance of inventors were grounded in considerations of right and wrong. Knighthood was so bound up with cultural norms that it was "almost indistinguishable from the ecclesiastical orders."[53]

Since the Napoleonic period the military has changed dramatically. Soldiers have become professionals. They have come to prize efficiency above courtliness. Their goal is not to fight well according to standards that are ultimately aesthetic but to win. Inventors have become professionals as well. Military research and development is a regular activity of organized groups of scientists rather than the sporadic product of ingenious individuals. Ideas of right and wrong still count for something. American scientists opposed the development of a fusion bomb on the grounds that it would, in the view of some of them, pose "extreme dangers to mankind."[54] Military men still have scruples about war in general and the weapons with which it is fought, including chemical weapons. In World War I "many military people found the notion of fighting with poison highly distasteful to their professional codes of behavior."[55] The most powerful restraints on weapons that have their origins in the armed forces, however, are of two different sorts.

One kind stems from bureaucratic considerations. Large organizations, bureaucracies, tend to operate so as to maintain themselves: The goal of self-preservation assumes an importance in the workings of the organization equal to, sometimes greater than, the task that it was created to perform. Modern armed forces are no exception. New weapons or practices that endanger the institution's well-being, that disrupt standard operating procedures, and especially that threaten to render the organization itself obsolete tend to provoke bureaucratic resistance. The U.S. Air Force, for example, has shown a tenacious fondness for the manned strategic bomber, whose comparative efficiency the advent of the intercontinental ballistic missiles has made dubious.[56]

The second modern institutional restraint involves considerations of military efficiency. A weapon may be discarded or never adopted at all by the armed services because the mission to which it is fitted is deemed unnecessary, or because that mission can be better performed in some other fashion. The medieval knight cared about the shape of the sword he brandished and the workmanship that went into its design. The modern general cares about how well the sword will cut, and also about whether there is a cheaper, more convenient, more reliable way to dispatch an opponent.

Bureaucratic momentum, at least in the United States, has worked *against* the restraint of chemical weapons. The army's Chemical Corps, which was created after World War I, has consistently lobbied for preserving and expanding the American stockpile of chemical munitions. The motive has been bureaucratic; without these armaments the Chemical Corps would have no role and might well disappear.[57] Its efforts have had some success. It brought the military as a whole, as represented by the Joint Chiefs of Staff, around to the position that the option to use tear gas ought to be preserved during the intragovernmental debate on chemical weapons and the Geneva Protocol between 1969 and 1975. The Joint Chiefs' support for chemical weapons was tepid, however, and the government adopted the contrary position. With little enthusiasm for them among military men in general, the cultural restraints on chemical weapons outweighed the pressure in their favor that the Chemical Corps was able to bring to bear. The military's lack of enthusiasm stemmed from the difficulties chemical weapons present for battlefield use, which is the second kind of modern institutional restraint on armaments.

As a battlefield weapon chemical munitions have several drawbacks. One was understood well before the First World War. An early proponent of chemical warfare was the British Admiral Thomas Cochrane. Several times during the first half of the nineteenth century he proposed that the Royal Navy use sulfur gas against Britain's enemies. His suggestion was consistently rejected, in part on the grounds that success would depend heavily on forces beyond the navy's control, like winds, tides, and currents.[58] When chemical weapons were actually introduced this proved to be a telling handicap. The effectiveness of chemical armaments depends particularly upon the weather. A current of wind blowing too weakly or gustily, or in the wrong direction, can carry away or dilute to harmless strength a chemical payload, or even send it back to poison the forces that have launched the attack. The weather cannot be controlled or even predicted accurately far in advance. So, advance planning – a staple of the military art – is difficult, if not impossible, for chemical warfare.[59]

The weather affects the use of weapons of all types. It is part of what Clausewitz called the "friction of war," the thousand small things that can go wrong on the battlefield to interfere with the carefully drawn plans of the commander. But of all weapons, chemical ones are the most strongly affected by friction, including the weather, and nuclear ones the least. Nuclear explosives are so powerful, and both the United States and the Soviet Union have so many of them, that neither errors, malfunctions, nor unexpected and unfavorable climatic conditions would prevent the infliction of enormous damage in a nuclear attack. By contrast, an ill wind could completely disrupt a chemical assault.

The use of chemical armaments, moreover, is incompatible with certain battlefield tactics. The site of a chemical attack is contaminated and so cannot easily be occupied by advancing troops. Chemical weapons are therefore not suitable for mobile warfare. (The chemical-equipped attacker faces a double pitfall: If he follows up his assault too soon, the lingering chemicals may keep him from making headway; if he advances too late the effect may have worn off and the enemy regrouped.)[60]

A nuclear battlefield would also be uninhabitable. Radiation would linger even after the blast and thermal effects had spent themselves. Chemical weapons, however, present some special additional strategic difficulties. Deploying them (as distinct from using them) is potentially dangerous. Chemical weapons are not conveniently portable. Imperfections in their containers can be fatal to those handling them. During World War I, workers in chemical munitions plants suffered high rates of disease and injury.[61]

Admiral Cochrane's suggestions for using sulfur gas prompted another reservation. Britain, it was objected, might not be able to retain a monopoly on the technique, once having introduced it.[62] The objection holds good today. The anticipated reaction of other military forces makes chemical weapons unappealing to military institutions. Here, too, there is a difference with nuclear weapons.

There have been historical dialectics between offense and defense for both types of armaments, but these dialectics have had opposite outcomes, which in turn have had different effects on the willingness of armed forces to adopt the two kinds of weapons. For chemical weapons, the defense has on the whole kept pace with the offense. More efficient ways of protecting soldiers against them have usually followed the appearance of deadlier poisons. The first chemical weapons were respiratory agents, which entered the body through the lungs. To withstand them, respirators, or "gas masks," were developed – with increasingly effective filters. So successful were the gas masks ultimately produced in World War I that by the war's end chemical weapons were regarded as only marginally useful in combat. Percutaneous gases, which seeped into the body through the skin, were also synthesized. Mustard gas is a percutaneous agent, and so are the newer, deadlier "nerve gases." But these too can be largely foiled by the use of protective clothing, shelters, filtered air intake valves on moving vehicles like tanks, and chemical countermeasures. Defense against attack with such gases is expensive, makes fighting awkward, and requires a high level of training and coordination. But it is possible – for soldiers, if not for civilians.[63]

One army contemplating a chemical attack on another might well reckon that the tactic was not worthwhile if it knew that the adversary had taken protective measures. The prospect would appear even less inviting if the other side could retaliate in kind. Chemical warfare between two armies equipped for both offense and defense would be a clumsy and slow engagement, with the soldiers rigged out like astronauts on the moon. Every battle involves uncertainty. In a chemical battle, however, not only would the outcome be in doubt but the decisions about which tactics to employ would be matters of guesswork without basis in experience. Like the lunar landscape, the chemical battlefield would be a forbidding environment, and commanders have never been eager to enter it.

Strategic restraints

Institutional restraints on chemical weapons apply chiefly to the United States and the Soviet Union, whose stores of chemical armaments, although not a match for their nuclear weapons stockpiles, are considerable.[64] Each country also sponsors an ongoing program of research and development in chemical munitions. The Soviets, in particular, seem to have made countermeasures against chemical attack a standard feature of the training that their forces in Europe receive, although this training is pertinent to nuclear attack as well,[65] and in the late 1970s NATO launched a major program to protect its forces against chemicals.[66] Other members of the international community have different reasons for abjuring a major commitment to chemical weapons. Some are political. Allies of the United States and the Soviet Union believe that they can call on the chemical arsenals of the two military giants if necessary. Western European nations could easily equip themselves with nerve gases; the British and the Germans, after all, were the pioneers in making chemical munitions. They rely, however, on their North American ally.

Not all countries can rely on Soviet or American protection. Many of those outside the penumbra of great power protection, however, do not have the technical sophistication to manufacture the deadliest chemical munitions. Most possess neither the requisite chemists nor chemical industries. These are important reasons why these states do not acquire nuclear weapons as well.[67] And one of the institutional restraints on chemical weapons is the same as the principal limitation on nuclear armaments: the anticipated response of other countries.

The nuclear weapons policy and the chemical weapons policy of the United States influence those of the Soviet Union, and vice versa. In both cases, each country deters the other. In the case of chemical weapons, however, deterrence takes place through the threat of effective defense as well as retaliation. And for chemical weapons, deterrence is effective earlier in the life cycle that runs from the scientist's idea to the soldier's weapon. Neither country is particularly well armed in chemical terms, at least in comparison with what either could achieve if it chose to emphasize chemical munitions. So although the United States and the Soviet Union deter each other from the use of nuclear weapons, what is deterred in the case of chemical weapons is in some measure their development and deployment.

The resemblance between the arrangements regulating nuclear weapons at which the world has arrived and the distribution and disposition of chemical armaments is plain. There is more than a resemblance between the two arrangements; there is a connection.. That connection is the final, and perhaps the most important, cause of the difference in the status of the two contemporary weapons of mass destruction.

In 1970 Denis Healey, the British Defence Minister, explained to the House of Commons the reason for NATO's disinterest in – and Britain's renunciation of – chemical weapons: "If the House really considers the situation, I believe that it will recognize that it is almost inconceivable that enemy forces would use chemical weapons against NATO forces except in the circumstances of mass invasion – in which event more terrible weapons would surely come into play."[68] Nuclear weapons overshadow – dominate – chemical weapons. Here history repeats itself. Before 1945 as well as after, the fate of chemical weapons was determined not only by the dialectic between cultural restraints and the exigencies of war, and between offensive and defensive developments, but by the dialectic between progress in chemical armaments and advances in other kinds of armaments as well. Then, as now, chemical weapons lagged behind.

Between the two world wars the development of the airplane and the tank dramatically widened the possibilities for mobile warfare. For defeating opposing armies and capturing defended territory they were much more effective than the gases that had been developed between 1914 and 1918. Thus they were better military investments. They were, to use the contemporary term, more "cost-effective" than chemicals.[69]

Nerve gases are powerful. Fusion explosives are much more powerful. The moment between 1918 and the present when the use of chemical weapons looked most promising came in the summer of 1945. Germany had surrendered, and the United States turned its full attention to the Pacific. The Americans had two goals. The first was the unconditional surrender of Japan. The second was to compel surrender without an invasion of the Japanese archipelago, which loomed as long, costly, and bloody. A shock, to persuade the Japanese that holding out would be not only futile but catastrophic, was required – a shock that could be administered without risk to Americans. A chemical attack might have served this purpose. The government of the United States chose instead the bombs that struck Hiroshima and Nagasaki.

The question of how far nuclear weapons dominate all other armaments, not just chemical ones, has been central to the strategic debate in the United States since 1945. One view has held that they completely overshadow lesser armaments, which are of little consequence in preventing war. This "absolute" definition of the character of deterrence led to a defense doctrine of "massive retaliation," which placed the emphasis of American military policy on nuclear armaments. The contrary view – that because the two giant nuclear stockpiles cancel each other out armaments of lesser potency remain important, a "graduated" or "proportional" estimate of the requirements of deterrence – yielded the doctrine of "flexible response," which posited the need for a NATO force capable of waging war with nonnuclear as well as nuclear weapons.

Early in the nuclear age, with the Eisenhower administration's "New Look," the first view held sway. The Kennedy administration made the second the reigning orthodoxy, and so it has more or less remained.[70] But even under this second definition of the requirements of deterrence, chemical weapons are not attractive candidates for deployment, both because of their battlefield drawbacks and because they are sufficiently different from the familiar weapons of war that their use might trigger the use of nuclear armaments.[71]

What would the world look like without nuclear weapons? Would chemical weapons receive more attention? Would they be central, or more central, to international politics? Would the United States and the Soviet Union have set aside the culturally rooted restraints that chemical munitions inspire and invested more heavily in research to overcome their disadvantages as battlefield weapons? There is, of course, no way of knowing.[72] Now, however, the two great powers "have so many other weapons, nuclear and conventional, deployed against each other that their chemical and biological weapons appear to be largely superfluous."[73]

What prospects do the restraints on chemical weapons hold out for further restrictions on nuclear armaments? How far, if at all, might the causes of such chemical disarmament as exists be enlisted to push nuclear weapons closer to disarmament than they now stand on the hypothetical scale that runs from acceptance to abolition? The answer appears to be not very far, if at all.

Insofar as the cultural revulsion to chemical weapons is contained in human chromosomes, it cannot be artificially implanted, at least not in less than a thousand or so generations. Insofar as it arises from shattering experience at first hand, a nuclear war might bring nuclear weapons up to the level of distaste in which chemical weapons are held, but such a war is scarcely to be desired for that reason.

As for institutional restraints, it is hard to see how nuclear weapons could acquire the unreliability that makes chemical armaments unattractive to the professional military. They pose the opposite problem. They are too devastatingly effective at producing death and destruction, rather than too inefficient at these basic military tasks, to risk using. Extensive experimentation has so far failed to produce effective defenses against nuclear weapons, and it is not likely that any defenses that are developed could be formidable enough to render the military value of these explosives negligible.

Domination is, in theory, a more promising route to the disappearance of nuclear weapons. It is the normal fate of armaments. Chain mail, the pike, the muzzle loader, and countless other instruments of mayhem of the past have been superseded and relegated to museums. The technical progress that has made possible the three modern military revolutions has speeded up the process of abandoning some weapons upon the creation of other, better ones. Revolutions by definition sweep away the old order and give birth to a new one. So it has been with the Napoleonic, the industrial, and the nuclear revolutions in warfare. Chemical weapons may be seen as a product of the second military revolution that has been rendered obsolete by the third.

Will the march of technical progress go on to produce yet another military revolution? Will human ingenuity, in its modern form, science, produce instruments of warfare that will stand in relationship to nuclear weapons as nuclear weapons stand to chemical ones? This seems unlikely. The laws of physics as they are presently understood do not leave room for a more potent reservoir of energy than nuclear fusion – which is, after all, the means by which energy is produced in what is for human beings its ultimate source, the sun. But even if there is another military revolution awaiting mankind, and even if it achieves at last what the Baruch Plan and its successors vainly sought – the abolition of nuclear weapons – its advent will be, at best, a mixed blessing.

3

The Balance of Power in the Nuclear Age

The balance of power

Like disarmament, the balance of power is a systemic response to the need for order. Unlike disarmament, the balance of power cuts with rather than against the grain of international politics. Disarmament would require the restructuring of the international system according to the principle of hierarchy. The balance of power takes advantage of the system's natural anarchy, and of the impulses for self-aggrandizement and self-defense to which anarchy lends itself. Rather than calling for a drastic change in the way that states conduct their affairs, the balance of power, defined as the tendency of the international system toward an equilibrium in which no single state dominates the others, is a means by which the characteristic behavior of states yields a kind of harmony.[1] It is an ancient feature of politics among sovereign political communities, which the nuclear revolution has helped to revive.

Thucydides records three occasions on which efforts to establish hegemony were thwarted. As his story begins, a coalition of Greek city–states has repelled an invasion by Persia. Then, when the Athenians bid to dominate Greece, other city–states coalesce to stop them.

So finally the point was reached when Athenian strength attained a peak plain for all to see and the Athenians began to encroach upon Sparta's allies. It was at this point that Sparta felt the position to be no longer tolerable and decided by starting this present war to employ all her energies in attacking and, if possible, destroying the power of Athens.

. . . .

People's feelings were generally very much on the side of the Spartans, especially as they proclaimed that their aim was the liberation of Hellas. . . . So bitter was the general feeling against Athens, whether from those who

51

wished to escape from her rule or from those who feared that they would come under it.[2]

The third instance in which the anarchical system arranges itself so as to prevent the dominion of a single power comes with the Athenian invasion of Sicily. Part of the enduring value of Thucydides's chronicle lies in the speeches he attributes to the leaders of the different states as they decide their policies – speeches that, in giving reasons for what is decided, spell out the logic of international behavior in general. The Sicilians' deliberations provide an example. Bitter political quarrels have divided their island's city–states. Hermocrates of Syracuse proposes that they put aside their differences and unite to fight against the Athenian invaders.

If we are sensible, we should realize that this conference is not simply concerned with the private interests of each state; we have also to consider whether we can still preserve the existence of Sicily as a whole. It is now, as I see it, being threatened by Athens, and we ought to regard the Athenians as much more forcible arguments for peace than any words that can be spoken by me ... We should realize that internal strife is the main reason for the decline of cities, and will be so for Sicily, too, if we, the inhabitants, who are all threatened together, still stand apart from each other, city against city. Having grasped this point, we should make friends, man with man and city with city, and should set out on a united effort to save Sicily as a whole.[3]

Hermocrates harbors no particular animus against Athens. Great powers, he says, always strive to dominate, "Now it is perfectly understandable that the Athenians should have these ambitions and should be making their plans accordingly. I am not blaming those who are resolved to rule, only those who show an even greater readiness to submit."[4] Hermocrates urges unity on his fellow Sicilians for the purpose of resistance. This is the logic of collective action: We must all hang together or assuredly we will all hang separately. In international politics it is the logic of the balance of power. Great powers assert themselves; others resist, to preserve their independence; the result is a kind of order.

The balance of power seemed a force of almost Newtonian precision, power, and regularity in the seventeenth century, when the term first came into common usage.[5] Rousseau described it as a kind of mechanical marvel:

The actual system of Europe has precisely the degree of solidity which maintains it in a constant state of motion without upsetting it. The balance existing between the power of these diverse members of the European society is more the work of nature than of art. It maintains itself without effort, in such a manner that if it sinks on one side, it reestablishes itself very soon on the other.[6]

The balance was not, of course, a work of nature. States do not act mechanically. They have motives, which produce foreign policies. A more appropriate metaphor comes from one of the intellectual giants of Rousseau's, not Newton's century – Adam Smith. Equilibrium in international politics is like Adam Smith's market. Both involve anarchical systems. In both cases individual acts have an overall consequence that differs from the intentions of any of the actors. The systemic result is a byproduct of what the constituent parts do. In the market, individual selfishness or, to put it as economists do, the tendency of each individual to maximize his economic position yields equilibrium – the optimal pattern of production and consumption. In the international system the self-assertion of the states similarly yields equilibrium defined as the absence of hegemony.[7]

Adam Smith's century, the eighteenth, was one of the great ages of the balance of power. From the Treaty of Utrecht to the French Revolution the principal powers of Europe were in equilibrium. This is not to say that foreign policies were invariably peaceful. Wars were fought, but they were limited in destructive violence, and no putative conqueror, like Louis XIV, appeared. The nineteenth century is commonly regarded as the other heyday of the balance of power. From the defeat of Napoleon to the outbreak of World War I no single state dominated Europe, and none truly threatened to do so.

With World War I the age when equilibrium could be achieved through the balance of power came to a close, or so it is often asserted. In the twentieth century such a system is commonly regarded as "inoperable."[8] It is true that in the years immediately following 1914 the international system knew little repose, and that twenty years after World War I another global conflict erupted. It is true, as well, that since the end of the Second World War international politics has been dominated by two mighty states rather than the several great powers of the eighteenth and nineteenth centuries.

Yet since 1945 the international system has achieved a kind of equilibrium that in important respects resembles its condition in the two previous centuries. Neither the United States nor the Soviet Union has pushed the other aside and dominated the international system. Each has striven to check the other's ambitions and to match its military might. The world has not been wholly peaceful since the end of World War II, but there has been no convulsive conflict like the Napoleonic wars or the two world wars of the twentieth century. If the balance of power is defined by the *condition* of the international system rather than its composition – in behavioral rather than formal terms – then the system since 1945 has been as "balanced" as it was before and after Napoleon.[9] Out of the same fundamental condition, anarchy, came the same general result – equilibrium, defined as the absence of preponderance.

Although the number of major powers distinguishes the twentieth- from the eighteenth- and nineteenth-century international systems, there is another important difference that sets the nineteenth- and twentieth-century systems apart from that of the eighteenth. In the eighteenth century, equilibrium came about in a haphazard fashion as the result of the uncoordinated policies of the European powers. In the nineteenth and twentieth centuries the leading states, even those that were adversaries, have cooperated to achieve it. In the eighteenth century no state managed to dominate the others. In the nineteenth and twentieth the major powers have taken limited steps to restrain their efforts to achieve domination. Since the Napoleonic wars there has been a conscious management of military might to forestall disequilibrium.

There is a second, related difference having to do with the prevailing attitude toward war. War was a part of the normal working of the eighteenth-century balance. It was one way, sometimes the only way, to keep one state from dominating the others. Armed conflict did not cease after 1815, but war ceased to be considered a routine part of international politics, as it had been previously. Neither the nineteenth- nor the twentieth-century balance of power systems has been free of war. But the leading states of both systems have been less eager for it, and have tried to limit it. Equilibrium has come to be more broadly defined than in the eighteenth century, to include not only the prevention of hegemony but also the avoidance of a general war – a war involving all the principal states – through the practice of mutual restraint in the conduct of foreign policy.

In the eighteenth century the balance came about through the natural, or at least the traditional, impulses of states in an anarchical system; in the nineteenth and twentieth centuries, although far from suppressing those impulses, nations have placed some limits on them. In the eighteenth century each state acted solely on the basis of its own interest, although this might lead to collaboration with another state in order to thwart a third. In the nineteenth and twentieth centuries they have acted partly, although far from exclusively, on the basis of some idea of the interest of the system as a whole, as if aware of the mechanics of the eighteenth-century system and resolved to make it work more smoothly. In the eighteenth century the favored instrument of the balance of power was war; in the nineteenth and twentieth centuries it has been diplomacy.[10]

The first modern military revolution – the Napoleonic – marks the break between the balance of power systems with and without conscious arrangements among the major powers to sustain equilibrium. Indeed, the series of dramatic and unexpected increases in usable military power that began with Napoleon caused the shift from one to the other. The modern military revolutions made general war – and therefore, insofar as it entailed general war, the unfettered workings of the balance of power – too costly to permit. In both the Napoleonic wars and World War II the balance worked, but at a terrible cost in life and treasure.

By 1812 Napoleon had made himself master of Europe. Only Britain continued to resist him. He had defeated Austria at Austerlitz and had struck an uneasy peace with Russia at the famous meeting with Alexander I on a raft at Tilsit. He was not satisfied. He tried to extend his reach, and reached too far. He invaded Russia but was battered and thrown back, as much by the murderous Russian winter as by the Czar's troops. After his rout from Russia, Prussia turned on him as well. Finally Austria moved from a tacit alliance with France to neutrality to membership in the grand anti-Napoleonic coalition. But the defeat of Napoleon took years – and several major wars. Although it worked, the balance of power worked in protracted, costly, and brutal fashion. Although they had won, the victors realized that another such victory would undo them.

In 1941 Hitler stood in Napoleon's shoes. He too struck against Russia. He too came close to victory; he reached not Moscow itself but the outskirts of the city. The Russian winter and the Russian army, in concert with Britain and the United States, finally defeated him. The victors of World War II understood that, devastating though that conflict had been, the next one would be infinitely more destructive if it involved the extensive use of the weapon that had been perfected too late for the war against Hitler and so had been used to attack two cities of Hitler's Asian ally, Japan – the atomic bomb.

The analogy with the market is useful for illustrating the effect of the Napoleonic and nuclear revolutions on the balance of power. The nineteenth- and twentieth-century balance of power systems stands in relationship to that of the eighteenth century somewhat as the managed economy of the twentieth century (which is often associated with the thought of John Maynard Keynes) stands in relationship to Adam Smith's laissez-faire market. For the liberal capitalist economies in the twentieth century as for international politics in the nineteenth, the unfettered workings of the system became intolerable. The economic analogy to the modern military revolutions is the business cycle, which led to a series of slumps culminating in the Great Depression of the 1930s. Keynes found an inherent tendency for these slumps to occur – for the economy, that is, to move out of equilibrium, with production dropping and people thrown out of work. Economic activity might eventually pick up and equilibrium at the level of full employment be restored. The cost in human suffering in the meantime, however, came to be regarded as intolerable, just as the victors – and survivors – of the Napoleonic wars and World War II believed that the next war would be too costly, even if equilibrium ultimately returned. Keynes prescribed limited governmental intervention in the economy to prevent the fluctuations of the business cycle. Similarly, in the nineteenth and twentieth centuries the great powers have resolved upon limited intervention in the workings of the international system, in the form of explicit cooperation, to avoid repeating the wars that they had just fought.[11]

The members of the victorious anti-Napoleonic coalition feared another war because they believed that the death and destruction that it would cause would be too great to sustain. They had seen what new and powerful armies like Napoleon's grand armée could do. Death and destruction on a large scale were not unprecedented. Europe had suffered terribly from war before the age of modern military revolutions – in the wars of religion, for instance. There were, however, two other motives for cooperating to sustain the international equilibrium. One was the danger that another Napoleon would arise and set off in quest of European hegemony. For the first half of the nineteenth century the other powers, particularly the British, continued to be wary of a revival of the French peril. Another consequence of war loomed as particularly dangerous in the wake of Napoleon: domestic revolution. Thucydides had observed it:

Practically the whole of the Hellenic world was convulsed, with rival parties in every state – democratic leaders trying to bring in the Athenians, and oligarchs trying to bring in the Spartans . . . revolutions broke out in city after city, and in places where the revolutions occurred late the knowledge of what had happened previously in other places caused still new extravagances of zeal.[12]

Napoleon had shaken the old order. By defeating him, the conservative powers had, just, managed to hold the forces of liberalism and nationalism at bay. Another such war, they feared, would mean the collapse of the ruling authorities all across

Europe, which almost everywhere on the continent were monarchical and dynastic, not liberal and national.

The order that the conservatives had sought to defend was
gone by 1945, swept away by World War I; so since 1945,
therefore, the incentive to cooperate in avoiding war so as to
forestall the forces that threatened the old order has been missing. There is one partial exception. Since 1945, the Soviet Union has re-created an illiberal multinational empire. It differs
from the vanished empires of the Habsburgs, Romanovs, and
Ottomans in that it has a stronger geopolitical position; it
dwarfs all but one other member of the international system; it
has a single predominant nationality and a formidable military force; it has a more attractive ideology (although the appeal of Marxism-Leninism is a rapidly wasting asset); and it
has a state apparatus whose resources for repression and self-
perpetuation exceed anything known to the nineteenth-century emperors.

Still, the signs of the decay that ultimately undid the empires that went to war in 1914 are evident: apathy in the domi-
nant nationality and discontent among the minorities, a lag-
gard economy, and an overweening, suffocating bureaucracy.
(It is no accident that one of the major literary forms of the
central European empires, the mordant satire of Gogol and
Kafka, has reappeared in the Soviet Union.) No doubt the Soviet leaders, if they think about the matter, worry that the rule
of the Communist Party in the Soviet Union and Eastern Europe could not survive World War III. But it is far from clear
what could survive a major nuclear conflict. The level of destruction that nuclear weapons can inflict is such that no social, political, or economic system, no matter how firmly
grounded in popular consent, could be certain of emerging
intact from a war in which they were used extensively. In the
nuclear age we are all Habsburgs.

If one achievement of the three modern military revolutions,
therefore, has been to bring to the fore of international politics
the impulse for disarmament, another is to have prompted a
shift from a laissez-faire to a managed balance of power system. Here the nuclear revolution has re-created the effect of its

Napoleonic predecessor. But in each case the shift was a two-step process. After both the Napoleonic wars and World War II the victors tried at first to go further, to create an even greater degree of order, through firmer solidarity and closer cooperation among the great powers, than a managed balance of power provides.

The Vienna system and the nuclear system: origins

The two managed balance of power systems had similar beginnings. Each grew out of a victorious coalition formed to fight a powerful state that threatened to dominate Europe and the world. In the early years of the nineteenth century Britain, Austria, Prussia, and Russia finally overcame Napoleon. In the twentieth the United States, the Soviet Union, and Britain defeated Hitler, the other European conquerer of modern times.

In both 1815 and 1945 victory yielded the impulse to perpetuate the coalition, and to elevate it to something more than a temporary alliance. The wish arose, in both cases, to turn the wartime partnership into a permanent instrument of peace, a kind of international police force to maintain the tranquility of the international system that Napoleon and Hitler had so thoroughly upset. After both great wars, the victors proposed to organize themselves into a kind of "league of the righteous" that would enforce order in the community of sovereign states.

The instrument of enforcement in the nineteenth century was the series of provisions for collaboration by the great powers that was written into the Treaty of Chaumont of 1814 and affirmed and extended at the Congress of Vienna the following year. The twentieth-century equivalent of these articles of collaboration was the 1945 Charter of the United Nations. Each went well beyond the eighteenth-century balance of power system in its aims and in the degree of coordination required to achieve them.[13] Both plans come under the heading of "collective security," a term coined in the twentieth century but applicable to the aspirations of the members of the anti-Napoleonic coalition as well. A scale of the ways of bringing order to the international system ranging from the least to the greatest degree of central coordination would have the laissez-faire balance at one end, then the managed balance of power system, then collective security, and finally world government with the abolition of sovereignty that is the necessary precondition, whether or not acknowledged, of disarmament at the other end. After both wars the victorious powers dreamed of the fourth way, aimed for the third, and achieved the second.[14]

As a practical matter collective security seems to have received the serious attention of governments for the first time in 1804, when British Prime Minister Pitt proposed to Czar Alexander I of Russia, in the course of negotiating an alliance to oppose Napoleon, "a general agreement and Guarantee for the mutual protection and securing of different Powers, and for reestablishing a general system of public law in Europe," which would automatically come into force in case of aggression.[15] Pitt's proposal did not come to fruition, but it was taken up a decade later by his colleague and disciple, the British Foreign Secretary, Lord Castlereagh.

Castlereagh caused to be included in the Treaty of Chaumont articles pledging the signatories to regroup in order to thwart French designs if these should revive after Napoleon had been defeated. The treaty also stipulated the specific quotas of troops to be furnished for this purpose. It was to remain in force for twenty years, with the possibility of prolongation.[16] The subsequent treaty forming the Quadruple Alliance of Britain, Prussia, Austria, and Russia reaffirmed the Treaty of Chaumont's terms – and also called for periodic conferences of sovereigns or their ministers to assure that the treaty was being executed and to "consolidate the intimate relations which today unite the four sovereigns for the good of the world."[17]

Castlereagh's favorable view of permanent arrangements for keeping the peace owed something to British war-weariness. Britain had been at war with France continually from 1782 to 1815, except during 1802–3. The Royal Navy had thwarted

Napoleon's attempts to cut off trade between Britain and the continent. Still, the British were eager for a respite. There was another reason for Castlereagh's position. It was easier for him to contemplate close cooperation with the continental powers because the self-restraint that a policy of collective security would require all parties to practice would not undercut ambitions for continental expansion. The British, unlike the other members of the Quadruple Alliance, had none. They required of Europe only that no state located there become powerful enough to threaten the British Empire.

Castlereagh's partner in trying to establish provisions for collective security after the downfall of Napoleon was Austrian Foreign Minister Clemens von Metternich. Austria had even stronger motives for seeking something more stable than the eighteenth-century laissez-faire balance than did Britain. Austria was weak and could gain greater influence through Metternich's diplomatic skill within a framework for the joint management of European affairs than its military might alone was likely to earn. Moreover, Austria required more for its survival than the absence of preponderance in Europe. Of all the major powers the Habsburg Empire could least afford more turmoil. During the nineteenth century the decrepit Ottoman Empire came to be known as the "sick man of Europe." For sheer shakiness Austria was not far behind. The stirrings of liberal and national feelings profoundly threatened the illiberal, multinational empire, which was a rickety, ramshackle affair built for a calmer world than the politically volatile nineteenth century. Continental domination by any single state threatened Britain's overseas interests; continental upheaval threatened Austria's very existence.

The United Nations was also intended to be an instrument of collective security. Its General Assembly appeared at first glance to be the embryo of world government itself. The UN Charter, however, gave considerable power to the Security Council, which was dominated by the states that, not coincidentally, had formed the victorious coalition in World War II. This was the twentieth-century equivalent of the Quadruple Alliance of 1815, from which, however, it differed in two respects.

The fundamental principles of the international system that the United Nations was supposed to guarantee were precisely those that Metternich had hoped, through the offices of the Quadruple Alliance, to suppress. The victors in the Napoleonic wars had sought to deny national self-determination and self-government to the people of Europe as well as to resist French expansion. By the end of World War II these principles had won universal acceptance, at least in theory. The UN Charter enshrined them. Even the Soviet Union paid them rhetorical homage.

In 1815 the idea of collective security was new. By 1945 it had won widespread approval – as an idea. In the nineteenth century the British government objected in principle to membership in a permanent international organization for peacekeeping.[18] In 1945 all accepted that the international system needed some version of what Castlereagh, in referring to the Quadruple Alliance, called "the great machine of European safety."[19]

The Quadruple Alliance and the United Nations both aimed, however, at creating a permanent association of powerful states to perpetuate, by force if necessary, international order. Both aspired to more, therefore, than the eighteenth-century balance of power system had achieved. Both relied on what the laissez-faire balance system had avoided – preponderance. The two schemes for collective security envisioned the preponderance of several states, not one, and for the sake of declared principles of international order rather than national self-aggrandizement. But preponderance – the dominion of the strong over the weak (which was supposed to coincide with the dominion of the law-abiding over the miscreant) – lay at the heart of both plans. Finally, the eighteenth-century balance presumed conflicts among nations – conflicts of purpose that occasionally translated into conflicts of arms. Conflict was what the authors of the Congress system and of the United Nations expected their creations to moderate, if not altogether eliminate.

Neither experiment in collective security succeeded. Both failed for the same reason – the absence of an underlying political consensus about the character of the postwar world. Both involved enforcing order in the international system, but in neither case was there an agreed-upon definition of the proper order to enforce once this ceased to mean the downfall of Napoleon and Hitler. War, and a common enemy, knit both coalitions together. Once peace came both fell apart.

The famous Hundred Days during which Napoleon returned from Elba to France, raised an army, and was ultimately and finally defeated at Waterloo illustrates the indispensable role of a common danger. When news of Napoleon's escape reached Vienna, where the four victorious powers had gathered, the coalition was already on the verge of dissolution. At issue was the question of how to dispose of the German province of Saxony and the territories that from time to time had composed the state of Poland. Prussia and Russia wished to incorporate them. Britain and Austria were opposed, and were in the process of making common cause with France – represented at Vienna by Foreign Minister Charles Maurice de Talleyrand – to resist the designs of their erstwhile allies. This would have reversed the wartime alignment as dramatically as did the Soviet–American split in 1945, and would have doomed forthwith the chances for a postwar order based on collective security.

The renewed danger reactivated the grand coalition. Even then, however, it did not endure, although it did not collapse immediately after Napoleon was defeated. The Congress of Vienna proved to be the high point of great power solidarity. In the subsequent meetings of the great powers, at Aix-la-Chapelle in 1818, at Troppau in 1820, at Laibach in 1821, and at Verona in 1822, the extent of their differences became increasingly clear. The year 1822 is sometimes counted as the end of the coalition, because it marks Castlereagh's last bow in European diplomacy. He died that year and was succeeded as Foreign Minister by George Canning, who had taken no part in the attempts to perpetuate the wartime alliance and who had little sympathy for the project. The failure of collective security was apparent well before then, however.

At Aix the terms of great power collaboration came into dispute. Britain disagreed with the other partners about the kind of international order to be created. Austria, Russia, and Prussia proposed a permanent crusade against radicalism, entailing intervention wherever dangerous strains of nationalism or liberalism flourished. Although Castlereagh placed considerable value on the solidarity of the coalition, he made it plain that Britain could not be part of such a grouping.[20] Britain's insular conception of security required simply preventing the hegemony of any single European power. For this the British were willing to fight. The continental definition encompassed the preservation of Europe's traditional social and political order against the challenge of the ideologies that the French Revolution had set loose. Austria, Russia, and Prussia were determined to defend this cause by force of arms; the British were not.[21]

Politics as well as geography conditioned these different outlooks. In 1815 Britain was the most liberal and most stable of the world's major powers. The British feared liberalism and nationalism less than the continental empires did, and had less to fear from them. The crucial year for the British political system in the nineteenth century is not 1848, as it is for the other states – each of whose political development was decisively influenced by the continent-wide revolution of that year and their respective reactions to it – but 1832, when an act of Parliament broadened the franchise. The British opposed the continental definition for reasons of foreign policy as well. They feared that intervention to quash uprisings against the established order would in practice be a way of extending Russian influence.[22]

After 1945 the wartime alliance proved even less durable than after 1815. The failure of the provisions for collective security after World War II was, in a sense, anticipated by the UN Charter itself, which gave each permanent member of the Security Council (the United States, the Soviet Union, France, Britain, and Chiang Kai-shek's China) the right to veto, unilaterally, any of its decisions. The anti-Napoleonic alliance fell apart gradually – and with less bitterness among its members than among those who formed the coalition that fought Hitler, which ruptured abruptly and with rancor. The breakdown of the wartime alliance led in the twentieth century, as it had not

in the nineteenth, to bitter hostility between the former partners. After the Napoleonic wars Britain declined to take a permanent part in European affairs. As midcentury approached,
Britain and France often took similar positions on diplomatic
issues, and were sometimes at odds with the three eastern empires, creating an alignment of "the two and the three."[23] But
the British and the French also differed on important issues.
After World War II the United States and the Soviet Union
switched almost overnight to firm opposition to one another's
international aspirations. At issue was not, as in the nineteenth century, whether the wartime allies would cooperate to
fight third parties; it was whether or not they would fight each
other.

In neither case, however, did the international system return to the wholly decentralized pattern of the eighteenth century. If not forward to collective security, neither did international politics move all the way back to a laissez-faire balance
of power system. If political differences pulled the major
powers apart, a common fear of war drew them together. Neither coalition disbanded completely. What emerged, after
1815 and 1945, was a modified, managed balance, with a measure of cooperation among the leading states and some rules to
govern their interaction that went beyond the avoidance of hegemony. The managed balance was, in both cases, a failed version of collective security. In neither was there a sufficiently
broad, firm consensus about the shape of postwar politics for
the victorious coalition to survive in peacetime. But there was,
in both instances, a consensus in favor of the two things that
set the managed apart from the laissez-faire balance: the need
for limited cooperation, along with inevitable and sometimes
fierce competition – and this was recognized even when cooperation was difficult to achieve – and the need not only for a
rough equilibrium of military might among the major powers
but for restraint in the conduct of their foreign policies as
well.[24]

The habit of consultation among the leading powers persisted even after the dissolution of the Quadruple Alliance.
Throughout the nineteenth century and into the twentieth

they came together, not regularly but when the peace of the continent seemed to require it. This habit was formed at the Congress of Vienna, and the nineteenth-century managed balance of power system may therefore be called the "Vienna system."

Similarly, the habit of collaboration between the United States and the Soviet Union, and the joint determination to keep their conflicts within bounds, survived even after it became apparent that, as an instrument for collective security, the United Nations was ineffective. The machinery of the United Nations, however, had little to do with this. The fact of nuclear weapons is the source of this cooperation. As their arsenals, and the mutual threats that these pose, have grown, so have Soviet–American habits of collaboration and common commitment to restraint. So the managed balance of power system since 1945 has been a "nuclear system."[25]

Between the Napoleonic wars and World War II, Europe was caught up in another violent conflict. The war of 1914–18 also produced a military revolution. In 1918, as in 1815 and 1945, the victorious coalition resolved to create international institutions that would prevent similar wars in the future. The result was another scheme for collective security – the League of Nations. The League, like the Vienna system and the United Nations, failed to fulfill the hopes that had launched it, and for the same reason: There was no consensus on the governance of the postwar world.

But the work of the peacemakers who gathered at Paris in 1919 did not lead to a managed balance of power system, as had happened a century before. Moderation, which is central to such a system, was in short supply at Versailles. The slaughter of war had inflamed popular passions, forcing the representatives of the victorious nations to try to extract from Germany terms of settlement harsh enough to justify the cost of victory. The Germans were never reconciled to these terms, and the Great Depression brought to power a German government dedicated to overturning the postwar settlement. Moreover, the United States withdrew and the Soviet Union (as Russia had become in 1917) was barred from active participation in European affairs, and Britain tried to stand aloof. Although Britain and the Soviet Union did move back into the thick of interwar international politics, the United States remained more or less in isolation until 1942. American power thus did not count in the balance. The fundamental requirement for a balance of power system, of either the laissez-faire or the managed variety, was therefore missing after World War I. The Vienna system and the nuclear system involved cooperation and self-conscious moderation among the major powers, as the eighteenth-century balance did not. But all three depended, in the first instance, on a distribution of military force favorable to equilibrium.[26]

The Vienna system and the nuclear system: workings

The conscious management of the distribution of power was central to both the Vienna and the nuclear systems. Calculating power and bargaining over its apportionment distinguish these managed balances from their laissez-faire predecessor. In the nuclear age effective power is difficult to define, let alone measure. This was true, although to a lesser extent, in the nineteenth century as well. To determine how powerful each of them was, the peacemakers at Vienna used a method upon which the principal states of the nuclear system came to rely as well: They made their yardstick one source of power, on which the most recent military revolution had been based, which contributed significantly to a state's military strength and therefore which symbolized that strength, and could be measured. In the nineteenth century the source of military might was territory and population. The larger the pool of manpower on which a state could draw, the more powerful its army was likely to be.[27] In the twentieth century the dimensions of the nuclear arsenals of the United States and the Soviet Union serve as the indices of their power.

Keeping the power of the major European states in some sort of equilibrium was a major preoccupation of the Congress of Vienna. The men who gathered there hoped to provide for the peace of Europe through collective security arrangements. But while trying to establish them they also made certain that the postwar territorial settlement gave no European monarch the means to follow in Napoleon's footsteps. So conscious was Metternich of the need for equilibrium that he was prepared to welcome France back into the postwar system in order to counterbalance any imperial ambitions Russia might harbor. He was even willing to countenance a France ruled by Napoleon, so long as the emperor relinquished his conquests and promised good behavior.[28] After the Hundred Days the return of Napoleon was out of the question. Still, by the grace of the victors France emerged from the Congress of Vienna larger than before the revolution.[29]

Metternich and Castlereagh's obsession with equilibrium provoked the dispute that almost split the coalition into two hostile camps until Napoleon's escape from Elba overwhelmed all other issues. The two believed that to grant Prussia's claims on Saxony and Russia's on Poland would make each too strong.

At Vienna and after, the sovereigns and their deputies apportioned territory and populations with mathematical precision.[30] They were mindful of the interests of the major powers and heedless of the interests of the lesser ones. The Vienna system was operated by and for the strong, always without regard for and sometimes at the expense of the weak, who often found chunks of their territory broken off and assigned to a different state, all in the interests of equilibrium.[31]

Inequality is also a feature of the nuclear system. The Strategic Arms Limitation Talks (SALT), like the great power conferences of the nineteenth century, serve as a forum for the close monitoring of the distribution of power that is central to a balance of power system. Only the United States and the Soviet Union take part. Inequality is less perilous for the lesser members of the international system than it was in the nineteenth century because crucial sources of military might lie within national borders. Neither the Soviet Union nor the United States needs to seize territory from a third country to offset the other's strength. The weak are further protected by the fact that inequality is a less readily accepted feature of international life in the twentieth century than previously. Every nation–state is now regarded as legally entitled to a full panoply of sovereign rights, although of course some are considerably more equal than others. In the nineteenth century, when Europe consisted of several hundred states (many of them tiny principalities like modern Monaco and Andorra), along with the major powers, equality was not even a polite fiction.

In SALT the United States and the Soviet Union have argued and bargained over how powerful each is, and ought to be, as did the congregants at Vienna. Because the two nuclear arsenals reside, for the most part, within the borders of the two countries, their dimensions have not always been as easily calculated as was the extent of the territory that the great powers of the nineteenth century possessed. Reconnaissance satellites, however, have given the two giants of the nuclear system the equivalent of the Vienna system's maps. In neither system of managed balance of power, it should be noted, was the allotment of power wholly determined by negotiation. Unilateral decisions – to occupy territory or to build weapons – counted for much more. Cooperation was for the purpose of making adjustments at the margin.

Although the apportioning of territory among the major powers in the nineteenth century began at the Congress of Vienna, the SALT talks did not start until twenty years after the Soviet Union first acquired nuclear weapons (which in turn was four years after Hiroshima). This was partly because the break between Hitler's conquerors after 1945 was much more acrimonious than the falling-out among Napoleon's opponents. Both the United States and the Soviet Union kept a close watch on the nuclear might of the other from 1945 on, but explicit cooperation to strike a balance between them was two decades in coming. The delay took place, as well, because two decades were required for the two sides to feel roughly equal in nuclear terms, equality being the necessary condition for equilibrium in a system of only two major powers.

The nineteenth- and twentieth-century systems differed from that of the eighteenth not only in that they involved a degree of conscious management but in what was managed in each case: not only the distribution of military power but the foreign policies of the leading states. In each case, there were two complementary modes of regulating foreign policies: meetings to resolve particular disputes and informal rules of conduct that the great powers observed.

During the nineteenth century the European heads of government met occasionally, and the foreign ministers more frequently, when territorial disputes threatened the peace.[32] The twentieth-century version of great power collaboration to keep minor crises from becoming major wars has been less formal. In the nineteenth century the main source of military power and one of the main causes of war were one and the same: the control of territory. A conference that decided the first went a long way toward preventing the second. Since 1945, however, the greatest danger of general war has not usually come from prospective imbalances between the American and Soviet nuclear arsenals. It has come from political disputes. But in a bipolar system these tend to be difficult to compromise, because one great power's loss is often the other's gain. Moreover, lesser countries are less malleable now than they were in the past. The eighteenth-century great powers could carve up Poland as they pleased; those of the nineteenth could hive off sections of the Ottoman Empire. It is far less easy to divide territory today.

Nonetheless, the United States and the Soviet Union have cooperated to manage troublesome political issues. They have participated in the division of Korea, of Indochina (for a time), and of Germany. They have even tacitly – indeed, explicitly since the 1975 Helsinki Accords – divided the entire continent of Europe. Their deliberations produced a neutral Austria in the center of that continent. They have colluded informally to keep the Middle East wars from drawing them into confrontation with each other.

As well as concerting to pacify troubled parts of the world the great powers of Vienna and the nuclear systems observed particular rules of interaction. These were not positive laws, which command obedience because an agency exists to enforce them. Neither, however, were they simply patterns that were produced by the unintended results of individual foreign policies pursued for other reasons, like the harmony of Adam Smith's market.[33] In both cases the norms of foreign policy qualify as rules because they did derive from common understandings, because they differed from normal international behavior – unchecked self-assertion, in contrast to the self-restraint that the rules prescribed – and because they did explicitly influence the behavior of states.

The nineteenth-century powers followed three related rules. There was, first, no general war among them – no war, that is, involving all the major states, like the Napoleonic wars. Indeed there was no war at all pitting any great power against another until the Crimean War of 1854. In the wars of German unification, Prussia fought with Austria in 1866 and with France in 1871; in neither case did a third party intervene. Perhaps the greatest threat of general war between the Congress of Vienna and the end of the century arose from the Russian attack on Turkey in 1877. The Congress of Berlin ended the threat by preventing the dismemberment of the Ottoman Empire.

There was also, and this was the second rule, no protracted and bloody conflict, like the Napoleonic campaigns, of the sort that could generate the kind of pressure, domestic and international, under which a monarchy might collapse. None of the wars of the nineteenth century after 1815 lasted long. This was partly fortuitous. The wars of 1866 and 1871 were brief because Prussia won them quickly. The same techniques that brought swift victory on those two occasions, when employed on both sides, contributed to a bloodbath in 1914.[34]

The observance of these two rules was not, however, entirely accidental, but was due also, in part, to the force of a third: The nineteenth-century wars were waged in the name of equilibrium. Equilibrium was the purpose for which Britain fought Russia in the Crimea. Bismarck was more the preserver than the destroyer of the Vienna system. He did not wish to

bring all Germans into a single political community, or to reduce to insignificance the other principal European states, as
his treatment of Austria after 1866 demonstrated. He took
upon himself the same task at which Metternich had labored
in the first half of the century, that of keeping at bay the forces
of liberalism and nationalism that menaced conservative Europe. He enjoyed some success. The German unity that he
achieved upheld the monarchical rather than the national
principle. It helped to keep Europe in equilibrium.[35] His victories were welcomed in some quarters as establishing a useful
bulwark against Russian ambitions. Other great powers did
not, on the whole, regard them as dangerous to peace or equilibrium.[36]

The central rule of the nuclear system holds that there shall
be no nuclear war. This is tantamount to a rule against general
war. It has been followed. Since 1945, despite the vast store-
houses of nuclear weapons that the United States and the Soviet Union have accumulated, and despite the manufacture of
nuclear armaments by at least three other states, there has
been no war in which such weapons have been used.

Two corollary rules have governed relations between the
United States and the Soviet Union. There has been no war of
any kind in the heart of the system, the "industrial circumference" that comprehends Europe and North America and divides the "primary" from the "secondary" balances.[37] Outside
the industrial circumference politics has been more turbulent
than inside. But even here a third rule has obtained: Although
the United States and the Soviet Union have competed strenu-
ously for influence, and although they have sponsored opposing sides in intensely fought wars, for example in the Middle
East, both have taken pains to ensure that their extra-European
rivalry does not touch off a direct test of arms between them.

Although meetings to resolve particular political disputes
were more formally organized in the Vienna than in the nuclear system, there have been more extensive attempts to put
the rules of great power behavior in formal terms since 1945
than before 1914, perhaps because specific disputes have
proved more intractable, perhaps because the penalty for mis-

conduct has become potentially so severe. In a "Text of Basic Principles" that accompanied the 1972 SALT agreements, for example, the United States and the Soviet Union officially recognized that "in the nuclear age there is no alternative to conducting their mutual relations on the basis of peaceful coexistence" and promised to "do their utmost to avoid military confrontations and to prevent the outbreak of nuclear war." They endorsed and pledged to continue the practice of "exchanging views on problems of mutual interest . . . when necessary at the highest level, including meetings between the leaders of the two countries."[38] The declaration was not a charter for a system of collective security. The United States and the Soviet Union did not promise to agree on important international questions, only to work to prevent such disagreements as arose from getting out of control. Nor did the fact that the rules were written down dispose the two great powers more favorably toward observing them. On the contrary, they were written down because they were already being observed.

For all their similarities, there are differences between the international system of the nineteenth century and that of the twentieth, differences that seem to have the potential for interfering with the working of a managed balance of power after 1945. Three particular characteristics of contemporary international politics are responsible for the view that a balance of power system is as obsolete in the nuclear age as divine kingship or serfdom.

The first characteristic is the number of major powers. From 1815 to 1945 the international system was multipolar; there were, counting France, five states upon which equilibrium depended. Now there are only two, the United States and the Soviet Union; the nuclear system is bipolar. This does not mean that equilibrium cannot be achieved, but it does mean that it must have different underpinnings. In a multipolar system states can maintain equilibrium by combining with others. In a bipolar system each of the major powers has to rely principally on its own internal efforts to balance the strength of the other.[39] The fact that it is a nuclear system has made the achievement of equilibrium in the postwar bipolar system easier than it might have been in another era of international politics. The two great powers have had relatively little difficulty in keeping up with each other in nuclear terms. In neither case has it been inexpensive, but neither has the cost of producing a huge nuclear arsenal been ruinous for either country. Moreover, the special properties of nuclear weapons dilute the importance of keeping precisely even, although both sides have endeavored to do so. Past a certain level of armaments, the point at which a nation can be sure of inflicting "unacceptable" damage on an assailant even after absorbing an all-out attack, additional nuclear weapons have diminishing value.[40]

General war can break out in either system, but the likely pattern is different. Miscalculation – uncertainty about which states will go to war under what conditions – poses the greatest threat to equilibrium in a multipolar system. There is less risk of miscalculation in a bipolar system. Both the United States and the Soviet Union know who the opponent is. The danger is rather overreaction: the possibility that a crisis involving both of them – and these are bound to occur – will escalate into a major conflict.[41]

The second potential obstacle to equilibrium in the nuclear age is the vastly enlarged scope of the international system. In 1815 the system included only Europe, at least so far as the obligations of equilibrium were concerned, and Europe's borders were precisely defined.[42] The present system is not only larger, it is more diverse. It has reached equilibrium, however, through a geographic and political distinction between the primary balance and its secondary counterparts. Within the boundaries of the primary balance, which encompass Europe and North America, the two great powers have monitored the distribution of power between them carefully, and have managed their political relations with supreme caution. In outlying regions the distribution of military might has been less stable, and relations among states less tranquil. In Africa, North and East Asia, and the Middle East, local balances have been the products of both the influence of the great powers, acting through allies or client states, and indigenous forces.

These local balances are related, but not wholly subordinate, to the central balance. The United States and the Soviet Union have not behaved with quite the restraint and circumspection that have governed their relations in Europe. But they have seen to it that their rivalry did not lead to a test of arms.

In this respect the nuclear system is not altogether different from the Vienna system. The extension of the European system began well in advance of the nuclear age. The railroad and the steamship were agents of expansion long before the day of the airplane and the intercontinental ballistic missile. By the end of the nineteenth century, competition among the major European powers had spread throughout the world. The scramble for Africa in the 1880s left Britain, France, and Germany owning large parts of that continent. The British dominated the South Asian subcontinent but faced a challenge at its borders, especially from Russia in Afghanistan – a rivalry called the "great game" in Kipling's novel *Kim*, for which it forms the political backdrop. The crescent of coastal provinces and archipelagos now known as Southeast Asia was parceled out among the British, French, and Dutch, and each of the major European powers carved its own trading settlements, called "Treaty Ports," out of the coast of China. Two new powers made their presence felt in East Asia. Both the United States and Japan demanded, and received, concessions from the European states. As for the Americas, for the first part of the nineteenth century the prowess of the Royal Navy made them a kind of British protectorate. In the century's final decades they remained off limits to the Europeans because of the surging power of the United States. First the British and then the Americans themselves enforced the Monroe Doctrine.[43]

The third impediment to equilibrium in the twentieth century with which the Vienna powers did not have to cope is ideology. Diplomatic flexibility was a hallmark of both prenuclear balance of power systems. In both, today's friend could become tomorrow's enemy if the maintenance of equilibrium required it.[44] The international alignments of the eighteenth century frequently crossed political and religious lines. Monarchies allied themselves with republics, Catholic states with

Protestant.[45] Equilibrium took precedence over considerations of domestic affinity.

At Vienna, as well, the leaders of the major powers put the achievement of international harmony above their preferences for the domestic constitutions of European states. This is sometimes counted as a heroic act of statesmanship, which made possible the century of peace that followed.[46] In truth it was not difficult for the men at Vienna to rise above ideological considerations because these did not deeply divide them. Britain was not as resolutely illiberal as the three eastern empires, but the British government in 1815 had little sympathy for continental rebels and retained a positive horror of Napoleonic ambitions, with which rebellion was associated. British prime ministers later in the century were more favorably disposed to the liberal cause than Castlereagh had been. Palmerston and Gladstone in particular were anxious to promote it, especially abroad. Not all prime ministers shared their disposition, however. Disraeli consistently supported the Turkish Empire against the national, Christian claims of some of its subject peoples.[47]

For most of the century, moreover, Britain had much in common with the three monarchies. All shared a sense of belonging to a single European culture. Almost all their diplomatic representatives continued to speak French. Popular opinion counted for little in shaping policy. The political class was larger in Britain than on the continent, but even with the widened franchise it did not reach very far down the social scale.

By contrast, the nuclear age is more emphatically an age of ideology. Ideological differences have fueled the rivalry between the Soviet Union and the United States, helping to rupture their wartime partnership and to incite the ensuing conflict between them. The importance of ideology has not, however, made equilibrium impossible to achieve, because it coincides with an international system that is bipolar. An ideological power cannot easily shift its allegiance from one partner to another; a major power in a bipolar system has no occasion to do so. The degree of commitment to ideological principles of the United States and the Soviet Union since 1945 might have made a multipolar balance of power system difficult to manage. It has not prevented the attainment of bipolar equilibrium.

The case of the People's Republic of China suggests that in the nuclear age even a multipolar balance of power system may function smoothly. Although far from indifferent to ideological principles, at least under the leadership of Mao Zedong, China drifted from solidarity with the Soviet Union to guarded friendship with the United States – a shift that bespeaks the triumph of considerations of equilibrium over those of ideology.

The Vienna system and the nuclear system: endings

It is of more than passing interest how the nuclear system might end, or be prevented from ending; or, if not prolonged indefinitely, how it might change in ways less abrupt than the manner in which one international system (or one phase of the ongoing international system) has succeeded another in the past.

The beginnings of the Second World War have shaped American thinking about that question. There are military reasons for harking back to December 7, 1941. The march of technology, especially the advent of nuclear weapons and the manufacture of intercontinental delivery systems for them, has brought within the realm of possibility a devastating surprise attack. The American strategic force is deployed so as to discourage a nuclear Pearl Harbor.[48] The origins of World War II have also deeply influenced the political dimension of American security policy since 1945. The United States has remained on guard against another Hitler – that is, against an aggressor bent on overturning the international order by any means at his disposal. The lesson Americans learned from the war was the importance of recognizing and opposing an aggressor early on: The earlier resistance is mounted, the greater are the chances for success at an acceptable cost. Failing to act on the basis of this maxim was the mistake the British and French made during the 1930s, or so Americans believed after 1945.

It is not, however, the present or likely future intention of either great power to follow the path of Germany in 1939 or Japan in 1941. Neither waits anxiously for a gap in the defenses of the other through which to mount an attack. Neither finds the present international order as intolerable as did the Third Reich and imperial Japan. On the evidence available, both are willing to tolerate it. This does not mean that there can be no World War III. It means that if there is another world war it will probably come as war came in 1914, *despite* the wishes of the participants, *despite* a system of collective management to secure equilibrium, and *despite* a history of restraint.

The nuclear revolution in warfare, like the Napoleonic revolution, has led to a managed balance of power system. How might it suffer, and how might it avoid, the fate of the Vienna system? Politicians and generals notoriously prepare for the last war. How likely is it that, in the last quarter of the twentieth century, they will find themselves caught up in a repetition of the next-to-last one?[49]

After World War I the question of how the Vienna system collapsed was the subject of exhaustive investigation, which continues in the present, although in a lower key. At first the investigation took the form of a trial: Which of the warring parties was guilty of starting the conflict? Subsequently, historical research became more like an autopsy, seeking the deep-seated causes.[50] This is where the instructive parallels are to be sought.

The chronology of disintegration is controversial. The year 1822 is often cited as crucial. It is true that in that year the Quadruple Alliance dissolved with the death of Castlereagh, its great British partisan. But these events, as noted, mark the end of hopes for a Europe governed according to the principles of collective security and therefore the *beginning* of the managed balance of power system of the nineteenth century.

It is true, as well, that crises and wars rocked the system from 1848 to 1914, and even the period from 1815 to 1848 was not wholly tranquil. What is striking in retrospect, however, is how long and how well it worked. The wars of the nineteenth century, especially the major wars between 1856 and 1870, reinforced rather than undercut equilibrium. They were fought in the name of the system. The Crimean conflict thwarted Russia without permitting Louis Napoleon to fulfill his dream of duplicating his uncle's conquests. Britain and France fought that war for the principle of extending the balance of power system to the Near East.[51] Bismarck's wars thwarted German liberalism. Certainly some of the forces that brought down the Vienna system had their roots in the outcome of these wars. But of the collapse of the balance of power system Bismarck was an unwitting agent. No stauncher champion of the European status quo existed, especially after 1871. When Russia proposed to annex large areas of Turkey in 1877, the European powers put on the most vivid display of the working of the system of managed equilibrium since the Congress of Vienna. They convened at Berlin to restrain Russia and to keep the Ottoman Empire a going, if feeble, concern.

Nor was the Congress of Berlin the system's last gasp. In 1895 Japan was compelled to relinquish gains made at the expense of China.[52] Even well into the twentieth century, as late as the Balkan Wars of 1912–13 that appear, in retrospect, a kind of prelude to the great explosion of 1914, the habits, practices, and attitudes associated with the managed balance system were evident in relations among the great powers. To be sure, there were changes in the way the system operated. Great power conferences convened less frequently toward the end of the century; but in moments of emergency, meetings were still held. Alliances formed, but these had defensive purposes, and the shared sense of the necessity of preserving the system, the common commitment to moderation and cooperation, persisted. Still, some changes in the system and in the foreign policies of the major powers did undermine equilibrium, and these bear on the life expectancy of the nuclear system.

The nature of military power changed, especially after 1870, and this contributed to the breakdown of the Vienna system. Steel production and railroads took their place beside territory and population as the sinews of military might. Although the Europeans did not fully understand the consequences of fighting an industrial war until the fall of 1914, the new preconditions for preparing for such a war – a substantial standing army, military alliances, and the soaring cost of defense – had become apparent well before that fateful year.[53]

Nuclear weapons remain crucial and calculable ingredients of military power in the last quarter of the twentieth century, but power is becoming more diffuse and "elusive."[54] The nuclear stalemate between the United States and the Soviet Union, the rise of economic issues that the distribution of military might does not decisively influence, and the growing ability of lesser countries to resist the entreaties and pressures of the major powers have combined to make the exercise of power more difficult and more problematical. Military might, although scarcely irrelevant, seems to do less for its possessor now than it did in the past, and is more difficult to measure.[55]

The nineteenth-century changes in the character of power were more dangerous to the Vienna system than the present changes are to the nuclear system. One reason is that the earlier changes shifted the relative balance of strength among the great powers. The changes in the nature of power also changed the distribution of power, which favored Germany at the expense of all the other major European states. After 1870 Germany forged ahead of the other powers in Europe, including the original leader, Britain, in the main categories of industrial development.[56]

The changes in the nature of power in the nuclear age, by contrast, seem to affect the United States and the Soviet Union equally. Neither appears to be drawing a clear advantage over the other from them.[57]

The Germans, moreover, pressed to capitalize on the shift in their favor. Britain and France, which they had passed in industrial terms, had vast overseas possessions. Germany wanted a comparable empire, and was predisposed to want one by the general climate of opinion of the time – a set of ideas about international politics that gained currency at the end of the nineteenth century that emphasized conflict. "Social Darwinism" is a convenient label for the way politicians and leading citizens in the principal European countries, especially Germany, came to see the imperatives of foreign policy – the inevitability of struggle and the need to expand or wither. Not everyone, of course, was a Social Darwinist, nor did these ideas determine the maneuverings that led up to the crisis of July 1914. They provided, however, a backdrop to those maneuverings, a framework within which foreign policy decisions were made. Germany was the power most responsible for the war in that, in keeping with the shifting distribution of power and the growing stress on the centrality of conflict and expansion in world affairs, the Germans attempted to use their military might to revise the international system's political arrangements.[58]

A different climate of opinion accompanies the changes in the nature of power in the nuclear age. The emphasis is on cooperation, not conflict. As Stanley Hoffmann put it, "the ultimate perspective is one of solidarity; the dynamics of the world economy, of world science and technology, is, for better (growth and welfare) or worse (population explosion, pollution, depletion, inflation, and recession) a dynamics of integration. If I push too far, your loss risks becoming mine."[59] The counterpart of Social Darwinism in the nuclear age is "interdependence." It has little or no currency in the Soviet Union, and even in the United States it cannot be called the foundation of foreign policy. Nonetheless the prominence of the view that force is becoming less, not more, useful does mean that the changes in the character of power are not taking place in the same atmosphere of urgency and danger that prevailed at the turn of the century.

The nuclear system has, however, the potential for an even more destabilizing change than the shift in the distribution of military might in favor of Germany that undermined the Vienna system. The emergence of another major nuclear power could be seriously unsettling. A change in the number of great powers in the system is, on the whole, more difficult to accommodate than a shift in the distribution of power among the same number – in the case of the Vienna system, among the same states. A change from two to three, moreover, represents the most far-reaching of all such changes in number, from a bipolar to a multipolar system. Foreign policy calculations vary considerably from one to the other.[60] Of all the possible multipolar systems, moreover, one involving three major powers might well be the most perilous, because the change of allegiance of any one of the principals would always be decisive, as is not the case in a multipolar system.

What are the chances that such an unsettling shift will occur? Gauging them depends, in the first instance, upon distinguishing between the spread of nuclear weapons to countries that do not now have them – nuclear proliferation – and the appearance of a third nuclear arsenal comparable to those of the United States and the Soviet Union. The first possibility is likely. Since 1945 the diffusion of these weapons has proceeded apace. In 1980 five states, the United States, the Soviet Union, Britain, France, and China, had officially declared and demonstrated that they had nuclear armaments, and two others, Israel and India, had impressive nuclear credentials if not the full-fledged status of a nuclear weapon state. The second possibility is less likely, at least before the end of the century. Two states towered over all the others in 1945. By 1949 they had both acquired nuclear weapons, and they continued to dominate international politics, despite the appearance of nuclear armaments in other hands, in 1959, in 1969, and in 1979. Their domination will likely still be a fact of international life in 1999.

How much nuclear might would be required to belong to the class of the United States and the Soviet Union? It is hard to say precisely, but it is plain that what the other nuclear weapon states have is not yet enough to qualify. None can be certain of surviving a preemptive attack by either of the nuclear giants with sufficient firepower to devastate the attacker.[61] None is formidable enough in nuclear terms to gain inclusion in the Soviet–American discussions that regulate the distribution of military force – the SALT talks. How much is enough to be a great nuclear power? There is no official threshold, but presumably the members of the international community, like the Supreme Court with obscenity, will recognize it when they see it.

There are three possible candidates for the status of great nuclear power. Japan has the second largest economy in the world, and the requisite industrial base and technological skills. Even if they decided to concentrate on acquiring a first-class nuclear arsenal, however, the Japanese could not have one overnight.[62] Such a decision is not likely. Japan enjoys the protection of the American nuclear arsenal and suffers, if that is the correct word, from an allergy to nuclear weapons that stems from the experience of Hiroshima and Nagasaki in 1945.

The nuclear force of a unified Western Europe could also be as large as that of the two great powers, for it could draw on the resources of an economic entity as big as the United States or the Soviet Union. The political prerequisite, European unity, is not, however, on the horizon. The People's Republic of China, by contrast, has the necessary political unity. It has the announced resolve to match the two nuclear giants. It even has the bomb. Ultimately, perhaps, China will make the international system tripolar. For the present, however, the People's Republic is poor, backward, and, in comparison with American and Soviet military might, weak.

The appearance of a third major power is not a pressing problem for the nuclear system. What is a problem is nuclear proliferation. There is a danger that, when it involves third countries that themselves have nuclear armaments, the unceasing and inevitable competition between the United States and the Soviet Union may get out of control. That danger would exist, however, even if no other countries had these weapons. Proliferation may make the task of managing their rivalry more difficult, but it will be the same task that has been theirs since 1945, which will not be the case if and when another country obtains enough nuclear might to match theirs. Until such time as the number of great powers goes from two to three, the prevention of World War III will depend less

upon maintaining equilibrium between the United States and
the Soviet Union than on their both observing the rules of
moderation and restraint that they have followed so far. This
was true of the Vienna system as well. The changes in the
character of military power that occurred after 1870 did not,
by themselves, touch off World War I. They put strains on the
system and created political tensions that the leaders of the
day failed to master. These leaders failed, in turn, because the
commitment to restraint that had formed such an important
part of the nineteenth-century balance of power system had
weakened.

This was a technical failure. European governments neglected to work out techniques for controlling force: "There
was a thought vacuum between the military technologist who
concentrated on how to obtain maximum kill and destructive
results in war and the civilian section which did not like to
contemplate the holocaust which would ensue."[63] Thus the
railroad timetables for mobilization could not be amended to
allow time for negotiation; Germany's Schlieffen Plan could
not be altered to avoid invading Belgium and making Britain a
belligerent; and battlefield tactics could not, or would not, be
changed to prevent the wholesale slaughter of advancing
troops by machine guns.

In the nuclear age the need for techniques to control force
has not gone unrecognized. The search for such techniques
has had, however, little success. There is no way of being certain in advance that, once begun, a nuclear exchange can be
kept short of a holocaust.[64] Hence there has been intense interest since 1945 in "escalation," and in delineating stopping
points short of the use of the most powerful of all weapons.[65]

The great powers of the Vienna system did not look for techniques for controlling force because they did not assume that
it was a matter of urgency to find them. They did not make this
assumption because the prevailing attitude toward war had
changed. War had ceased, by 1914, to be regarded as a horror
to be avoided at any cost. War, even a general European war,
had come to seem a useful instrument of national policy under
the proper circumstances. In the summer of 1914 the Germans

believed that these circumstances had arrived. This shift had three causes.

First, the continental perception of the relationship between war and domestic politics changed. Governments, even imperial governments, began in the latter part of the nineteenth century to try to capture, rather than to throttle, nationalist sentiment. War ceased to be regarded as a poison that would arouse people against their rulers and began to seem an elixir for enlisting the populace in the service of the regime. The behavior of Austria–Hungary, Russia, and arguably Germany in the July crisis arose in part from such considerations. The point is controversial.[66] Whether or not the view of war as a way out of domestic difficulties was present, however, the conviction that the war would overturn the existing order and so had to be prevented, which had been an article of faith at the Congress of Vienna and for decades afterward, was missing.

This is not a likely danger to the equilibrium of the nuclear system. It is hard to imagine a widespread belief that nuclear war could be politically useful. Neither Soviets nor Americans would retreat to their shelters in case of World War III with the panache with which young Europeans trooped to the colors in 1914.

A second reason for the weakening of the European distaste for war was ignorance. None of the great powers had any clear idea of what World War I would be like. None anticipated its carnage. All presumed that it would resemble the swift, decisive, Franco–Prussian War. A more accurate harbinger turned out to be the longer, bloodier American Civil War, but this no one realized in 1914. Whereas the Vienna system existed *before* the full flowering of the mechanical revolution in warfare, the nuclear system has come into existence *after* the nuclear revolution. The effects of this second revolution, unlike those of the first in 1914, are plain. They are not likely to be forgotten.

The third cause of the relaxation of the rule against general war by 1914 is pertinent to the nuclear period. With the passage of time the memory of the last great war had grown dim.

The Congress of Vienna and Napoleon were as remote to the men of 1914 as Lincoln and Shiloh were to the officials in charge of the Cuban missile crisis, and as the Congress of Berlin was to SALT II. Men forgot the horror of the Napoleonic wars and then forgot the memory of the horrors that had been handed down to them. "Peace, if it ever exists," it has been said, "will not be based on the fear of war, but on the love of peace."[67] But such peace as the Vienna system and the nuclear system have achieved has been based on the fear of war. Insofar as that fear is a product of human memory it necessarily fades over time. The longer the nuclear system succeeds in maintaining equilibrium, the more precarious, in this sense, it will become.

The point of comparison is not reassuring. Neither is one final feature of the Vienna system. It ended. This greatest and most successful balance of power system, moveover, which avoided a major war in a stubbornly anarchical international system for a century, which produced the golden age of European civilization, finished, not gracefully and gradually, but with a terrible, bloody, catastrophic bang. The nuclear system has a long way to go to match the longevity of the Vienna system; and the Vienna system, the pattern of international conduct that had its roots in the meeting of the anti-Napoleonic coalition that took place in that central European city, ended in disaster.

4

Arms Competition: the Nuclear Arms Race and the Anglo–German Naval Rivalry

Three arms races

Thucydides records that when the Spartans and their allies resolved to go to war they decided to assemble a fleet of ships to rival the navy of the Athenians, the masters of naval warfare in ancient Greece.[1] Building armaments is a logical, indeed *the* logical, way to prepare for war. It is logical even in peacetime. The logic stems from the character of the international system. Because it makes war possible, anarchy produces insecurity, which places a premium on military strength. States have sometimes tried to protect themselves by changing the system – either radically, through disarmament, or in more modest fashion, through the establishment of a balance of power.[2] Short of the first, and even in the event of the second, they have invariably found it advisable to provide themselves with other forms of protection. There is a story about a visitor to Israel who asks an Israeli why so many of the people of the Bible, which preaches peace and tranquility, go about carrying guns. "It is true that the Bible says that on the day of days the lion shall lie down with the lamb," he is told. "But it isn't the day of days yet. And even then, I'd rather be the lion than the lamb."

Most states have preferred to be lions. They can draw strength from external sources, by forming alliances with others, or they can use their own resources to build up their military might. (The two are not, of course, mutually exclusive. Both the Athenians and the Spartans did both.) How a state strengthens itself depends upon the resources at its command, the technology of the moment, and its security requirements.

In arming themselves, states often imitate their putative adversaries. This, too, is logical. Each side wants the most potent weapons available. In this way the competitive acquisition of armaments, like the impulse for disarmament and for a balance of power, springs from the structure of international politics. The competition between Athens and Sparta is the first recorded example of it; that between the United States and the Soviet Union in the acquisition of nuclear weapons is one of the most recent. It is the feature of the nuclear age whose effects are most tangible, having produced thousands of giant intercontinental-range ballistic missiles sunk in concrete bunkers in the heartland of each country, hundreds of jet airplanes capable of transoceanic nuclear bombing excursions, and tens of thousands of assorted nuclear-capable rockets, aircraft, and artillery of lesser range, as well as thousands of nuclear explosives that these vehicles can deliver. The competition in acquiring these weapons is probably the longest-lasting in history. Its root causes, however, are the same as for all previous arms competitions: Anarchy promotes political rivalry and both breed insecurity, which encourages self-strengthening, which in turn often becomes a competitive exercise – a nonviolent version of, as well as a preparation for, open warfare. The advent of nuclear weapons has led to one of the oldest and most familiar features of international politics – an arms race.

Arms races, then, are recurrent features of international politics. But they have occurred more often since the latter part of the nineteenth century[3] than they had before. The reason for their increased frequency is the industrial revolution. The arms competition between the United States and the Soviet Union is itself an industrial (as well as a nuclear) arms race, because nuclear armaments are industrial products.

Here, a difference between the nuclear revolution in warfare and the Napoleonic and mechanical military revolutions that preceded it is important. In the two earlier cases a revolution in social life took place, of which the military revolution was a part. The harnessing of nuclear energy was equally momentous for war and diplomacy. Its nonmilitary effect, however, has been comparatively small. Nuclear weapons have changed international politics, as the sources of the previous two military revolutions did; nuclear energy has not changed the world.

Behind the Napoleonic revolution in warfare lay the democratic revolution in Western society, which marked the rise to political importance of the common man, as distinct from the nobles and the clergy. The French Revolution replaced the subject with the citizen, who claimed the full complement of political rights, most notably the right to participate in political life. An army of citizens made possible Napoleon's conquests, and the French army, in turn, spread the message of democracy across Europe and beyond. The old regimes tried to stem the democratic tide, setting up, among other things, the nineteenth-century balance of power system as a barrier against it. In the end they were overcome and swept away.

In our time the democratic revolution has triumphed, at least rhetorically. The people are almost universally proclaimed sovereign. Self-government has become a reality in many parts of the world, and is a slogan virtually everywhere. No regime any longer defends inequality, although many practice it. Even those governments that give their people no say in politics concede that they owe them a certain standard of well-being. And even the least liberal regimes recognize that they need more from their people than passive acquiescence in their rule, if only to reap fully the benefits of the second great upheaval in human society, one of whose consequences was a military revolution – the industrial revolution.

The second revolution was an even greater earthquake in human affairs than the first. The democratic revolution altered the way many political communities were governed. The industrial revolution affected the daily habits of a large fraction of the planet's population. It changed where people lived, how they worked, and what their world looked like. It pro-

duced the greatest change in human existence since the Neo-
lithic age, when packs of hunters and gatherers gave way to
agricultural settlers.[4] The industrial revolution involved "the
substitution of machines for human skill and inanimate power
for human and animal force."[5] It was not, and is not, an isolated event, but an ongoing process. The history of the industrial revolution is the history of one industry rising to serve as
the engine of the economy and then giving way to another:
textiles, iron, steel, chemicals, and electronics. It is also the
history of successive kinds of power sustaining these industries: wood, steam, coal, hydroelectricity, oil, and most recently, nuclear energy. So, nuclear power is simply the most
recent stage in a progression that stretches back almost two
centuries. Nuclear weapons, relying as they do on nuclear
power and on sophisticated electronics, are the latest in the
sequence of industrial products.

Outside the military realm the uses of nuclear energy have
so far proved limited. Controlled fission and fusion constitute
a revolution in international politics like those that emerged
from the Napoleonic wars and from World War I. In nonmilitary terms, however, in its effect on social life within political
communities, nuclear energy is simply another stage of the
industrial revolution.

Evidence of the industrial character of the nuclear arms race
is its marked resemblance to a previous competition in armaments in the industrial period, between imperial Germany and
Britain in the construction of capital ships – that is, large bat-
tle-ships – in the years leading up to World War I. Next to the
American–Soviet rivalry this is the best-known of all arms
races.[6] Like the ship-building competition between Athens
and Sparta, the two industrial arms races had their roots in the
anarchical structure of the international system. All three
grew out of political rivalries. Just as Sparta set out to challenge Athenian domination of the sea in ancient Greece, so
Britain and the United States were the leaders, and Germany
and the Soviet Union the challengers, in their respective arms
races – although the first challenge, unlike the other two, com-
menced after war had been declared. Both industrial competi-

tions, moreover, were formally arms races; each country officially geared its weapons programs to match the arsenal of its rival. In fact, three of the four competitors assembled their arsenals according to a specific formula that calculated military adequacy in terms of the dimensions of the opponent's arsenal, a formula that was the equivalent for each arms race of a formal declaration of war.[7]

A comparison of the Anglo–German naval rivalry and the nuclear arms race demonstrates the effect of nuclear weapons on one of the commonest features of politics among sovereign states – competition in weaponry. The similarities between them testify to the extent to which the nuclear revolution has *not* changed international politics, but rather has simply brought another industrial innovation to weaponry. The differences between the two, specifically the differences in the outcomes of the two political rivalries that spawned them – war in the first instance, the avoidance, so far, of war in the second – show how nuclear weapons *are* different from all other armaments.

Both the American–Soviet and Anglo–German competitions were industrial arms races first of all in that the weapons the rivals competed to build were machines. The heart of the industrial revolution was the triumph of the machine. Machines, like democratic ideas and institutions, had of course existed long before the nineteenth century. There were windmills before there were steam engines, just as the citizens of ancient Athens controlled their city's destiny long before the French assembly seized power from Louis XVI. There were even formidable machines of war centuries before the industrial revolution.[8] Only then, however, did the superiority of the machine become a fact of daily life. Machines that could perform a wide variety of tasks, including the tasks of warfare, far better than men could without them became available in vast numbers.

War has always had four parts: the operational, the social, the logistical, and the technical.[9] In the eighteenth century the first was paramount. The best-drilled troops and the field commander displaying the highest tactical virtuosity usually won the day. Napoleon shifted attention to the second part. He put an entire society in arms and, fired with the fervor of revolutionary belief, that army subdued most of Europe. Napoleon's legacy to the nineteenth century was the mass army. The European powers began to conscript citizens into their armed forces and to worry about their comparative rates of population growth. The industrial revolution made the last aspect of war crucial. Technology became the dynamic element. Industrial backwardness increasingly appeared a dangerous handicap; it contributed to the defeat of Austria–Hungary and Russia in World War I.

Machines were adapted less quickly to military purposes than to other social tasks. The industrial revolution did not come with full force to warfare until 1914, more than a century after it had begun. Its uses were recognized sooner for war at sea than on land. Even navies, however, did not take note of its possibilities immediately. Through the first half of the nineteenth century the British Admiralty scorned steamships in favor of the familiar sail-driven vessels. By the last quarter of the century, however, industrial discoveries were being systematically applied to the building of warships.

There are further similarities between the nuclear arms race and the Anglo–German naval rivalry, which arise from the second principal feature of the industrial revolution. This is change, and change in a particular direction. Not just new sources of inanimate power, but increasingly large sources became available. Not just machines, but more and more powerful machines for bigger and bigger tasks came into use. Previously, progressive change had been sporadic and accidental. In the nineteenth century, for the first time, it became regular and predictable. The century's most important invention, as Alfred North Whitehead put it, was the method of invention.[10] The regularity with which existing machines were improved and entirely new ones created made for a characteristic industrial cycle: first a technological invention; then its application to some social task, like warfare, in the form of a new machine; and finally the displacement of this machine by a better one, as the pattern was repeated. This industrial cycle left a common imprint on both the Soviet–American nuclear competition and the Anglo–German naval rivalry.

The industrial arms races

Each arms race was both a quantitative and a qualitative contest. In each case, both sides strove both to deploy greater numbers of weapons than the other and to make technical advancements more swiftly. Each wanted both more and better weapons than the other.

The quantitative character of both rivalries stems from the first major feature of the industrial revolution, the supremacy of the machine. Machines reduced the importance of human skill in warfare. The shift from sail to steam-powered warships meant that adroitness at catching the wind no longer affected the outcome of battle at sea. The accuracy of a ship's guns came to depend less and less on the experience, steadiness of hand, and instinct of the gunner. In the nuclear period virtually all the human ingenuity goes into the design, and almost none into the use, of weapons. Nuclear war, should it be fought, might well be almost exclusively an exercise in the competitive pushing of buttons.

The tendency of technology to diffuse, and for one country to be able to imitate the technical achievements of another, means that the machines of war tend, over time, to be equally efficient. Victory goes not to the better fighters but to the better fighting machines; when fighting machines tend to be equally good, victory increasingly seems to belong to the side with more machines. Napoleon observed that God was usually to be found on the side with the bigger battalions. The industrial revolution made the side with more weapons even surer of the favor of Providence, and competitors in industrial arms races equipped themselves accordingly.[11]

The qualitative aspect of both the Soviet–American and the Anglo–German arms races springs from the second cardinal feature of the industrial revolution, the regularity of improvement. New models incorporating these regular improvements made existing warships and nuclear armaments obsolete, because less capable.

For navies at the end of the nineteenth century and the beginning of the twentieth, "the improved engines, powerful boilers, irresistible projectiles, and impenetrable armor of one year were relegated to the scrap heap of the next."[12] Progress was perhaps not quite that swift, and in neither arms race were older weapons simply discarded. But it is true that the technology of naval warfare changed almost as much between 1850 and 1900 as it had in the previous ten centuries. Dramatic improvements occurred in the propulsion of ships. When steam engines replaced sails, fleets gained in speed and maneuverability and became, for the first time, independent of wind currents.[13] The guns mounted on battleships became larger, with greater range, and had even more explosive projectiles to fire. Defenses against shells also improved. Ships acquired progressively thicker, tougher armor plating, but the means to shield a battleship against their fire did not keep pace with the improvement of naval guns.

In the nuclear age the fission bombs of 1945 gave way to fusion explosives less than a decade later, and both the United States and the Soviet Union devised ways to make these hydrogen bombs both vastly more powerful and more compact than the prototypes. The delivery vehicles for these bombs changed even more dramatically. Jet aircraft were replaced by ballistic missiles that could be fired either from land or from submarines patrolling the bottom of the ocean. In the 1970s the United States began to develop pilotless drones called "cruise missiles," which were not as technically elegant as ballistic missiles but which for that very reason were cheaper to produce and deploy in large numbers.

The regularity of technical improvement made both the Anglo–German naval rivalry and the Soviet–American nuclear race a series of numerical competitions within increasingly sophisticated categories of armaments: The sequence of quantitative arms races in each case made up a qualitative contest. The expectation that improvement would be regular gave each another common feature: what might be called the "innovation imperative." Each rival shifted its emphasis from old to new weapons as a matter of policy, no matter where the competition stood. The leader was as anxious to innovate as the challenger. Preemption is a logical tactic in an inevitably qualitative arms race. It did not become standard practice, however, until well along in the Anglo–German competition. The Royal Navy had followed, throughout the nineteenth century, the policy of always being the second to innovate, so as not to render existing ships obsolete unless absolutely necessary.[14] This policy assumed that technical progress would be gradual, and that if another navy introduced a technical refinement Britain would have ample time to match and surpass it.

The rapid progress in warships in the nineteenth century undercut these assumptions. In 1905 the British Admiralty decided to build the first all-big-gun battleship, the *Dreadnought*. Critics questioned the wisdom of erasing the advantage in warships that Britain had accumulated by introducing a ship that, because it surpassed all others in fighting potential, started the competition again from scratch. Sir John Fisher, the First Sea Lord, maintained in response that the *Dreadnought*-style ship was inevitable, and that by having it first Britain was gaining as much advantage as was available.[15]

By the time nuclear weapons arrived the innovation imperative was a matter of course. Some American scientists did suggest in 1950 that the United States *not* be the first to develop the hydrogen bomb. Their opposition was based not on the assertion that the Soviet Union could not soon fabricate a fusion explosive of its own, however, but rather on the hope that the Soviets would not do so; the belief that the United States should not create a weapon of such terrible destructive power; and the confidence that, because the already existing fission bomb was so mighty that even a Soviet lead in hydrogen explosives would not present a threat, the United States need not be the pioneer in this new kind of weapon.

The innovation imperative led to the reversal, for military machines, of the original industrial cycle. In that cycle, first an invention would appear, usually as the result of the skill, or luck, or both, of a solitary tinkerer; then somebody would grasp its usefulness for war; and finally there would be a new weapon for military use of it. By the third decade of the nuclear age the military in both the United States and the Soviet Union were specifying the missions that had to be carried out, and a small army of scientists and engineers was then setting to work to design the appropriate machines.

The regularity of innovation, and the consequent expectation that innovation would be regular, led to another characteristic common to both arms races: stage skipping. Because it was possible to see what needed to be invented it was possible to imagine the sequence of inventions, the order of the successive quantitative arms races that would make up the overall qualitative competition. Thus it became possible to skip stages in the sequence. The appeal of stage skipping to the challenging power is that it provides a shortcut to equality. For neither imperial Germany nor the Soviet Union was this easy to accomplish. The successive numerical competitions together made up a sequence precisely because each required a greater degree of technical skill and engineering experience than the one before. Nonetheless, both Germany and the Soviet Union did manage to skip stages, and so make their challenges more formidable. The advent of the *Dreadnought*-class battleship gave Germany the chance to compete with Britain on an even footing, and the Germans did try to match the British fleet from 1906 to 1912. Similarly, the Soviet Union did not bother to build a substantial fleet of intercontinental-range jet aircraft in the 1950s, as did the United States. Instead, they concentrated their efforts on perfecting ballistic missiles, and after launching the first earth-orbiting vehicle in 1957 they seemed to lead the United States in this weapon for a few years.

The anticipation of regular improvement and of preemption produced another common industrial feature of both arms races: the danger zone. This was a period when one side anticipated being dangerously inferior to the other, when the balance of forces was expected to be so unfavorable as to make the inferior power vulnerable to a knockout blow.

Military inferiority has never been a happy circumstance for the inferior state. The memory of the British attack on the Danish fleet in Copenhagen harbor in 1807, long before the industrial revolution came to naval warfare, haunted the Germans as they mounted their challenge. Inferiority became more dangerous in the machine age, however, for a number of reasons. It became more readily calculable; tactical virtuosity had less power to overcome it; machines were more capable of striking sweeping, crippling blows than preindustrial weapons; and finally, in an arms race, the period of inferiority was finite – knowing that it would eventually disappear, the leader might be tempted to strike while enjoying an advantage.

In 1908 the British feared that they were entering a danger zone, that the German schedule for building *Dreadnoughts* would put the Royal Fleet in jeopardy. In the late 1950s fear of a danger zone gripped the United States. Americans worried that the Soviet Union would achieve a decisive lead in ballistic missiles in the early 1960s.

Both fears proved unfounded. It was the challengers who faced severe difficulties. Both went about coping with inferiority in similar fashion. They resolved to build steadily to escape the danger zone. Their motives in both cases were initially unclear to their rivals and may in fact have been mixed. From 1897 to 1905 Germany ostensibly built capital ships according to the "risk" theory, which held that the capacity to damage, although not to defeat, the British fleet would bring Britain to terms, because even a victorious engagement with Germany would leave the Royal Navy weakened and vulnerable to France and Russia.[16] The risk theory may have been intended to camouflage the ultimate aim of parity.[17] Whatever Germany's true aims before 1905, afterward the *Dreadnought* made equality seem a feasible objective, and the realignment of European politics, with Britain forging ententes with France and Russia, made the risk theory irrelevant.

For a time in the 1960s, it appeared to some American officials that the Soviet Union had become resigned to having lesser numbers of nuclear weapons than the United States.[18] By the 1970s, however, for most purposes, the Soviets had caught up, and in a few categories of weaponry had forged ahead in numerical terms.

Achieving equality, both Germany and the Soviet Union realized at the outset of both arms races, would take time. Each tried to buy it in two ways. One was political dissembling. Each made gestures of friendship to its rival to try to mute the hostility between them. The Germans more than once began private discussions with the British without really intending to resolve their differences.[19] The Soviets periodically launched "peace" campaigns in the West in the late 1940s and early 1950s and tried to win support for banning nuclear weapons altogether. The other means of keeping the leading power at bay was a military strategy short of equality in armaments. For Germany this was the risk theory. In the first years of the nuclear arms race the Soviet Union was thought to hold Western Europe "hostage" to American nuclear restraint with its nonnuclear forces. The size of the Soviet army and its proximity to the European allies of the United States were regarded as a counterbalance to the American nuclear advantage.[20]

The presumption of regular innovation in weaponry, combined with the long periods required to manufacture elaborate industrial armaments and the swiftness with which these armaments could strike decisively, made for a final common feature of the Anglo–German and Soviet–American arms races: worst case planning.

In both arms races neither side could know how many weapons – how many capital ships or nuclear-equipped airplanes, missiles, and submarines – its rival intended to acquire. By the time the other's intentions became apparent in both instances, it might be too late to match them. The construction of weapons had to begin well before the appearance of the threat that they were designed to meet. Without knowing what it *would* do, it was natural to proceed on the basis of the worst that the other side in the arms race *could* do. Overestimates could, and did, lead to weapons in excess of what turned out to be required.[21] In 1909, under the impression that Germany had embarked on a secret program of accelerated battleship construction, the British Parliament voted a larger number of *Dreadnoughts* than had originally been authorized, only to discover that the Germans were proceeding at a more modest pace than had been feared.[22] Similarly, in the early 1960s the United States, anticipating a missile gap, built many more intercontinental ballistic missiles than were needed to match the numbers that the Soviets managed to deploy, in part because of previous fears that the Soviets enjoyed an advantage in these weapons.[23]

The democratic arms races

The democratic revolution also left its mark on the Anglo–German and Soviet–American arms races, for it reshaped the political systems that conducted them by broadening the base of politics. Since the French Revolution the number of people who have a say in the governance of many political communities has grown. Before the nineteenth century the decision for war and preparations to fight were the business of the monarch, or the few people who had charge of public policy. They commanded that soldiers be recruited and that bows, lances, cannons, and catapults be fashioned. Since then, two other sources of influence have arisen: organized groups, outside and lately even within the government, which seek to advance their interests; and the public as a whole, which is often politically inert but which can sometimes be galvanized on behalf of a particular cause and whose opinions, actual or potential, governments now habitually weigh.[24]

The democratic broadening of politics created restraints on the building of armaments.[25] The idea gained currency that weapons cause war and so should not be acquired. Other claims on public resources received political voice. The perennial public choice between guns and butter stems from the democratic revolution. The radical wing of Britain's Liberal Party at the time of the arms race with Germany regarded large naval expenditures as misappropriations of taxpayers' money, money that could otherwise support the cause of social reform. In budget debates these "economists" regularly clashed with the "navalists," who favored defense spending.[26] Democratic government permitted dissent on foreign policy. Both Germany and Britain in the first decade of the twentieth century harbored proponents of reconciliation, rather than naval competition, with the other.

Where the two great industrial arms races were concerned, however, the expansion of politics cut both ways. As well as developing resistance to the accumulation of armaments, the democratic revolution, in concert with the industrial revolution, created social forces that profited from, and therefore favored and encouraged, the construction of weapons, forces that affected both the Anglo–German naval rivalry and the nuclear arms competition. So each arms race was the product of three things: the competitive implications of the anarchical international system; the supremacy of the machine and the regularity of innovation that were the hallmarks of the industrial revolution; and the influence of the principal results of the democratic revolution, economic and political interests and public opinion.

In the United States, pressure to sustain the continuous manufacture of armaments comes from the armed services, whose existence is bound up with modern weapons. There is a tendency within ever-larger modern governments for "partial allegiances" to develop.[27] Different sections of the government, especially the military, press for generous allocations of resources for their own programs. Without ships the Navy loses its reason for being. Without airplanes and missiles the role of the Air Force shrivels. The services have lobbied for the production of the weapons that belong to them, with some success since 1945.[28] It is not only the military that behaves in this fashion. Nor is the tendency of the military to do so necessarily sinister, or improperly motivated. It is natural for people who have devoted their professional lives to a particular armed service to believe that its mission is crucial to the national welfare.

Political pressure to build weapons in the United States comes, as well, from the private industrial firms that produce them. Without military orders these firms would suffer financially; some depend on government patronage so heavily that they could not survive the loss of government weapons contracts. The aerospace industry is a good example.[29] The industrial revolution has created these interests in building weapons; the democratic revolution has opened political channels through which they can be advanced. The result, in the United States, is what has been called the "military-industrial complex."[30] How much influence the military-industrial complex has, how this influence compares with that of similar groups composed of different interests, and whether or not such influence as it wields subverts the public weal are all contentious and extensively debated questions. Whether it is good, bad, or neither, however, the American military-industrial complex is certainly not the first of its kind.

A British version preceded it by more than half a century. Capital ships rather than nuclear weapons were the armaments that the British military-industrial complex lobbied to promote. The Admiralty was skillful at putting forward the case for naval expenditures. Sir John Fisher, the First Sea Lord at the time of the *Dreadnought* decision, was especially adept at presenting the navy's point of view to Parliament and to the country. The British ship-building industry also pressed for high naval expenditures, both directly and through members of Parliament who represented districts where shipyards and ports were located.[31] Cities like Woolwich and Portsmouth, whose livelihood depended on the navy, played the same role in the British economy, and their elected representatives similar parts in British politics, as Seattle, the site of the Boeing Company, and St. Louis, the home of McDonnell-Douglas, in the United States. Both the British and American governments worried that slackening arms budgets would throw large numbers of men out of work.[32] (As with the American aerospace industry, orders from foreign countries to the British shipyards helped to keep them active.)

The German military-industrial complex before World War I was more formidable than the other two in that the German navy was a less logical and less popular part of national policy than the American nuclear arsenal or the British fleet. An international system of two major powers imposes strong pressures on each to become the rival of the other. Neither the United States nor the Soviet Union could easily have declined to compete with the other in building nuclear weaponry. The Royal Navy was vital to Britain's well-being because it knit together what was by the end of the nineteenth century the farthest-flung empire since Roman times, and because it served as a lifeline for the economy of the home islands, which depended upon selling manufactured goods abroad and importing raw materials and food.

Neither condition was relevant to Germany at the turn of the century. The international system had at least five major powers, and Germany traded mainly with other European states and had, in any case, done without any navy to speak of for centuries. When, twice in the twentieth century, the Germans *did* make a bid for empire, they turned east, over land. The British "economists," the parliamentary critics of the Admiralty's plans, conceded the importance of the fleet and even the necessity for British superiority over all other powers, quibbling only about the costs of naval construction and urging that the government try harder to reach some sort of accommodation with Germany. The opponents of naval construction in Germany, the Social Democratic Party, by contrast, stoutly resisted military spending of all kinds.

Much of the initial impetus for a German high seas fleet came from the navy, which was as interested in promoting its own special weapon as in opposing Britain.[33] Its success in building ships that challenged British predominance at sea was due in large part to the political skills of Admiral Alfred von Tirpitz, the father of the German battle fleet.[34] Tirpitz craftily guided naval authorization bills through a reluctant and suspicious Reichstag.[35] He won an important ally in the Kaiser, who became an enthusiast for capital ships. He received support, as well, from shipbuilders, the suppliers of the materials from which ships were made, especially steel, and the members of the Reichstag sympathetic to these industries.[36] On behalf of the German program of battleship construction, in short, there assembled a formidable version of the same coalition that promoted the manufacture of armaments in Britain before 1914 and in the United States after 1945.

The democratic revolution had less effect on the Soviet Union, a country that cannot be called democratic in the ordinary sense of the word, than on the other three participants in the two industrial arms races. The rhetoric of democracy is abundant there; popular participation in the governance of the country, however, is negligible. As for extragovernmental groups like the industrial firms that pressed for large military budgets in the United States, Britain, and imperial Germany, these not only do not exist – the state controls virtually all economic activity – they are considered illegitimate. The proletariat, according to Soviet doctrine, is the bearer of the interests of society as a whole; the Communist Party, and it alone, represents the proletariat.[37]

During Stalin's time Soviet practice appeared to conform to this doctrine. The government seemed monolithic, a pyramid with the dictator sitting at the top and brooking no independence below. In the twenty-five years after Stalin's death, signs of change appeared. Western interpretations of Soviet politics reflected these perceived changes. Whereas in the 1950s the "totalitarian" image held sway, in the 1960s the "Kremlinological" school of analysis, which posited differences among the top Soviet leaders – differences ultimately grounded in personal ambition but involving matters of policy as well – became popular. In the 1970s, Western students of the Soviet Union began to ask whether divisions within the government did not go deeper than the personalities of Politbureau members. They began to debate the extent to which the concept of interest groups – which has become so influential in the understanding of Western industrial politics and which applies to the military-industrial complexes of the United States, Britain, and Germany – has become relevant to the Soviet Union.[38]

The military is well placed to exert independent influence within the Soviet system. It is heavily represented in the upper echelons of both the Communist Party and the government. Since Stalin's death military affairs have become more complicated. Here the military has an advantage because, according to a careful study, it "seems to control far more of the information relevant to making policy in its specialized realm

than do its counterparts in the West."[39] Stalin could personally supervise the design of weapons, the promotion of officers, and the tactics of battle. Even if he had had the political
authority to dominate military affairs in this fashion,
Brezhnev would not have had the technical expertise to do so;
he seems in fact to have had neither.[40]

There is reason to believe that the Soviet military has asserted itself. The choice between guns and butter is a particularly significant one for the Soviet Union. Such active loyalty
among the populace as the Communist Party commands
comes in large measure from its success in raising living
standards. The components of the standard of living – consumer goods, housing, and food – compete for resources with
military production. Yet, despite some sweeping changes in
the allocation of resources – agriculture's share increased dramatically in the 1970s – the level of military spending has
remained high.

There is some direct evidence for the independent influence
of the military as well. Military leaders have publicly emphasized the need to devote a generous share of the national
wealth to armaments, and they have sometimes seemed to be
taking issue with civilian officials on this score, although the
Communist Party has traditionally given high priority to defense for its own purposes. Policy debates were sharper and
more open in the Khrushchev era than in the Brezhnev period.[41] Nonetheless, military publications in the late 1970s insisted on high levels of investment in heavy industry, the industrial sector vital to defense, and warned of the continuing
threat from Western imperialism even in an era of detente.[42]
Individual politicians may have made personal alliances with
military figures, offering assurances of a sympathetic hearing
for requests for defense expenditures and perhaps even personal advancement in exchange for support in the jockeying
for supreme political power. Khrushchev and Marshal Zhukov
seemed to have close ties; Brezhnev and Marshal Grechko may
also have struck up a special relationship.

Behind Soviet nuclear weapons programs, therefore, stand
groups that in some although by no means all ways resemble

the politicians, industrial managers, and military officials who encouraged the production of armaments in the United States, Britain, and imperial Germany. In the Soviet political system and for Soviet participation in the nuclear competition with the United States, the democratic revolution's second contribution to modern politics – public opinion – has had little effect. The differences in policy that do exist, the battles over the allocation of resources that are fought, remain within the narrow precincts of the party and the government.

In the United States since 1945 and in Britain before 1914, by contrast, public opinion did help to shape public policy. Regular elections made the public the ultimate repository of sovereignty. In both countries popular sentiment raised the level of arms production by reinforcing the tendency to worst case planning. In each country, the public became alarmed at the prospect of falling into a danger zone. The resulting outcry forced the government to build more weapons than had originally been planned.

In the United States the launching of Sputnik and the fear of a missile gap created a wave of public concern that John Kennedy rode to the presidency in 1960 but that impelled him, once in office, to authorize a larger increase in intercontinental ballistic missiles than the dimensions of the Soviet nuclear arsenal, which satellite reconnaissance had fixed precisely for the first time, seemed to warrant.[43] The British equivalent of the missile gap scare was the *"Dreadnought* panic" of 1909. Grim rumors floated through London that many more German capital ships were being built than had previously been suspected. Newspapers agitated for an accelerated British program of construction. The Liberal cabinet split on the issue, and from outside the government the Conservatives called for more ships. The number finally authorized went beyond what any of them had wanted. As Winston Churchill put it, "In the end a curious and characteristic solution was reached. The Admiralty had demanded six ships; the economists offered four. And we finally compromised on eight."[44]

Public opinion played a different role in Wilhelmine Germany. The imperial political system was a curious hybrid, part autocratic and part democratic, with a parliament grafted on to the Prussian monarchy. Rather than public opinion pushing the government to build more ships, the reverse was true: The government worked to drum up popular support for the fleet. Tirpitz orchestrated a campaign of naval propaganda.[45] A Navy League was created to inform Germans of the benefits of a high seas fleet,[46] and Tirpitz and others endeavored to shape public sentiment through the newspapers.[47]

The effort to win support for a program of naval construction had a larger purpose: The fleet was to serve as a symbol of national pride, and as a focus of support for the Kaiser and for imperial rule, with which it was identified. It came to be seen by its champions as a means of patching up the deep divisions in the German political system, or, failing that, of undercutting support for the Socialists. German armaments policy before 1914 was less the result of popular opinion than a tool for controlling it.[48]

The nuclear arms race

The nuclear arms race between the United States and the Soviet Union has been the product of the age-old competitive impulse that springs from the anarchical structure of the international system and the two great social revolutions that made modern society – and that, in doing so, touched off the first two modern revolutions in warfare. In this sense the advent of nuclear weapons has simply re-created the results of the mechanical revolution in warfare, as its similarities with the Anglo–German naval rivalry demonstrate. The Soviet–American nuclear competition and the Anglo–German naval rivalry have followed similar patterns because both were industrial arms races. Is there any way in which the Soviet–American contest is distinctively nuclear?

The two industrial rivalries have not had identical histories. The outcomes differ. Since 1945 the United States and the Soviet Union have reached negotiated agreements placing limits on their nuclear arsenals; before 1914 the Germans and the British, despite efforts to do so, failed to agree on limiting arms. The political rivalry of which the Anglo–German arms race was a part ended in war; this has not been true, so far, of the rivalry between the Soviet Union and the United States. What, if anything, do these differences owe to the special properties of nuclear weapons?

As they armed, each pair of adversaries talked about limiting their arms, both in public multinational forums and in private direct talks. Naval restraints formed part of the agenda of the 1907 Hague Disarmament Conference, which both Britain and Germany attended. The two sides held a series of bilateral discussions of matters outstanding between them, of which those arising from the mission of the British Minister of War, R. B. Haldane, to Berlin in 1912 held the most promise of success. All came to nothing. Similarly, representatives of the United States and the Soviet Union debated disarmament at the United Nations beginning in 1946 and then, in the late 1950s, met privately to try to find some formula for stopping the testing of nuclear weapons, without success.

The reasons for failure were the same in both cases. Neither side was willing to modify the political goals that had animated the rivalry in the first place. Germany was prepared to contemplate naval restraints, but only in exchange for British assent to German freedom of maneuver in Europe. The British were not willing to allow Germany to dominate the continent and insisted on naval supremacy, which not all Germans were inclined to concede.[49] Similarly, the first American disarmament proposal, the Baruch Plan of 1946, which would have placed nuclear weapons under international supervision, would have left the Soviet Union, which had not yet set off a nuclear explosion, at a disadvantage in relation to the United States. And the supervising body, if the newly formed United Nations was a precedent, would likely be dominated by the United States. The Soviet counterproposals, on the other hand, for disarmament without (or at least prior to) international control, for nuclear-free zones, and for nonaggression pacts would have given the Soviet Union, with its large non-nuclear army, the kind of military advantage on the European continent that the Germans had sought before World War I.

In historical perspective the paths of the two negotiations run parallel for a time, then diverge. The United States and the Soviet Union concluded a series of formal arms control accords, beginning with the Limited Test Ban Treaty of 1963 and including the Nonproliferation Treaty of 1968 and the Strategic Arms Limitation (SALT) accords of 1972 and 1979. Britain and Germany reached no such agreements.

What accounts for success in negotiations in the one case and failure in the other? One factor was the number of major powers in the international system. Because before 1914 there were several, Britain could not deal with Germany without taking into account the effects on Russia and France. The United States and the Soviet Union have each been freer to bargain with the other than Britain or Germany were because no other member of the international system approaches them in power and therefore in importance.[50]

The world's principal maritime powers did finally join in a comprehensive agreement to limit capital ships, but this took place *after* World War I. The United States, Britain, France, Italy, and Japan subscribed to the Washington Naval Treaty of 1922 and the London Treaty of 1930. Each signatory was assigned a tonnage total, and the quotas varied from nation to nation. Britain and the United States were allotted more than Japan, which in turn had the right to a larger fleet than Italy.

Two conditions prevailed after 1918 that had been missing before. The technology of battleships had become familiar. As long as the potential of a new technology is uncertain there is likely to be a reluctance to constrain weapons that use it.[51] The post-World War I naval accords did not ban the newest kind of fighting ship, the submarine, as Britain had hoped they would. Similarly, by 1963 atmospheric testing, which was prohibited by the Test Ban Treaty of that year, had become unnecessary for the improvement of the American and Soviet nuclear arsenals. The first SALT agreements did not cover multiple warheads, which were just being deployed, and the second placed only loose restraints on the most recently developed weapon, the cruise missile. The obsolescence, or at least the familiarity, of a weapon seems to be a necessary condition for agreements to limit it. To put it another way, one quantitative stage of a qualitative arms race can be circumscribed when the contestants have moved on to the next one.

Furthermore, whereas Britain and Germany had been political adversaries, the parties to the Washington Treaty were not. They had been allies in World War I. Neither Germany nor the new Bolshevik regime in Russia, the two international outcasts of the immediate postwar period, signed the treaty. It was possible to agree on armaments because there was rough agreement on the political issues on behalf of which armaments might be used.

Since 1945 the United States and the Soviet Union have never reached the kind of political consensus that united the signatories to the two naval treaties after 1918. They have, however, found grounds for nuclear accommodation despite the deep political differences that divide them. Three common interests have formed the basis for the arms control agreements that they have signed.[52]

One has been the avoidance of war. The formal accords that they have concluded have served as vehicles for expressing their common resolve to cooperate at least far enough to avoid catastrophe.[53] The presence of this common incentive for negotiated agreements after 1945 and its absence before 1914 no doubt have something to do with the toll in lives and resources that a nuclear war would take. World War I, however, was itself enormously destructive. So the timing of the pertinent military revolutions was as important as, perhaps more important than, the differences between the principal weapons of the day. The dimensions of the nuclear revolution were apparent in August 1945, whereas the import of the industrial revolution was not fully understood until after August 1914.

Another interest common to the United States and the Soviet Union that their nuclear agreements have served to promote is nonproliferation. The Test Ban Treaty and the Nonproliferation Treaty were designed, indirectly in the first case and directly in the second, to keep nuclear weapons from countries that did not already possess them.[54] The absence of a comparable common interest before 1914 may be due, however, not only to the extraordinary power of nuclear armaments but also to the structure of the international system then and now. Nonproliferation is, among other things, an exercise in the preservation of bipolarity. Before 1914 there was no bipolarity to preserve.

The third common interest that underlies the arms control agreements that the United States and the Soviet Union have signed is the relationship of "mutual assured destruction," wherein each has and understands that the other has the capacity to devastate the other beyond all precedent even after absorbing the most powerful initial blow that the other can strike. Each holds the society of the other hostage to its good behavior. The 1972 treaty prohibiting the deployment of antiballistic missile systems ratified this relationship, and by signing it both sides implied that they regard it as the basis of stability. Bipolarity lends itself to this relationship. So, too, does the main feature of nuclear weapons – extraordinary destructive power, enough power to give each side the ability to inflict damage that will be unacceptable to the other no matter what the attendant circumstances. In this sense the fact that the Soviet–American rivalry is a nuclear arms race has contributed to the agreements they have reached to regulate it. The extraordinary force of nuclear weapons, and the stable relationship on the basis of a mutual assumption of a devastating response to an attack that this makes possible, have also contributed to the second difference between the two arms competitions: war in 1914 and the absence of war, so far, since 1945.

As with their attempts at cooperation, the conflict between each pair of rivals runs parallel up to a point, then diverges. After the initial challenge a series of crises unfolded in each case. The mutual suspicion between Britain and Germany rose a notch after the first Moroccan crisis in 1905, and then again after the Austrian annexation of Bosnia and Herzegovina in 1908, the Agadir incident of 1911, and the Balkan wars of 1910 and 1912. It boiled over in the fateful crisis of July 1914, which began when Serbian nationalists assassinated the Austrian Archduke Franz Ferdinand. Austria first made a series of demands on Serbia and then declared war. Russia mobilized to protect its Balkan ally. Germany struck to support Austria. Finally, when it was certain that Germany would not only fight but would attack Britain's tacit ally, France, by marching through Belgium, whose independence Britain was party to guaranteeing, the British entered the war.

A comparable sequence of events stretches forward from 1945: the collapse of the American-sponsored Baruch Plan for the international control of atomic energy; the forcible incorporation of Eastern Europe into the Soviet orbit; the civil war in Greece; the blockade of Berlin; the North Korean attack; the Hungarian uprising; Suez; Berlin again; and finally the gravest moment of all, the Cuban missile crisis of 1962, when the United States discovered that the Soviet Union was setting up nuclear-capable ballistic missiles in Cuba, demanded that they be removed, and placed a naval blockade around the island that was lifted only when the Soviets agreed to withdraw them. The missile crisis was similar to the July 1914 crisis in that although neither was a direct attack by one rival upon the other, both were provocations by the challenger that turned into tests of will from which graceful exits were difficult to find. In both crises, troops were mobilized and diplomatic messages exchanged.

War broke out in 1914 and not in 1962. All other things being equal, the Soviet–American conflict seems likelier, in retrospect, to have led to warfare than the one between Britain and Germany. Wars, after all, grow out of political rivalries, and the rivalry between the United States and the Soviet Union was fiercer, the rift between them deeper, the common ground between them narrower than was the case for Germany and Britain. The British and the Germans had been allies in the still-remembered past. So had the United States and the Soviet Union, and even more recently, but important sectors of public opinion and members of the governing classes in both countries were well disposed toward the other, which was not true for the Soviet Union and the United States. The Kaiser was even related to the British royal family. Far fewer common bonds linked the United States and the Soviet Union. Their mutual ideological animosity ran deep. Nor did the assassination of the Austrian Archduke and the events that followed necessarily constitute a graver provocation than the emplacement of Soviet intermediate-range nuclear-capable ballistic missiles ninety miles from the Florida coast. The American government gave every indication of being willing to go to war over the Cuban missiles. As late as the end of July 1914, Lord Grey, the British Foreign Secretary, was trying to mediate the dispute that the assassination had touched off. He had little thought of becoming involved on one side of it.

The weapons that the two sets of rivals competed to acquire played different roles when peace hung in the balance. In the July 1914 crisis the European powers scarcely gave a thought to capital ships. The naval race had in fact subsided two years earlier, when Germany had turned its attention to continental matters. Britain's naval superiority proved decisive at the very end of the war, when a blockade helped to bring about the final German collapse, but it hardly mattered before 1918. The one important naval engagement of World War I, the Battle of Jutland, confirmed British mastery of the seas, but Germany almost won the war all the same; indeed, the Germans did win the war in the east. In great power crises since 1945, by contrast, nuclear weapons have never been far from the thoughts of the American and Soviet leaders. The Cuban missile crisis unfolded in an atmosphere of nuclear-induced foreboding and mortal dread. Both sides maneuvered to avert open warfare, and each signaled to the other its wish to keep the shooting from starting.[55]

So the power of nuclear armaments helped to keep the peace after 1945, whereas battleships played no such role before 1914. Here again, however, the contrast may be due not so much to differences in destructive power between the two types of weapons as to differences in the timing of two military revolutions: the mechanical coming in full force only after World War I had begun, the nuclear before World War III could commence. If the German Chancellor Bethmann-Hollweg, Lord Grey, and other European leaders in the summer of 1914 had been as clear about the devastation that the war they were starting would unleash as Kennedy and Krushchev were of the consequences of war between them in 1962, the outcome of the July crisis might more closely have resembled the *dénouement* of the missile crisis.

There is, however, one clear and relevant difference between the industrial armaments the British and the Germans competed to acquire and the industrial but also nuclear weapons the United States and the Soviet Union have raced to build. They have affected differently the underlying political rivalries. At first each arms race exacerbated political relations between the nations involved; neither leading power was happy to be challenged. Ultimately, however, the two competitions in weaponry had opposite effects. The naval challenge from Germany was one of the principal causes, perhaps the most important cause, of the realignment of European politics at the beginning of the twentieth century that saw Britain move closer to France and Russia, and ultimately to treat the ententes with these two countries as virtual alliances – a realignment without which a world war might not have begun in 1914.[56] The nuclear competition has had a less inflammatory impact on Soviet–American relations; it has in some ways had a pacifying effect. The reason has to do with the basic difference between the perceived political purposes of capital ships before World War I and of nuclear weapons after World War II. The purposes of the first were, or at least appeared at the time to be, offensive; the second have come to seem, in general, inherently defensive. Germany's high seas fleet was a tool for upsetting the international status quo; the Soviet and the American accumulation of nuclear armaments have increasingly, with some exceptions, appeared to be instruments for preserving it.

In World War I the mechanical revolution in warfare favored the defense. Hundreds of thousands of soldiers died struggling for possession of a narrow strip of territory in northern France. Before 1914, however, mechanical military developments seemed to favor the offense. In the wars of German unification one of the two principal innovations in land warfare, the railroad, made swift victory possible. The other major innovation, the machine gun, was preeminently the weapon of conquest, enabling Europe to bring all of Africa and much of Asia under its rule.[57]

If the mechanical revolution in land warfare appeared to improve the odds of the attacker, its effects at sea, where the machine age came sooner in full force, seemed even more emphatically advantageous to conquest and expansion. Naval battles with modern ships produced sweeping victories in the Sino–Japanese War of 1895, the Spanish–American War of 1898, and the Russo–Japanese War of 1905. Moreover, in each of them a state without a history as a great power but one that had assiduously applied the fruits of the industrial revolution to naval warfare defeated a traditionally great but industrially backward nation. Their navies achieved for the United States and Japan what Germany wanted – empires won from historic great powers.

Germany in fact regarded a first-class navy as an instrument of imperial expansion. The Germans took to heart the writings of the American naval officer Alfred Thayer Mahan, whose best-known book, The Influence of Sea Power Upon History, attempted to demonstrate that great empires had usually been founded on, and the important wars won by, naval supremacy, or at least that sea power had had greater importance than was ordinarily assumed.[58]

Maritime supremacy meant "command of the sea," which entailed control of the major sea lanes through the capacity to destroy or to blockade – to defeat or to deter – rival navies.[59] Before the days of submarines and combat aircraft, command of the sea belonged to the nation with the most powerful fleet of battleships. So the German decision to acquire a high seas fleet could only be interpreted by the British as a bid to wrest command of the sea from the Royal Navy.

Still, countries other than Germany were constructing fleets of capital ships in the first decade of the twentieth century. The navies of both Japan and the United States were growing. The British were not particularly happy about these naval programs but were able to accommodate them in a way that was not possible for the German battleships. For if, in 1914, industrial weapons in general and industrial navies in particular seemed threatening, a German industrial fleet posed the greatest threat imaginable to Britain. Command of the sea, indeed the projection of any sea power at all, depended in the first instance on control of the home waters; without it a fleet would not be able to leave its home port. For Germany and Britain – and this was the crucial point – the home waters were the same, the North Sea.[60]

Either Britain or Germany could control the North Sea, but not both. So security in maritime terms for one meant insecurity for the other. Their naval contest was, to use a phrase that has become popular in the study of strategic affairs since 1945, a "zero-sum game." One side's gain was automatically the other's loss. For Britain, the loss of the North Sea would have put the empire and the trade routes – that is, the nation's supreme interests – at risk. This the British could not afford to do.

Because it improves the deterrent and therefore defensive capacities of both sides, the Soviet–American nuclear arms race, by contrast, has become a "positive-sum game." The goal of assured destruction, the capacity to inflict devastating punishment in reply to any attack, is available to *both* sides. Security is defined in such a way that both the United States and the Soviet Union can achieve it. Before 1914, the more ships Britain and Germany built the more likely it seemed to each that the other would use them to advance its own and subvert the other's interests. Since 1945, the more nuclear weapons each has accumulated, the less likely, on the whole, it has seemed that either would use them.[61]

In this sense, the sense that it has given each side the capacity for assured destruction and so promoted a stable relationship between the United States and the Soviet Union, the nuclear competition has a final feature that sets it apart from all previous arms races. All others have ended and ordinarily, in one of two ways. Either war has broken out, or the political relations underlying the arms competition have shifted, through reconciliation or a change in alliance partnerships.[62] By making each side too powerful – because too secure in the where-withal for retaliation – for the other to attack, the nuclear arms race has prevented war. It has frozen political relations between the United States and the Soviet Union as well. The growth of their respective nuclear arsenals has forestalled reconciliation by giving each the means to resist the threats of the other, and has made alliance switches less important than in the past by keeping the two more powerful than any third country. Without the customary ways of ending it the nuclear competition continues, a series of quantitative contests in nuclear explosives with increasingly diverse and sophisticated – that is, qualitatively different – delivery vehicles. In this way the nuclear arms race, because it is nuclear, is self-perpetuating.

5

Arms Competition: The Nuclear Arms Race and Tariff Competitions

Optimizing doctrines

The United States and the Soviet Union have each accumulated weaponry with an eye on the other's nuclear arsenal for the same reasons that have underlain previous arms races: They have had different and opposed political goals and have regarded nuclear weapons as useful for reaching, and for preventing the other from reaching, those goals.

The pattern of rivalry between the two nuclear giants has had features common to other industrial arms races, notably the Anglo–German competition in capital ships before World War I. So far, the Soviet–American political rivalry has stopped short of war, unlike the rivalry between Britain and Germany before 1914, in part because of the nuclear character of the Soviet–American arms race. Its nuclear character has also helped to make the competition between the United States and the Soviet Union, unlike previous ones, self-perpetuating.

The Soviet–American arms race has another property, stemming from the unprecedented destructive capacity of nuclear weapons, that runs counter to its self-perpetuating character and sets it apart even more dramatically from all other arms races in all of recorded history. That property is a logical stopping point. The American government has reckoned that it needs to be certain of being able to inflict a certain amount of damage in response to Soviet aggression in order to prevent such aggression. The capacity to inflict that much damage is

117

the standard that the United States has adopted for effective deterrence. It has been given the name "assured destruction." Assured destruction has two singular features that make it a logical point for both the United States and the Soviet Union to stop acquiring nuclear weapons.

First, as a standard it is absolute. The capacity for assured destruction not only represents more destructive force than any country has ever had before, it represents the point beyond which additional destructive force simply serves no purpose at all. The United States set the requirements for assured destruction at the annihilation of between a fifth and a third of the Soviet population and between half and three-quarters of the Soviet industrial capacity. Why did American officials choose these particular figures? It was not just that they believed that "amounts of damage substantially below those levels might not suffice to deter irrational or desperate leaders"; they also saw that "beyond these levels very rapidly diminishing damage would be achieved for each additional dollar invested."[1] Up to those levels, nuclear destruction was relatively cheap. Beyond them, it looked expensive. In theory the capacity to destroy 80 percent of the industrial facilities of the Soviet Union might deter what the ability to lay waste to only 75 percent would not. Beginning in the mid-1960s however, the American government assumed that 75 and even 50 percent was adequate.[2]

Nuclear weapons beyond those required to ensure the requisite levels of damage are, by the terms of this standard, of no military or political value. This is not to say that the Americans assumed that the capacity for assured destruction would by itself keep the Soviets from doing anything nasty or threatening; rather, they believed that the ability to inflict the designated levels of damage would prevent everything that could be prevented by *nuclear* threats. More deterrence might be available, but more *nuclear* weaponry could not purchase it.

As a military capability, moreover, assured destruction is more or less unassailable; that is its second cardinal feature. Neither the United States nor the Soviet Union has any hope of undercutting the other's capacity for destroying appreciable portions of its society. There are two ways that either might do so. One is to launch a preemptive strike, crippling the adversary's nuclear weapons before they can be used. The fleets of nuclear-equipped submarines that both sides field prevent this. A surprise attack might conceivably knock out the land-based missiles of either side and catch the bomber aircraft assigned to targets in the other country on the ground. Submarines are a much more elusive quarry. They patrol the vast regions of the world's oceans. They are difficult to hit because difficult to detect. Without a breakthrough in the techniques of antisubmarine warfare neither side could prevent the submarine force of the other from delivering a blow of devastating, unprecedented proportions.[3]

The other way to deprive the adversary of the capacity for assured destruction is to be able to intercept incoming nuclear explosives. This is a formidably complicated task. Even a few nuclear weapons, even one, could take an enormous toll in lives and property should they (or it) strike either the United States or the Soviet Union. Could either great power ever construct defenses against incoming missiles that could offer substantial protection in wartime? The question is difficult to answer. Since 1972 it has been moot. In that year the two countries signed a treaty renouncing systems of ballistic missile defense.[4]

If either preemption or defense were possible, each side would have an incentive to continue building its nuclear stockpile beyond the level necessary for assured destruction: to have enough explosives to destroy the other's arsenal, to survive an attack, or to saturate systems of defense. Because preemption is technically infeasible and defense is illegal, neither side has such an incentive.

Once having provided itself with a nuclear arsenal powerful enough to kill half the population and devastate three-quarters of the industrial plant of the other, to use the upper ends of the specified ranges, neither the United States nor the Soviet Union stands to gain from having more nuclear weapons, according to this way of thinking. For nuclear weapons, to the question "how much is enough?" there is a definitive and final answer. Assured destruction is enough. Beyond it, as former Secretary of State Henry Kissinger once said, "the term 'supremacy,' when casualties will be in the tens of millions, has practically no operational significance."[5] Or, as a Soviet military officer put it, "when both sides possess weapons capable of destroying many times over all life on earth, neither the addition of new armaments nor an increase in their destructive power can bring any substantial military – and still less political – advantage."[6]

By the logic of assured destruction, the United States and the Soviet Union should have expanded their nuclear arsenals as rapidly as possible until they reached the capacity for assured destruction, and then stopped. Below the level of assured destruction nuclear superiority may bring real advantages and inferiority may pose genuine risks. Above this level, both sides are beyond disadvantage, beyond danger, at least so far as these depend upon nuclear weapons.

Here the nuclear competition has no parallel in any arms race of the past. All other kinds of armaments are infinitely fungible, in the sense that they can always be put to military use.[7] The natural stopping point that assured destruction provides suggests a different kind of comparison, with the movement of commodities across national boundaries – that is, with international trade.

International economics and international politics have marked similarities. Factors of production move freely within but not between sovereign states; similarly, governmental authority is exercised within but not between states.[8] The purpose of authority is security; the purpose of economic activity is welfare.[9] Armaments are agents of security; trade is an agent of welfare. For each there is an "optimizing doctrine," which prescribes levels of armaments and trade that will yield the greatest possible security and welfare, respectively.[10] For armaments it is the doctrine of assured destruction. For trade it is the doctrine of comparative costs, or comparative advantage.

The doctrine of comparative costs holds that with an international division of labor each state should throw open its borders to goods from all others. Assuming that each state specializes in the goods for the production of which it has the greatest comparative advantage or relative efficiency (even if it is absolutely less efficient than all other states in producing all goods), all states will benefit if goods flow freely across national boundaries. Moreover, if nation A puts obstacles in the way of goods from nation B, B is still better off welcoming all that A wishes to export than retaliating in kind. By imposing a tariff in response, B simply further diminishes its own well-being (as well as A's.)[11]

The theory of comparative advantage was first demonstrated in 1817 by the English economist David Ricardo. For purposes of illustration he assumed an economic universe composed of only two countries, England and Portugal, and of two products, wine and cloth. The theory has been shown to hold true, however, for all countries and all products. The doctrine of assured destruction, and its implications for the acquisition of nuclear weaponry, may not be so plainly applicable to more than two states. But there are, for the moment at least, only two for whom assured destruction is relevant. The universe of nuclear powers, for these purposes, includes only the United States and the Soviet Union.[12]

The doctrines of assured destruction and comparative costs are optimizing doctrines not only in the sense that they prescribe levels of tariffs and arms that are optimal from the point of view of security and welfare but because their prescriptions run counter to widely held ideas of how states become more secure and richer. The prescribed levels are *lower* than what the conventional wisdom has often judged desirable. Optimizing security and welfare, according to these doctrines, does *not* mean *maximizing* arms and tariffs. In most political communities, however, where arms and tariffs were concerned, more has been considered better. This has been so even for nuclear armaments and even since the doctrine of comparative costs was first presented.

So the parallel between nuclear weapons and international trade goes further: The prescribed level of armaments – what is necessary for assured destruction – and the prescribed barriers to trade – none – are regularly exceeded in practice. Despite Ricardo and his successors, the history of international economic relations in the nineteenth and twentieth centuries is studded with obstacles to the movement of goods across national boundaries. Similarly, although the point at which the requirements for assured destruction is satisfied is difficult to fix precisely, and although both the United States and the Soviet Union have undoubtedly approached the fulfillment of those requirements in conservative fashion,[13] by the end of the 1970s both sides had gone well beyond even a generous definition of those requirements in their nuclear acquisitiveness.

Why did they do so? Why has the nuclear arms race continued? Why, to put it another way, has the nuclear arms race been similar in this respect to arms races of the past when the special properties of nuclear weapons ought to have made it different? The history of international trade is instructive and pertinent. It is a far longer history than that of the nuclear arms competition between the United States and the Soviet Union. The circumstances in which tariffs have risen and fallen shed light on the forces that determine the dimensions of the nuclear arsenals that the two great powers deploy, and hence on the future of the nuclear arms race.

Competing doctrines

Why would a country impose a tariff knowing that, according to the doctrine of comparative advantage, this will reduce its own welfare? It might simply not accept the theory. Until Ricardo presented it, no one had heard of it. The body of "scientific" or "classical" economic thought, of which comparative advantage is a part, has come into being only in the last two hundred years. For the two previous centuries European governments were under the influence of an economic doctrine quite different in its implications from comparative advantage. This was mercantilism, which stressed the importance for a sovereign state of a surplus of exports over imports. European governments tried to sell as much and buy as little as possible abroad. Tariffs were among the devices they used to restrict imports. They believed that a nation's wealth depended crucially upon its supply of precious metals. The more of its goods a nation could sell to others, and the less it had to buy from others, the more gold and silver it would receive in payment.

Mercantilists believed, as one economic historian put it, that "the quantity of wealth in the world was a constant, and a country could gain only at the expense of other countries." By the lights of modern economic thinking they "grossly misunderstood the true means to and nature of plenty."[14] One reason for this misunderstanding was that mercantilist thinking took hold during the period of European history when war was not only a normal but a constant national undertaking. Without conscription and the extensive and generally reliable powers of taxation that modern governments possess, the size of a state's army depended on its supply of gold and silver. The larger the store of precious metals, the more soldiers it was possible to recruit and the better the state could therefore expect to fare in the continual rounds of warfare. War is inevitably a competitive enterprise, and because the importance of national wealth lay in its contribution to war, the accumulation of wealth became competitive as well.

"Mercantilism" may be defined as a doctrine that recognizes no fundamental difference between international politics and economics. Similarly, the strategic equivalent of mercantilism – the rejection of assured destruction as an absolute standard of nuclear adequacy – does not recognize the fundamental difference between nuclear weapons and all other kinds of armaments that the strategic optimizing doctrine, assured destruction, assumes.

In its purest form strategic mercantilism rests on the conviction that one side can deny to the other the capacity for assured destruction; that nuclear weapons, like all other weapons, can be used to "win" wars in the sense that the goals attained are in some kind of rough balance with the damage suffered.[15] This view had some currency in the early years of the nuclear age, especially in the ranks of the American and

perhaps also the Soviet, military. In the 1970s the treaty prohibiting defensive systems and the impressive dimensions
both arsenals had attained deprived it of much of its plausibil-
ity, and hence its appeal, although officials on both sides presumably still go about the task of making plans to win a nuclear war.[16]

A version of strategic mercantilism that is more widely
shared holds that, short of "victory" in a nuclear exchange,
asymmetries in the nuclear arsenals the United States and the
Soviet Union deploy can lead to significant political consequences even when both sides possess the capacity for the assured destruction of the other. The *ratio* of strategic nuclear
forces over and above the level of assured destruction, according to this version of the doctrine, does count. The United
States and the Soviet Union continue, after all, to be rivals.
Their rivalry has brought them in the past, and will likely
bring them again in the future, into confrontation with each
other. In a confrontation, in a moment of tension and uncertainty, one side may be able to draw some advantage from its
larger nuclear stockpile even if its rival has the undeniable
power to destroy a third (or more) of its population and half
(or more) of its industry.

Mercantilists believe that equality between the two strategic
forces matters, in the words of former Secretary of Defense
James Schlesinger, "for symbolic purposes, in large part because the strategic offensive forces have come to be seen by
many – however regrettably – as important to the status and
stature of a major power."[17] Either the opposing great nuclear
power or other countries might take conspicuous gaps in one
of the two giant nuclear arsenals as a sign of weakness, and act
accordingly.[18]

Strategic mercantilists worry not just about the overall appearance of the two principal nuclear forces but about specific
weapons and capabilities that they deem especially important
even where the capacity for assured destruction exists. The
wherewithal to destroy some of the other side's missiles in
their concrete subterranean bunkers – the capacity, that is, for
counterforce attacks – received particular attention in the sec-

ond half of the 1970s from Americans who credited the ratio of strategic forces above the level of assured destruction with political importance. Their concern arose from a particular "proportional" definition of deterrence, which held that "to be credible, and hence effective over the range of possible contingencies, deterrence must rest on many options and on a spectrum of capabilities."[19] In the 1950s and 1960s this definition lay behind suggestions that the North Atlantic Treaty Organization needed to muster enough nonnuclear force to thwart a Warsaw Pact attack in Europe without resorting to nuclear weapons. In the absence of adequate Western nonnuclear, or "conventional," strength, the argument went, a Soviet invasion could present NATO with the terrible choice of either accepting defeat or bringing nuclear weapons into play to stave it off, thereby risking Soviet nuclear retaliation. Similarly, the lack of a counterforce capacity on the American side could, according to Schlesinger, "bring into question our ability to deter limited and selective attacks."[20] The proponents of a graduated concept of deterrence in the 1950s and 1960s suggested that the Warsaw Pact might actually launch a nonnuclear attack on Western Europe; seizing the city of Hamburg was a popular scenario. Those who applied it to the balance of counterforce capacities between the two great powers in the late 1970s feared not so much that the Soviet Union would launch a sudden strike at the American land-based missile force as that the theoretical capacity to do so might give the Soviet Union "ways of exercising coercion and extracting concessions without triggering the final holocaust."[21]

Strategic mercantilism rests on the conviction that for nuclear weapons, as for all other kinds of armaments, more is better. If this is true, if more nuclear weapons are always useful no matter how many are already on hand, they are not useful in the same way that increments of nonnuclear armaments can be put to use. For all other weapons, the more a state has, the greater is its capacity both to defeat another, with whatever benefits – territory, treasure, influence – accrue from victory, and to defend its own country. The second, for nonnuclear armaments, is the automatic consequence of the first. A nonnuclear nation whose army is destroyed cannot harm the people of the victorious country.

With nuclear weapons at the level of assured destruction and beyond, this no longer holds true. The power to hurt another is divorced from the capacity to protect oneself. No matter how much damage country A inflicts on country B, B can still devastate A in return. A must depend on B's forbearance (which will be influenced by the fact that A can destroy B as well) for its safety. A's superiority in some category of weaponry, even though both possess the capacity for assured destruction, may discourage or demoralize or frighten B and pave the way for political or military gains on the part of A. But the protection that superiority can give in such situations is psychological, not physical. A counterforce war between the United States and the Soviet Union, for example, would be a contest of wills, because however effective the counterforce attacks that either managed to mount, the other would still have the capacity to deliver a crushing blow in return.[22] A nuclear war between the United States and the Soviet Union would be unlike any war in the past, not only because each side could damage the other far more extensively far more quickly than was ever before possible, but because either could inflict such damage *no matter what* the other side did. In all past wars force was used, sometimes exclusively, sometimes in part, to affect the enemy's *capacity* to fight; in a nuclear war (or a war of any kind) between two states with the means for assured destruction it would be used almost entirely to affect the enemy's *will* to fight.

Whether ratios of nuclear strength beyond what is required for assured destruction affect policy in wartime is a question for which there is no evidence, because there has been no war between the United States and the Soviet Union. On the effect of differences above the level of assured destruction in circumstances short of war the evidence is not conclusive. The Cuban missile crisis is often cited as evidence in favor of the truth of strategic mercantilism. The American nuclear arsenal was certainly larger than its Soviet counterpart in October 1962. The very size of the gap between the two, however, calls into question the relevance of the missile crisis. Both sides subsequently assembled so much more nuclear firepower than they had in 1962 that it is unlikely that either could achieve the same ratio of superiority that the United States then enjoyed. It is not at all clear that the Soviets had the capacity for the assured destruction of the United States.[23] Moreover, the outcome of the crisis was not unambiguously a victory for the United States. The Soviets did agree to withdraw their missiles from Cuba, but received concessions from the American side in return.[24]

If the arguments for additional nuclear weapons beyond those required for assured destruction are less firmly grounded than are those for superiority in other varieties of weaponry, however, the case for observing the optimizing doctrine is less compelling for armaments than it is for trade. The reason has to do with the difference between what is being promoted in each case: material welfare by trade and security in the case of nuclear weapons. The first can be readily measured, the second cannot. Assured destruction is further from being a positive law of politics than comparative advantage is of economics. An economist can characterize most economic arguments in favor of protection as "gross fallacies"[25] because he can give a mathematical demonstration of these fallacies. A strategist cannot validate the case for assured destruction and its implications with comparable precision. Furthermore, a country stakes more on its security than on its commercial policies. The costs of being behind if strategic mercantilism is right are likely to be higher than the price of free trade if economic mercantilism is valid. A state may become poorer in the second instance. It can cease to exist altogether in the first.

The combination of these two differences works in favor of accepting strategic mercantilism. Because its opposite, the optimizing doctrine, cannot be precisely demonstrated, and because the price of being wrong is potentially so high, it has generally seemed prudent to err on the side of caution and to risk possessing too many rather than too few nuclear weapons.

There is, moreover, an even more powerful argument in favor of strategic mercantilism: The other side believes in it. Belief in it may be misguided, even foolish. Nonetheless, because deterrence exists in the minds of those governing the state being deterred, for one side to give credence to strategic mercantilism makes it true. If A believes it to be true and accumulates more weaponry than B even though both have the capacity for assured destruction, and challenges B on the basis of this belief, B must meet the challenge no matter how erroneous the belief. Its psychological essence makes the requirements for deterrence a kind of elastic clause: The amount of force that is arguably necessary for deterrence in any particular situation may be infinite, depending only on how headstrong, foolish, or maniacal the party being deterred is taken to be. When A is the Soviet Union, where secrecy surrounds all official policy, particularly foreign policy – and most particularly foreign policy having to do with nuclear weapons – it is difficult to know what the reigning strategic doctrine is, and tempting to act on the assumption that it is strategic mercantilism.

The Soviets have plainly accumulated nuclear weapons in excess of the requirements for assured destruction. Americans have frequently ascribed this to a Soviet hope of drawing political profit from these weapons.[26] The Soviets, for their part, may believe that the doctrine of strategic mercantilism exercises a powerful influence in the United States.[27]

If each side believes that the other values nuclear superiority even above the level of assured destruction, then both may continue to build their arsenals in order to thwart the other, thereby confirming the other's perception. The result of such mutually reinforcing misperceptions is to push the two nuclear stockpiles higher and higher. It takes, however, only one communicant in the faith of strategic mercantilism to produce an arms race between two countries that already possess the capacity for assured destruction. The psychological character of deterrence forces the other to behave as if it were a believer even if it is in fact a skeptic.

There is another set of reasons why states might exceed doctrinally prescribed levels of armaments and tariffs. A state may accept the truth of the doctrine of comparative advantage but value other benefits more highly than achieving the greatest possible welfare. A state may decide that what it loses in welfare through a tariff is worth the concomitant gain in employment, redistribution of wealth, the allocation of resources, or government revenue.[28]

Ironically, each optimizing doctrine is most often violated in the name of the benefit that the other is supposed to promote. States depart from the practice of free trade for the sake of national security. They cannot, they say, afford to depend on foreigners for their steel, or petroleum, or computers, for that would risk being cut off in time of war and blackmailed in peacetime. Similarly, nuclear weapons are occasionally justified by the contribution that building them makes not to the nation's defenses but to its economy. Assembling them, and the intricate and expensive vehicles to deliver them, provides work for large industrial firms with thousands of stockholders and employees. These firms, and the armed services that have custody of the weapons in both the United States and the Soviet Union, have an interest in the ongoing deployment of nuclear armaments, and they habitually make their preferences known and felt in the political system of each country. As well as promoting the doctrine of strategic mercantilism, the military-industrial complex in both the United States and the Soviet Union contributes to the persistence of the nuclear arms race between them, despite the level of destructive power they both have achieved. Here, too, there is a parallel with international trade.

Competing interests

According to the doctrine of comparative advantage, a tariff diminishes the welfare of the state that imposes it (as well as the welfare of all its potential trading partners). Its net effect is to make each state poorer. But not every person or group within the state does worse as a result of a tariff; some do considerably better. By raising the price of the protected good, a tariff leaves most people slightly worse off than they would be otherwise, because they will have to pay more for the good in question. But the domestic firms in the protected industry benefit. With higher prices their profits rise. They can afford to produce more, and therefore they will hire more workers than if the good were available from abroad at lower cost. These workers, too, are obviously better off than they would be if foreigners, and not they, were employed to produce the good.[29] Tariffs work to the advantage of those with a direct stake in protected industries.

Their distributive effects are more important than their net impact in determining whether or not there are tariffs. Tariffs are set through politics. In politics, (at least politics in open societies), interests that are concentrated do better than those that are diffuse. Those who gain from them have stronger incentives to promote tariffs than have those whom tariffs penalize to oppose them. A tariff on steel, for example, may mean the difference between employment and joblessness for a steelworker. This is a considerable difference. For anybody else it means the far less cosmic difference of, say $10 in the purchase price of a new automobile. The sum of the $10 increases may exceed the total salaries of the steelworkers affected. But the lesser sum will be translated into greater political effect.

Those in the first group are intensely interested in a favorable outcome. They will ordinarily devote more time and money to getting their way than will those in the second group. The expression of time and money in politics is organization. In open political systems, organization is the vehicle for success. Organized groups have great influence upon the workings of government and the distribution of public resources. They lobby, they provide information, they offer support during political campaigns. Occasionally they employ the ancient practice of bribery. Those who have organizations advancing their interests usually do better than those who do not.

Security is not unevenly distributed, like welfare. It cannot be parceled out in different shares. Each citizen of the United States and the Soviet Union is equally protected against a foreign military threat by his country's nuclear arsenal. But the manufacture of nuclear weapons has an effect upon a nation's welfare as well as its security. The economic effects of the construction of nuclear weapons, including of course weapons that are superfluous for the purpose of assured destruction, like the consequences of tariffs, vary from person to person and from group to group. Most citizens reap no benefit. Those whose business it is to manufacture these armaments, however, realize substantial gains.

If the level of tariffs for every country and the level of nuclear weapons for the United States and the Soviet Union were decided by popular ballot in which each citizen had one vote and each understood and accepted the doctrines of comparative advantage and assured destruction respectively, the level of armaments and of tariffs would be lower than is the case for each. They are not decided in this way. No country sets its tariffs by a system of direct democracy, nor does the United States or the Soviet Union fix the dimensions of its nuclear arsenal in anything like this fashion. Both are shaped by the bargaining and compromise of politics.

Some of the champions of nuclear weapons in excess of what assured destruction prescribes have other than economic reasons for promoting their production. The armed services have organizational interests that the weapons serve – prestige and a wider role in the nation's defense. Similarly, firms sometimes favor tariffs not in order to increase profits but to maintain the integrity of the organization – by sustaining a high volume of production, for example. Lobbyists for tariffs play the same role for international economics that the two military-industrial complexes do in international politics.[30]

Political contests rather than the simple application of doctrine set the levels of tariffs and nuclear weapons. In neither case do pure optimizers alone face mercantilists and interest groups. Both kinds of political contests take place in the context of possible international agreements regulating the levels of armaments and tariffs. Where potential agreements are involved, the coalition for low levels is broader than where restraint must be unilateral.

Not every economist subscribes to a pure version of comparative advantage. Some have shown that there are circumstances in which a tariff can redound to the benefit of the state that imposes it. When that state has a large share in the trade of a commodity, for instance, a tariff may improve its terms of trade and therefore increase its welfare, although the net welfare of the international community will decline.[31] Whether or not a tariff is advantageous depends upon the commodity and the country in question.

A country almost never increases its own welfare with a tariff, however, if its trading partners retaliate with tariffs of their own. Then all are likely to be worse off than they would be if trade flowed unimpeded.[32] For two countries, therefore, three trading relationships are possible. One may impose a tariff whereas the other doesn't; neither may do so; or both may do so. Optimizing calculations might well favor a tariff in some cases where political reckoning would argue against this, on the grounds that other countries would reciprocate. A "conditional optimizer" would then favor the second relationship, on the grounds that trying to achieve the first would inevitably produce the third. Conditional optimizers' support for free trade – and especially for free trade *agreements* – stems not only from economic but from political calculations. Tariffs may not be counterproductive in theory, according to the conditional version of comparative advantage, but they are likely to be self-defeating in practice. The assumption of a reciprocal response to the erection of tariff barriers is well supported by the history of trade policies, especially in the twentieth century.

Although pure optimizers are willing to support free trade no matter what other countries do, conditional optimizers insist upon "multilateral tariff disarmament."[33] The conditional position has attained broad popularity since 1945. The existence of an institutional embodiment of a multilateral commitment to free trade, the General Agreement on Tariffs and

Trade (GATT), testifies to the acceptance that the conditional position has achieved.

There are few pure optimizers for nuclear weapons. It has occasionally been suggested that the United States confine itself to a nuclear arsenal of a few submarines carrying nuclear-tipped missiles, but the suggestion has never carried much political weight. One reason is that although a successful challenge to either side's capacity for assured destruction is not likely, neither is it wholly unimaginable. Improved techniques of antisubmarine warfare, of ballistic missile defense, of preemptive attacks on missiles and airplanes – or a combination of these – could conceivably make it possible for one side to "win" a nuclear war against the other. It is scarcely likely that this will happen, but both the Soviet Union and the United States have been inclined to hedge against it.

Strategic mercantilism is particularly appealing because the price that a country must pay if the doctrine is wrong – if superiority brings no benefit or if its rival reciprocates by increasing *its* arsenal – is not high. The worst that is likely to occur is an accelerated arms race. Nuclear weapons are so powerful that when both sides have the capacity for assured destruction neither is likely to be either confident enough, even on the basis of a favorable asymmetry in the two arsenals, or frightened and desperate enough, because of an unfavorable difference, to start a war. Strategic mercantilism holds that in a crisis, when events force a confrontation, the side with more weapons may enjoy an advantage in bargaining and maneuvering. Few mercantilists assert that more weapons produce eagerness for such confrontations. In a crisis the relative sizes of the two arsenals may tell. In normal circumstances the absolute capacities of both sides are forbidding.

As in the case of trade, conditional optimizers for nuclear weapons may accept the idea that superiority in nuclear weaponry even above the level of assured destruction can yield political dividends, but believe that superiority cannot be achieved in practice. Neither side, conditional optimizers assume, will permit the other to gain a quantitative advantage in weaponry. Each will build to match the other. The result of an attempt to gain an advantage, therefore, will be equality at a higher level of armaments. Neither side will be better off strategically, and both will be poorer.

As with trade, three relationships between two arms race competitors are possible where a particular weapon is concerned. One may have it and the other not; both may have it; or neither may have it. Conditional optimizers for nuclear weapons prefer the third relationship because they assume that trying for the first will produce the second. Not just strategic assessments but also assumptions about the behavior of states lie behind this preference.[34]

The conditional version of the optimizing doctrine for weapons has become, as it has for trade, popular enough to give rise to what is in effect a permanent forum for negotiation. For the first decade of their existence, however, the SALT negotiations involved only the United States and the Soviet Union. Their counterpart for trade, GATT, has had the participation of most of the countries of the industrialized West.

Both sets of negotiations, however, faced the problem of comparability. Because the Soviet and American arsenals are composed of different weapons in different combinations, it did not prove easy to equate them for the purpose of limitation. The SALT negotiations between 1972 and 1979 centered on just this task. Tariffs seem, on the surface, simpler and therefore easier to tally. The GATT deliberations, however, have in many cases been as complicated as the SALT talks. Tariffs on primary products, for example, affect the costs of secondary goods. A tax on flour raises the price of bread. The tariff rate on bread alone does not register its full social impact, which economists call the "effective rate of protection,"[35] and which is not always simple to compute. There are, moreover, numerous types of nontariff impediments to imports. These can be formal, like quotas, or informal, like business practices that discourage the merchandising of foreign goods.[36]

Tariffs, of course, are public in character, and the results of informal nontariff barriers become publicly evident. Nations often wish to keep their arms deployments secret. Satellite reconnaissance, however, has exposed the Soviet nuclear arsenal to American inspection. (The reverse is equally true.) Satellite reconnaissance as a means of monitoring compliance has in fact become the bedrock of arms control agreements, indeed the starting point for negotiations. What cannot be inspected cannot be formally limited. Where formal agreements are concerned, therefore, nuclear weapons are as visible as trade restrictions.

The level of nuclear armaments that the United States and the Soviet Union deploy, like the level of tariffs in open political systems, is determined by political contests in the context of international accords that restrain the levels of both. These contests pit similar contestants: pure and conditional optimizers on the one hand against mercantilists and interested groups on the other. The two parts of the mercantilist coalition certainly overlap. Members of the armed services often subscribe to the tenets of strategic mercantilism out of genuine conviction rather than hypocritical self-interest.

There are occasions when the two wings of the optimizing coalition may part company. Once committed to negotiations it is logical for a state to behave as if it subscribes to mercantilist principles; otherwise there is no point in bargaining to obtain concessions from the other side. One way to win concessions, to persuade the other side to put limits on a particular weapon, is to authorize and begin to deploy that weapon. This is known as the "bargaining chip" tactic. Country A starts to build weapon X to show country B that it will pay a penalty for failing to agree to control it, offering to cancel or limit the weapon if B agrees to do the same. A pure optimizer may oppose the tactic for fear that it will fail and that both countries will in the end deploy the weapon. According to the conditional version of assured destruction, this outcome is preferable to one in which B has the weapon and A does not. By the lights of the pure version, however, it is better to abstain no matter what the other side does. Such a disagreement arose over the Nixon administration's proposal to construct an antiballistic missile (ABM) system in 1969. Those who opposed

the ABM then joined with many of its proponents in support
of the 1972 treaty that prohibited the system for *both* the
United States and the Soviet Union.[37] Because tariffs are more
easily put up and taken down than arms can be deployed and
removed, the same tension is far less pronounced in free trade
coalitions.

A different issue sometimes divides pure from conditional
optimizers in both the international economic and international political arenas. This is the contention that agreements
do not, in the end, restrict the levels of weaponry or protection
very much because of the concessions that must be made to
pressure groups in both cases to form the political consensus
in favor of a formal accord.[38]

The mercantilist coalitions for both tariffs and armaments
are diverse. Those who belong to these coalitions want the
same *kind* of thing, but not precisely the *same* thing. Shoe
manufacturers, for instance, have no particular reason to want
protection for wheat. On the contrary, they stand to lose from
wheat tariffs because they are consumers of flour and bread.
Similarly, at least in the United States, the Air Force will want
one weapon and the Navy another. With limited resources
available their interests, on the face of it, conflict. Sometimes,
however, they form tacit alliances as they lobby for their pet
projects. Each agrees to support the other's requests and re-
ceives support for its own in return. This practice has a parallel in the way tariffs have been set in the United States. The
representatives of different industries have followed, toward
each other, a policy of "reciprocal non-interference: a mutual-
ity under which it is proper for each to seek tariffs for himself
but improper and unfair to oppose tariffs sought by others."[39]
This tactic has helped to make mercantilist coalitions formidable even when negotiated agreements for restraint are in prospect. What determines when those nogotiations succeed and
when they fail?

Political prospects

Ideas have lives and consequences of their own. They have a
way of capturing imaginations. People believe in them and act

on them. The doctrine of comparative advantage scarcely belongs among the most powerful ideas, but it has had some influence. Nations have traded freely because their leaders believed what Ricardo and others wrote about the benefits of free trade. The general lowering of tariff barriers in Europe between 1848 and 1873 was due in no small part, according to one historian, to the "strong, widely-shared conviction that the teachings of contemporary orthodox economists, including Free Traders, were scientifically exact, universally applicable, and demanded assent."[40]

The optimizing doctrine for nuclear weapons, assured destruction, has also influenced American public policy. Presidents and secretaries of state and defense have proclaimed American adherence to it and have geared the design of the American nuclear arsenal to its requirements – or at least have often tried to do so.[41] The loci of political support for both optimizing doctrines in the United States have been the central organs of the federal government. On trade matters the President has opposed protectionist economic interests; on armaments the President has bargained with the armed services.[42]

Comparative advantage has made political gains through its association, in the public mind, with other valued goals. In the nineteenth century an influential school of thought regarded commerce as the royal road to international peace. Today's economic optimizers do not believe as fervently in the connection between the two as did Richard Cobden and John Bright, free trade's foremost British champions, but the perception that the two are associated remains. Continental leaders in the mid-nineteenth century saw free trade as the means to more specific ends. Bismarck hoped that it would promote German friendship with France. Napoleon III sought to conciliate Britain with commercial ties.[43]

Free trade won acceptance in the United States after 1945 because it was bound up with widely and strongly held anti-communist feelings. It became an American article of faith that the economic and political systems of Western Europe had to be fortified to resist the challenge, from within and without, of communism. This required sacrifices from the

American people, first in the form of direct assistance, then by shipping American goods and opening American markets to the Europeans. A popular slogan of the time was "trade, not aid." By equating the two it suggested that trade with Europe entailed economic sacrifice for the sake of a larger purpose, just as foreign aid had.[44]

Arms control has been tied in public thinking to peace, although the substance of the agreements that the United States and the Soviet Union have signed has had little to do with the likely causes of war between them. Opposition in the United States to defense spending, including the building of more nuclear weapons, arose in the late 1960s and 1970s out of dissatisfaction with American participation in the Vietnam War, of which the defense budget became a symbol,[45] and the opposition translated into support for negotiated agreements. Although evidence on the point is scarce, the Soviet leaders may regard arms control agreements in the same light in which Bismarck and Louis Napoleon saw trade: a vehicle for the achievement of specific political purposes, notably the improvement of political relations with the United States.

Ideas do not spread in historical vacuums. Events, sometimes traumatic events, have lent urgency to both optimizing doctrines. Protectionism became identified in the public mind with the Depression of the 1930s. The beggar-thy-neighbor policies that the Western countries adopted to cure their common economic distress seemed in retrospect to have worsened it, and this helped to discredit the presumption that tariffs were good for national welfare. The decline of mercantilism after the eighteenth century was due not only to belief in the theory of comparative advantage but also to the belief that mercantilist policies led to war.[46]

Similarly, the shock of the Cuban missile crisis spurred the leaders of the United States and the Soviet Union to an energetic search for nuclear agreement that culminated in the Limited Test Ban Treaty of 1963. There is a sense in which the continuing fear of nuclear war, muted and even subconscious though it may often be, serves as the functional equivalent of a traumatic memory. Fear of nuclear war has certainly inspired the efforts to secure agreements on restricting nuclear armaments that began shortly after Hiroshima and have continued more or less constantly since then.

The politics of tariffs does not simply pit ideas against interests, altruistic optimizers against greedy protectionists. "A good cause seldom triumphs," John Stuart Mill once said, "unless someone's interest is bound up with it."[47] The cause of free trade has had interested proponents. Free trade coalitions have included not only convinced optimizers but those who profit from unrestricted commerce – who benefit from cheap imports or who want to sell abroad and fear that other countries may put up tariff barriers of their own.

States that outstrip their trading partners across the board in innovation and efficiency, and that therefore have a comparative advantage in a wide range of goods, will find free trade an attractive policy. Britain in the nineteenth century and the United States after 1945 fit this description. Ordinarily, however, national economies are too diverse for everyone to profit from the same trade policy. Who does well from free trade and therefore favors it and who is hurt by and therefore opposes it will vary according to time and place. Sometimes the divisions over trade correspond to the principal political cleavages in a society – as between North and South in the United States in the mid-nineteenth century. At other times, free trade (and protectionist) coalitions are heterogeneous groupings.

The largest social and economic category that stands to profit from unrestricted commerce is that of consumers, for whom tariffs increase prices. Consumers seldom think or act as an organized group, however. That is what makes tariffs possible even in the face of the optimizing doctrine of comparative advantage. Another group with an institutional interest in promoting free trade is economists, who are, in a sense, the proprietors of the doctrine itself. Governments have taken their advice to heart in the last two decades. Before that, however, they were usually politically feeble. In 1928, 1,028 economists signed a petition calling for rejection of the Smoot-Hawley tariff without noticeably affecting congressional enthusiasm for passing it.

Military strategists play a role in international security similar to that of economists in international trade. Strategists have had, on the whole, more influence than economists because the leaders of the central institutions of the federal government, to whom they have had access, have had more control over security than economic policy. This is because nuclear strategy is an arcane and complicated matter, in which the layman is willing to defer to the expert, whereas issues of the pocketbook, like trade, are not; and because the overriding importance of security policy gives the overall national interest greater weight against particular interests than is the case for economic matters. Although not all nuclear strategists in the United States subscribe to the theory of assured destruction, there is a community of specialists that does, and that energetically lobbies for arms control measures.[48]

The equivalent for nuclear weapons of broadly based free trade coalitions that bring together those who benefit from low tariffs would include individuals and groups that compete for resources with the military. If investment in military might in general and nuclear weapons in particular comes to be seen as preventing expenditures on pressing social welfare needs – housing, schools, pensions, and the like – a political coalition may form to press for buying more butter and fewer guns.

The history of trade policy suggests, then, that the optimizing doctrine for nuclear weapons, assured destruction, will shape nuclear arsenals – often through negotiated agreements – if the doctrine itself has wide currency or if competitors for resources organize themselves and press their claims effectively. What does the record of the Soviet–American competition show about these influences? How have they affected in the past, and how might they affect in the future, the nuclear arms race?

In the United States the idea that the accumulation of nuclear weapons can stop when the capacity for assured destruction is achieved has had, as noted, some influence. The optimizing doctrine for strategy was conceived and developed in the United States, where almost all of the public thinking about the special implications of nuclear weapons has taken place. Organized interests pressing for limitations on expenditures for these weapons, however, have been comparatively weak.

A formidable equivalent for nuclear weapons of a broadly based free trade coalition did not, at least in the first three decades of the nuclear age, really take shape in the United States. The reason is that the choice between guns and butter was not particularly painful. The United States has been able to afford both. Guns, at least nuclear guns, have been relatively cheap. Of course the American nuclear arsenal cost billions of dollars to assemble. But paying for it placed little strain on the social, economic, and political fabric of the United States. Exact comparisons are difficult to draw, but a case can be made that the social burden of being a great power, especially a great power in nuclear terms, has been lighter for the United States than for the great powers of the past – fifth-century B.C. Athens, for instance, or nineteenth-century Britain.

The instruments of great power status – military hardware – have, it is true, grown more and more expensive. The capacity of societies to produce complicated weaponry, however, has grown enormously as well, through the industrial revolution in its various stages. No country has benefitted more from the industrial age than the United States, which has the largest output of goods and services of any country in the world, and therefore has some claim to being the richest country in history.[49] The requested defense budget for the fiscal year 1979 came to about 5 percent of the American gross national product. Of that, about one-tenth was earmarked for strategic nuclear weapons. So the cost to the United States of being a nuclear power in that year was around 0.5 percent of the total social product.[50]

Admittedly, 0.5 percent of the trillion-dollar American gross national product is no small sum. But as the cost of preparing for war has risen, so has the government's capacity to prepare. The resources that a government can command for military as well as for other purposes have increased astronomically since the French Revolution. In the eighteenth century the size of a monarch's army depended crucially on his personal wealth and credit. In the nineteenth century, governments relied heavily on tariffs to produce revenues. In the twentieth century the state has established claims on personal and business incomes, and in open societies puts levies on commercial transactions. In closed political systems, like the Soviet Union, the government has a claim, which is liberally exercised, to everything.

The base of taxation has broadened over the last two centuries. Societies are far more affluent now than before. So the same fraction of a nation's wealth confiscated in taxes is apt to be less burdensome in the last decades of the twentieth century than it would have been one hundred or two hundred years before. The relative cost of the necessities of life has declined. Citizens of the United States today have more of what economists call "discretionary income" than did their forebears. Most of them do not have to choose between guns on the one hand and butter on the other, but between guns and things that they may want but do not need in order to survive. A taxation rate of one-third of a person's income is less onerous when food and shelter also require one-third of his earnings than when they take two-thirds of it. This is not to say that, like Justice Holmes, every American signs his yearly check to the Internal Revenue Service with a smile, knowing that he is purchasing civilization. It is to say that Americans, at least, do not have to starve themselves to feed the appetite of the armed services for nuclear weapons.

Among the more popular words in the political lexicon of the United States since World War II has been "priorities." Those who use it in political discourse usually want more spending on butter and less on guns. But words are not deeds, and formidable political pressure to shift resources from one to the other has not accompanied the use of the term. The relative share of national resources devoted to defense did decline in the United States in the 1970s.[51] The decline came about, however, because of the end of the Vietnam War. Strategic spending within the defense budget declined as well, but this was because the most expensive part of the deterrent force, the delivery systems, had been built in the 1950s and 1960s and did not need to be replaced. By the 1970s, the principal capital investments necessary for nuclear deterrence had already been made. When expenditures on nuclear weapons were higher, government spending on other things was lower. When it was highest, in the 1950s and early 1960s, the arsenals on both sides were small enough, and the American estimates of Soviet capabilities subject to such uncertainty, that no one considered the weapons being acquired excessive.

It is true, as well, that opposition to defense spending did grow in the 1970s. But its political weight remained limited, and it had as its target the defense budget in general rather than simply nuclear weapons in excess of the requirements of assured destruction. It was inspired not by the popularity of the optimizing doctrine but by dissatisfaction with the Vietnam War, with which defense spending was linked in public thinking. By the end of the 1970s, with the war in the past, public opinion had grown better disposed to defense expenditures.[52]

The relative weakness of organized interests favoring the diversion of resources from guns to butter is not the main reason for the difference between what is needed for assured destruction and what the Soviet Union has. The armed services and the representatives of heavy industry do seem to exercise some influence in the higher councils of the Soviet government, and they have reason to resist the optimizing doctrine, which threatens their institutional importance.[53] Moreover, a bias in favor of the manufacture of large industrial products is deeply ingrained in the Soviet political system. It might almost be said that the Stalinist system, which survives in modified form to the present day, was created expressly for the purpose of managing an economy geared to the production of heavy industrial goods like nuclear and other armaments.[54]

But it is also true that the price of being a first-class nuclear power has been considerably higher for the Soviet Union than for the United States. The Soviet economy is about half the size and the Soviet nuclear arsenal roughly the equivalent of their American counterparts. So in per capita terms the Soviet force has been twice as expensive to build as the American one, perhaps more so given Soviet inefficiencies. Its commitment to raise the living standard of Soviet citizens gives the Soviet government a powerful incentive to redirect the flow of investment from military to civilian purposes. The Soviet leaders have far more power than their American counterparts to do so. In the 1970s a sweeping shift of resources to agriculture, at the expense of other sectors of the economy, took place.[55]

Support for the optimizing doctrine for nuclear weapons is weak in the Soviet Union. There is no clear, officially endorsed version of assured destruction. There is no public equivalent of the American literature on nuclear strategy and arms control. There is no comparable private and independent community of strategists. Scientists, who have played a role in forming American nuclear weapons policy, and especially in counseling restraint and propagating the optimizing doctrine, do not enjoy a similar status in the Soviet Union.[56]

For some American strategic thinkers, assured destruction defines the requirement for adequate deterrence, and nuclear force above that level connotes either foolishness or aggressive intent. For the Soviets, in contrast, superiority in nuclear terms, even when both sides have the capacity for assured destruction, may seem a way to reinforce deterrence. The more they have, they may believe, the more effectively they can keep their enemies, including the United States, at bay.[57]

Moreover, an aversion to the optimizing doctrine, and to the attitude toward international politics that underlies it, has roots in Soviet history and culture. Assured destruction is a counsel of restraint, of trust in others to be rational, and of moderation. To Soviet leaders, the axiom that no level of military strength is ever truly high enough is likely to seem more plausible. They are, after all, the heirs of a small conspiratorial party that had to struggle constantly with mortal enemies, and that succeeded in seizing and holding power because it relied on the ruthless exercise of force more fully than any other branch of nineteenth-century socialism. They are, as well, the rulers of a country that has been invaded and all but conquered twice in the twentieth century, and many times before. Official Soviet rhetoric reflects the Bolshevik and the Russian past; it is strident, defensive, and military.

Nor is the Communist Party's fearfulness entirely unjustified, even – perhaps especially – after more than sixty years of Communist rule in the Soviet Union. The United States sets its nuclear arsenal to deter the Soviet Union. The Soviets must reckon with China, a minor nuclear power in this century (although hardly to be discounted for that reason) but perhaps a formidable one in the next, as well as with Britain and France. They must worry, as well, about Germany and Japan, neither equipped with nuclear weapons but both potentially powerful if they should choose to acquire them.

There are signs of change in both countries. The optimizing doctrine may be making headway in the Soviet Union. Official pronouncements increasingly bear what seems to be the stamp of the doctrine of assured destruction.[58] In the 1950s, a debate over the relevance of Marxist–Leninist canons to nuclear weapons took place within the Communist Party between those who believed war with the capitalist–imperialist states remained inevitable, as the founding fathers had said, and those who thought that the control of nuclear fission for military purposes had invalidated at least one of the sacred teachings. The heretics won. The party admitted that the atomic bomb did not conform to the class principle, and that nuclear war would set back the cause of world revolution.[59] Perhaps the question of how much nuclear force it is necessary to deploy will follow the same pattern, and the Soviet Union will put aside the prejudices and fears that have contributed to a nuclear arsenal far in excess of the demands of assured destruction.[60]

On the American side, the 1980s may see the rise of the kind of optimizing coalition, calling for a shift in public investment from military to civilian purposes, that did not appear in the first thirty years after Hiroshima. A confluence of three developments has the potential for bringing it into being. One is the sharp increases in strategic expenditures that are in prospect to replace the principal delivery vehicles of the American strategic nuclear force – the submarines, missiles, and bomber aircraft – that were produced in the first two decades of the nuclear age. Their useful lives are drawing to a close, or so it is argued. When they were built the American economy was growing rapidly. When they are being replaced – and this is the second development – the economy is likely to be growing at a snail's pace, or perhaps not growing at all. Third, as the economic pie is shrinking, or failing to grow, more people will be demanding larger shares of it. There were far fewer organized demands on the social product in the 1950s than there are likely to be in the 1980s. The appearance and growth of these demands is one of the major changes in American society since World War II.

If assured destruction wins favor among the leaders of the Soviet Union, and if shrinking resources and rising demands for them create a coalition with real political power that is opposed to the purchase of more nuclear hardware in the United States, then the nuclear arms competition may taper off. Negotiations between the two great powers may yield broader restrictions on their respective arsenals than they produced in the first decade of serious discussion on the subject. It is conceivable that the two sides will begin to reduce their stockpiles of nuclear armaments toward the level, difficult though it is to fix, at which each has just enough firepower for the assured destruction of the other, and no more.

The nuclear competition over three decades, however, has had a different, and paradoxical, history. Because it has been nuclear the arms race has been the only one in history to provide a clear standard of military adequacy, which in turn yields a natural stopping point, beyond which weapons can be plainly and unambiguously regarded as excessive. The competition has been carried beyond that point, however, because it has involved two countries that have been predisposed – the United States by affluence, the Soviet Union by extreme defensiveness – to excess.

NATO: The nuclear alliance

The Atlantic alliance

Anarchy breeds insecurity, which fosters the impulse for self-protection. This is the logical chain that connects the structure of the international system with the behavior of states, from antiquity to the present. Members of the system can and do draw upon their own resources for protection. When rival states fortify themselves in explicitly competitive fashion, the result is an arms race. States reach out to others, as well, when they feel threatened, seeking to strengthen themselves through alliances, which are as familiar in international politics as arms races.

In Thucydides's account of the Peloponnesian War both Athens and Sparta do both. As they prepared for war, in addition to arming themselves, both "planned to send embassies to the King of Persia and to any other foreign Power from whom they hoped to obtain support, and they tried to ally themselves with other Hellenic states who were not yet committed to either side."[1] Questions of who would ally with whom take up much of the first part of the account. Alliance politics is a theme that runs throughout the story. Alliances are not only common, they are commonly marriages of convenience. In arms races, interests of particular groups may influence the types and numbers of weapons with which states equip themselves;[2] the necessary condition for any arms race, however, is the rivalry that springs from the structure of the international system. Similarly, alliances may unite states with political or cultural affinities, which can reinforce their mutual commitments. The *basis* for those commitments, however, is the need for protection, which arises from the anarchical character of international politics. Without friendship between allies an alliance will be more fragile than when there are affinities between them; without a common enemy there will be no alliance at all. The two coalitions that fought for control of Sicily, Thucydides records, "stood together not because of any moral principle or racial connection; it was rather because of the various circumstances of interest or compulsion in each particular case."[3]

How have nuclear weapons affected alliances? At first glance, the period of international history beginning with the end of the Second World War appears to be a great age of alliances. There are as many sovereign states as at any time in the past, and almost all participate in a broad range of diplomatic activities – exchanges of cordial visits by heads of state, declarations of friendship, and formal documents pledging the signatories to various kinds of cooperation. Of course, only 2 of the more than 150 sovereign states have been major nuclear powers. But these 2, the United States and the Soviet Union, each stand at the hub of a network of ties to other countries, many of which are security commitments. Of these many ties, however, only two truly qualify as nuclear alliances: the American connection with Japan, which is embodied in the Security Treaty of 1950 between the two countries, and the North Atlantic Treaty Organization, which binds together the United States and the states of Western and Southern Europe.

Other American international ties have proven flimsier than these two. During the 1950s, the United States signed treaties of friendship with nations in South and Southeast Asia and in the Middle East as well. Neither the Southeast Asia Treaty Organization (SEATO) nor the Central Powers Treaty Organization (CENTO) committed the United States to the defense of the other signatories as emphatically as was the case with NATO and the Japanese Security Treaty. These less binding treaties were not so much promises to fight side by side as attempts by the United States to win influence by extending assistance, usually military assistance, somewhat as Britain had sent money, but not soldiers, to warring continental powers in the eighteenth century. American military assistance did not always serve its intended purpose. Tanks and planes went to Pakistan, a member of SEATO, to counterbalance the military power of the People's Republic of China. The Pakistanis used them against India, a country whose favor the United States was simultaneously courting and that itself received a generous supply of American armaments.

As for the Warsaw Pact, the joint military organization of the Soviet Union and the Communist-governed states of Eastern Europe, it is not truly an alliance in the sense of a voluntary association. Membership is not voluntary. Soviet troops are stationed in Eastern Europe not only, perhaps not even mainly, to protect these countries from the West but to make certain that the ruling Communist parties remain in power. The relationship between the Soviet Union and the other signatories to the Warsaw Pact is arguably less an alliance like those that the Greek city–states formed just before the Peloponnesian War than a system of indirect rule, of the kind with which Britain dominated parts of Asia and Africa in the late nineteenth and early twentieth centuries. The indigenous rulers retained the trappings of sovereignty and some genuine sovereign prerogatives. Ultimate power, however, rested with the British, who could always force the local chieftains to follow their wishes.[4]

In what sense, then, is NATO a nuclear alliance? How have nuclear weapons made it different from alliances before 1945? It is a defensive peacetime alliance that has endured for three decades, longer than most alliances of the past. In the eighteenth century, for example, states allied for the purpose of fighting, not preventing, wars. Alliances were transitory, forming on the eve of war and usually dissolving soon after the fighting stopped. They were often established secretly.[5]

The main reason for the differences between alliances before the French Revolution and after Hiroshima is the changing nature of war.[6] Two hundred years ago, war was a normal and familiar part of international politics, a continuation of politics by different – but not dramatically different – means. Since 1945, war has come to be regarded as abnormal, horrible, even unthinkable.

This sea change in the character of war stems, of course, from the dramatic expansion of the military force available to states since the eighteenth century. As armed combat has become more destructive, states have become more interested in preventing wars and less interested in fighting them. The goal of avoiding war lends itself more readily to formal peacetime alliances than to the *ad hoc* secret arrangements of the eighteenth century. For a state that aims simply to defend itself, not to attack others, or not to have to fight at all, it is as useful to *look* powerful before the outbreak of war as to *be* powerful afterward.[7]

Disposable force for military purposes has been expanding for almost two centuries. The harnessing of nuclear energy for warfare marked an upturn in that long-term expansion sharp enough to qualify as a military revolution. But it was the third, not the first, military revolution of modern times. Logically, the previous revolutions, the Napoleonic and the mechanical, should have shifted the purposes of alliances away from fighting and toward deterring war. Historically, this was so.

The alliances among the great powers of Europe in the nineteenth century were more enduring, and geared more to stability, than had been the case before 1789. (Of course, the Concert of Europe was as much a system of international management as a series of bilateral security commitments, and its purpose was not just the prevention of war but the enforcement of domestic stability on the continent.)[8] The Triple Entente and the Triple Alliance, the military coalitions that went to war in 1914, were more firmly tied together than previous alliances, although neither was as closely integrated or as patently defensive as NATO.[9] After 1918, the British and French joined together explicitly to try to enforce the settlement. Their purpose was the same as NATO's – deterrence – of Germany rather than the Soviet Union. Nuclear weapons have made NATO a defensive peacetime alliance. In so doing, however, they have helped to continue a trend that has been underway since the French Revolution, and to which the other revolutionary advances in military might have also contributed.

NATO has been a contentious alliance, frequently consumed by intramural crisis and controversy.[10] Dissension among the allies is a feature of all alliances. This is because alliances are limited partnerships. The partners ordinarily agree on one important thing – who their most dangerous enemy is – but not on everything.[11] So there is always tugging and pulling, or, to use the language of politics, threatening and negotiating between and among allies (as between and among adversaries), just as there is, for example, in a coalition government drawn from more than one political party in a parliamentary political system. The cohesiveness of alliances has varied according to the perceived seriousness of the threat being faced, the domestic similarities among the allies, and the range of their common interests. In none, however, has disagreement been wholly eliminated. Every alliance has to some extent been, in Winston Churchill's words, "an exercise in mutual recrimination."

Allies may quarrel about anything. The most serious, most basic, and most common source of friction, however, is what is after all the heart of any alliance: a state's commitment to fight for its ally. That commitment poses two dangers; every member of an alliance has, potentially, two fears. One is that the alliance will not work, that he will be abandoned in his hour of need. The other is that the alliance will work too well, that he will be entrapped in a war he does not wish to fight.

Thucydides records both fears. When Corcyra seeks an alliance with Athens, the Corinthians, the enemies of Corcyra, warn the Athenians that accepting the Corcyrians as allies will lead to entrapment: "You will force us to hold you equally responsible with them, although you took no part in their misdeed."[12] This is exactly what happens. The Athenians try to limit their commitment to Corcyra, but find themselves drawn into battle with Corinth.[13] Later, in the debate over the wisdom of invading Sicily, the Athenian general Nicias argues against the same danger: "Let the Egestaeans, in particular, be told that, just as they started their war with the Selinuntines without consulting Athens so they must themselves be responsible for making peace; and in the future," he adds, "we are not making allies, as we have done in the past, of the kind of people who have to be helped by us in their misfortunes, but who can do nothing for us when we need help from them."[14] The outbreak of World War I offers a more recent illustration of the danger of entrapment. Britain, Germany, Russia, and France were drawn into war by the quarrels of their lesser allies.[15]

If entrapment is one of the painful lessons of the first great war of the twentieth century, abandonment is part of the history of the beginning of the second. Britain and France left their erstwhile ally Czechoslovakia to be partitioned, and then swallowed entirely, by Germany. Similarly, in fifth-century B.C. Greece, Thucydides records, the Corinthians pleaded with the Spartans to fulfill their obligation to stand with them against Athens. "Your inactivity has done harm enough. Give your allies, and especially Potidaea, the help you promised, and invade Attica at once. Do not let your friends and kinsmen fall into the hands of the bitter enemies."[16]

The perennial fears of abandonment and entrapment have lain at the heart of NATO politics, especially during the 1960s. The fact that NATO has been a nuclear alliance, both deploying and facing nuclear weapons, has given particular urgency to these fears. The costs of nuclear war are so high that abandonment becomes powerfully attractive if is means avoiding them: Entrapment is extraordinarily dangerous when it means being swept into a nuclear conflict. Besides aggravating them the nuclear character of the alliance has affected these perennial fears in two other ways. The first is that they have been bound up with, and expressed in, debates about nuclear weapons doctrine, deployment, and control.[17] The second arises from the distribution of nuclear firepower within the alliance. In theory, each ally must fear both abandonment and entrapment. Because NATO's nuclear arsenal rests almost entirely in American hands, however, each of the two fears has been marked on one side of the Atlantic and not the other. It has been the Europeans who have worried about abandonment; entrapment has been largely an American concern.

Another effect of nuclear weapons on alliances, therefore, can be seen in the politics of the Western alliance in the 1960s. The disputes over nuclear strategy stemmed from European fears that at the moment of truth the military and political arrangements on which they relied for their safety would not work, and from American anxieties that the alliance *would* work – not wisely, but too well.

The fragile alliance

NATO began life in 1949 as a guarantee pact. The United States guaranteed the safety of Western Europe by pledging to come to its defense if necessary. This was a natural arrangement. America was powerful; Europe, recovering from the devastation of war, was weak; and the Soviet Union seemed menacing, especially in the wake of the Berlin blockade of 1948. The United States had come to the rescue of Britain and France twice in the twentieth century. Both world wars had begun, however, with the Americans standing aloof. Three years were required in the first instance, and two in the second, for American help to arrive. In a third war the Europeans would not have the luxury of being able to wait. NATO was, in effect, a promise that they would not have to do so, a promise that would not have to be honored if the Soviet Union believed it and refrained from aggressive behavior accordingly.

Then, in 1950, came the Korean War. The mere promise of American assistance seemed inadequate to protect Europe from militant communism. From a simple pledge of help in time of war, NATO turned into a full-fledged peacetime military organization. The United States dispatched troops to Europe. Each NATO nation fielded its own army, but allied military planning was unusually closely integrated, and a supreme commander, invariably an American, presided over all forces.

In the early 1950s the allies made plans for a large land army, comprising ninety or more divisions. They did not come close to reaching this goal. Instead, they continued to rely on the promise of full-scale American assistance to deter the Soviets. What made the guarantee credible was the American nuclear arsenal. If the Soviet Union attacked Western Europe the United States could visit nuclear destruction on the Soviets in response. The prospect was thought both grim enough and likely enough in Soviet eyes to keep the Soviet army at bay.

Still, the Europeans worried about whether the United States was a truly reliable protector. They fretted that for all the solemn pledges that came from the other side of the Atlantic, the Americans would abandon them in their hour of need. In the early years of the alliance the Europeans also felt some anxiety about entrapment, which probably reached its zenith during the Korean War, when the British in particular feared that the conflict would become nuclear. This did not happen, and when the United States sent several hundred thousand troops to fight in the ongoing civil war in Indochina, few Europeans believed that they themselves would be dragged into it. General nuclear war, whose consequences the Europeans could scarcely hope to avoid, seemed likely to begin not in Korea or Vietnam but in Europe, over an issue like Berlin. The Europeans, then, worried not about being entrapped in Asia but about being abandoned in Berlin. The United States, after all, had a history of isolation from European affairs, which the American political tradition, beginning with George Washington's Farewell Address, had elevated to a principle of statecraft. The Atlantic Ocean was a formidable barrier between protector and protected, even in the jet age.

The history of NATO from its beginning, therefore, was a history of American efforts to reassure Europeans troubled by the prospect of abandonment. One way to reassure them that the United States would defend them was to say so. This high officials of the American government did, and repeatedly. John Kennedy's 1960 declaration "Ich bin ein Berliner" is probably the best-known American proclamation of dedication to the terms of the alliance, but it is far from the only one. Another sign of reassurance was the garrison of American troops in Europe. Their value was thought to lie not so much in their fighting efficiency as in the symbolic expression of American intentions that they represented. They served as hostages to the Americans' willingness to honor their commitments. If the Soviets attacked in Europe, the United States, with all its wealth and power, would have to come to the rescue of its soldiers, and hence of the Europeans. Or at least, in the European view, the presence of American troops improved the chances that the United States would step in to repulse a Soviet attack. The American troops, and indeed NATO as a whole, came to be seen by the Europeans as a "trip wire," set in place to serve as a trigger for the alliance's truly effective military force – the American nuclear arsenal.[18]

None of these expressions of good faith, however, sufficed to allay the fears of abandonment that a development in the second decade of the nuclear age produced. This development was the attainment by the Soviet Union of the means to launch nuclear attacks against the continental United States.

The credibility of NATO's military arrangements for deterrence for the first decade of the alliance's existence rested on an asymmetry between the United States and the Soviet Union. From bases in Western Europe the United States could launch nuclear attacks against Soviet cities and military installations. The Soviet Union had no way to reach the United States. By the end of the decade this had changed, and the change called the reliability of the American commitment to protect Europe into question. Although immune from Soviet reprisal, the United States risked relatively little by threatening to attack the Soviet Union, even with nuclear weapons. When the Soviets could threaten to bomb American cities in return, however, the American threat seemed to become hollow. In the event of a Soviet assault on Western Europe, would the American leaders really authorize the use of nuclear force against the Soviet Union, knowing that this could bring on terrible devastation to the United States? Would the Americans truly put their own cities at risk to protect Europe's? It was not easy to believe that they would. Americans and Europeans wondered whether the Soviets would believe it.

The development of a Soviet intercontinental nuclear striking force seemed to create a barrier that, although psychological in nature, was even more formidable than the Atlantic

Ocean between North America and Western Europe. It seemed
to close off the possibility of an American rescue of a be-
leaguered Europe just as emphatically as the German remili-
tarization of the Rhineland in 1936 had blocked the path between France and its Eastern European allies, the members of
the "Little Entente."[19] The nonnuclear forces of the Soviet Union and the other communist states of Eastern Europe were
widely believed to be far superior to NATO's. So a Soviet
thrust along the central front in Europe would confront
NATO, and especially the United States, with a choice between humiliation and holocaust: either to accept a nonnuclear defeat or to bring nuclear weapons into use, with the risk
of incurring fearful retaliatory damage as a result.

The development of a Soviet intercontinental nuclear striking force coincided with the removal from Europe of the main
part of the American nuclear arsenal, and this further undermined European confidence in the sturdiness of deterrence. In
the 1950s, only American airplanes and medium-range missiles stationed within the borders of the European members of
NATO could reach Soviet cities. But the 1960s saw the advent
of two new weapons that could be based outside the continent. The Minuteman missile could reach targets from Minsk
to Vladivostok within minutes of its launch from the middle
of the United States. The nuclear weapon-bearing Polaris submarine was on station at sea; most of the time it needed no
land base at all. The Americans promised that an attack on
Europe would bring these weapons into play if they were
needed. But Minuteman and Polaris would be far from Europe
when a Soviet attack came, and their distance from the scene
of battle reinforced European skepticism that they could be
counted on to arrive at all.

A Soviet capacity to visit nuclear destruction on the United
States was predictable well before it came into being.[20] By the
end of 1957, that capacity seemed to exist. The Soviet Union
tested an intercontinental ballistic missile (ICBM) in August
of that year and then, in October, launched the first earth-
orbiting satellite, Sputnik. Suddenly the Soviets appeared to be
the masters of space, from whence they would be able to bom-

bard the United States. There was, however, a lag between the
moment when the vulnerability of the United States to Soviet
attack became obvious and the launching of serious efforts to
adjust NATO's military arrangements to compensate for this
vulnerability. It fell to the Kennedy administration, which
took office in 1961, to try to protect NATO from the consequences of the extended reach of Soviet striking power.

The solution to this problem that the Kennedy administration proposed was to turn NATO from a trip wire into an effective fighting force, by building up its nonnuclear forces to the
point at which they themselves could repulse a Soviet attack.[21] The alliance could avoid the choice between humiliation and holocaust by being strong enough to avoid humiliation in nonnuclear combat. The idea was not new in 1961. It
simply revived the still unmet expectation that some Americans had held for NATO at its founding. The failure to have
strong nonnuclear forces cost little in the early 1950s because
an alternative to nonnuclear forces equal to those of the Soviet
Union was readily available – the American nuclear arsenal.
By 1961, however, the Soviet and American striking forces
canceled each other out, and a decisive advantage seemed
available to the side that was better equipped to fight a nonnuclear war. The idea of preparing to engage the Soviet Union
and the Warsaw Pact at levels of violence below the nuclear
threshold came to be known as the policy of "flexible response."

The Europeans opposed it. Their objections arose in part
from domestic political considerations. They did not wish to
raise taxes or increase conscription into their armed forces.
Their chief objection, however, had to do with the logic of the
policy itself. Flexible response involved being ready to fight a
nonnuclear war in Europe. The Europeans did not want to
fight a war of any kind there. World War II had been enough
for them. After 1945, moreover, the expansion of nonnuclear
force continued apace. The nuclear revolution tended to ob-
scure it, but the extension of the mechanical revolution in warfare after the Second World War placed much greater military
power in the hands of governments than they had had before,

apart from the development of fusion and fission explosives. When Hitler's army invaded the Soviet Union, it relied heavily on the same mode of transport that had carried Napoleon to Moscow – the horse. There are no horses on the central front in Europe today. If the spread of the nuclear revolution in warfare to the Soviet Union made flexible response seem necessary to the United States, the continuation of the mechanical revolution on the continent made it appear dangerous to the Europeans.

No doubt they would have armed themselves more resolutely if no other form of protection had been available. But there was an alternative to making ready to fight a nonnuclear war as a means of protecting Europe: threatening to fight a nuclear war. The Europeans feared that a policy of flexible response would undercut that threat. Flexible response was designed to give NATO the means to fight a war in Europe that would not immediately become nuclear. The Europeans wished to cultivate the impression that rapid escalation to the nuclear level *would* follow a Soviet attack, because they believed that this impression was what deterred the Soviet Union.[22] Flexible response, the Europeans feared, would give them the worst of all possible worlds: Without a firmly nuclear American guarantee deterrence might be weakened to the point that the Soviets would be tempted to attack. Such a war, even if free of nuclear exchanges, even if the United States stood shoulder to shoulder with the Europeans, was bound to be brutally destructive.

What they feared in the early 1960s was not precisely abandonment. The United States was prepared to contribute to the improvement of NATO's nonnuclear forces. They feared, rather, that the American nuclear arsenal would not be seen automatically as ready to defend Western Europe. The term that came to express this fear was "decoupling." It connoted separation – of nuclear from conventional weapons – for the purpose, the Europeans suspected, of separating North America from Europe as a theater of war.[23]

If the Europeans feared that flexible response would undercut deterrence, the Americans believed that only flexible response could make it credible. Only by being prepared to fight a war of a particular type, they argued, could NATO deter it. If the Soviets knew they could not win a nonnuclear war they would not launch one. If they were confident of their chances at the nonnuclear level, however, they might gamble that NATO would not dare try to save its position by nuclear means.

Their distaste for flexible response did not mean that the Europeans favored reducing the nonnuclear NATO forces that were already in place in 1961. That, they reckoned, might signal a diminution of American determination to keep its commitments to Europe. They therefore favored deploying precisely the level of forces that NATO currently had, no more and no less.

The disagreement about flexible response had the makings of an impasse. The growth of Soviet nuclear power appeared to subvert the arrangements for protecting Europe by deterring a Soviet attack, arrangements that had been put in place in the early 1950s. What the Americans proposed for buttressing deterrence was unacceptable to the Europeans. One European, however, offered a different solution to the problem.

The entangling alliance

The European in question was Charles de Gaulle. His response to the growth of Soviet long-range nuclear striking power and the impact that this was widely believed to have had on the effectiveness of NATO's policy of deterrence in the 1960s was the creation of national nuclear arsenals by the alliance's European members.

In the drama of NATO politics in the 1960s the Americans cast de Gaulle as the villain. They came to see him as arrogant and misguided, bent on sacrificing alliance unity for a dream of French grandeur that had, understandably, arisen from the humiliation of World War II, but that that war, and its aftermath, had put forever beyond France's reach. The French President was scarcely a warm, friendly character. He harbored a deep personal distrust of the "Anglo-Saxons" – the

Americans and the British. His troubles with the United States did not, however, stem from personal incompatibilities between himself and his opposite numbers on the other side of the Atlantic. Nor did they arise from misunderstandings about the aspirations of the two countries or the workings of the two political systems, although misunderstandings there certainly were. On the contrary, de Gaulle was a thorn in the side of the American government above all because he shared American assumptions about the shakiness of deterrence in Europe, from which, however, he drew different conclusions. He was, above all, the expositor of the nuclear logic of the European members of NATO, and that logic made the Americans as uncomfortable as flexible response had made the Europeans.

De Gaulle accepted the reasoning that underlay flexible response. He agreed that the credibility of the threat upon which Western Europe's safety rested needed to be reinforced. His skepticism went further. He doubted the worth of *all* formal alliances. Abandonment, in his view, was normal. Because alliances were marriages of convenience, he believed, when they ceased to be convenient no ally could be depended upon to fulfill its obligations, no matter how solemnly it had undertaken them. States, according to de Gaulle, pursue their own interests and only these. If it suits the interest of state A to come to the aid of state B then A will come, whether or not a formal promise has been given. If not, the tug of alliance ties will not be powerful enough to overcome the pull of self-interest in the other direction.

This would certainly be the case, in de Gaulle's judgment, for NATO. In the wake of the vulnerability of North America to Soviet nuclear attack, the question arose as to whether American leaders would put New York at risk to protect Paris. De Gaulle had no doubt that they would not. Nor could the Soviet Union be depended upon to believe that they would. But if the United States would not use nuclear weapons in defense of Europe, the Europeans themselves would certainly use them, and the Soviets would certainly believe that the Europeans would use them. So, national nuclear arsenals were necessary for deterrence.

Whereas the United States wanted one center of authority with several military options, de Gaulle proposed several centers of authority each with the same single nuclear option. Accordingly, de Gaulle presided over the beginnings of an independent French nuclear arsenal, whose formal origin dates from 1960, when the first French nuclear test took place.

Even short of protection in a moment of ultimate danger, nuclear weapons had their uses, and de Gaulle appreciated these. They conferred prestige upon their owners. They ensured, in the British phrase, a "seat at the top table" of diplomacy, which de Gaulle coveted for France. An independent nuclear arsenal, even a modest one, seemed both a symbol of and a means to a whole range of prerogatives. Here ornamental and instrumental purposes merged. The most basic prerogative for any state is mastery of its own destiny, and for Europeans in the nuclear age, as de Gaulle saw it, only the possession of nuclear weapons could secure this prerogative.[24]

De Gaulle was the most obstinate and outspoken proponent of the logic of independent national nuclear forces. This was far from being his private obsession, however. Other Frenchmen shared it. France's nuclear weapons program both preceded and survived his presidency. In time, political parties from all points on the French political spectrum came to endorse the independent *force de frappe*.[25]

The British were not entirely unsympathetic to de Gaulle's views. They whispered their doubts about American reliability, whereas the French President trumpeted his. They preferred to conciliate the Americans, whereas it suited de Gaulle to quarrel with them. Despite these differences of style, however, the British had their own small independent nuclear striking force, and their motives for acquiring it were similar to de Gaulle's.[26]

There were reasons why the American government might have endorsed de Gaulle's thinking, and his nuclear policy. The acquisition of independent nuclear forces by the Europeans offered several advantages. It promised to increase NATO's military strength – the basic purpose, after all, of any alliance. It could ease the burden, both psychological and military, of protecting Europe. The Americans were constantly urging the Europeans to contribute more to the alliance's defenses. And it had the potential to contribute to European unity, which had long been a professed American goal; the Europeans might be expected to pool their nuclear resources, which could, in turn, lead to other forms of political integration.

Quite to the contrary, however, the American government adamantly opposed the development of independent European nuclear forces. In fact, the word the Americans used to describe the spread of nuclear weapons, a word of Latin origin that sounded like a disease (which was the way the United States saw the matter), perfectly expressed this position: "proliferation." The Americans pressed their opposition despite the potential advantages of national nuclear arsenals, even when it became obvious that to do so was to widen a crack in the alliance. American disapproval of proliferation aggravated a feud with France, to which the United States refused nuclear assistance even when de Gaulle made it clear that he would proceed with his weapons program unaided. The American position ruffled relations with the British as well, which reached their nadir when the Kennedy administration abruptly decided to cancel production of the Skybolt missile, which the British had been counting on to prolong the useful life of their nuclear-equipped bomber aircraft. The ostensible reason for the cancellation was economic. But the fact that the missile was to contribute to the maintenance of another national nuclear arsenal made it easier to put considerations of economy over the claims of alliance solidarity.

The American government argued that independent European nuclear forces were unnecessary; the American striking force was adequate for NATO's purposes. The Americans charged, in addition, that separate European forces were bound to be inadequate. They would not be able to meet the standard of assured destruction that, in American eyes, was the measure of strategic usefulness. A force of hundreds of hardened, dispersed intercontinental missiles and dozens of nuclear-equipped submarines such as the United States was assembling was beyond the means of any single European country.

An independent European nuclear arsenal was, in the American view, not only unnecessary and inadequate, but liable to be dangerously provocative. Its owner would be more, not less, vulnerable to the Soviet Union, because in the event of war a small nuclear force would be first on the Soviet list of targets.

The Europeans could, and the French did, reply that independent nuclear forces were not as self-evidently useless, and worse, as American objections to them claimed. True, the technical definition of strategic adequacy – assured destruction – was not easy to achieve, especially for a country without the resources of the United States or the Soviet Union. But neither was a "survivable" striking force wholly beyond the reach of the Europeans. Over time they might hope to build enough missiles – perhaps making these mobile or concealing them or putting them on submarines in order to avoid a preemptive blow – to be confident of being able to reply in kind to a Soviet nuclear attack.

Even a small nuclear arsenal not absolutely certain of surviving a knockout blow, the Europeans could argue, might look dangerous enough to spare its owner a Soviet attack in case of war. If the European country could not be sure of being able to strike Moscow after a Soviet assault, the Soviets, for their part, would not be certain that this would not happen. And even a few hydrogen bombs, even one, could do more damage to the Soviet capital than Napoleon or Hitler had managed. Moreover, insofar as the effectiveness of a deterrent depended partly upon the perceived will of its owner to use it, national nuclear forces were highly effective, because France would undoubtedly be more willing to respond in nuclear terms to an attack on France than the United States would be.

Whatever its shortcomings, a national nuclear arsenal certainly seemed better than nothing for a European member of NATO. And de Gaulle, at least, professed to believe that the alternative to an independent striking force, no matter how vulnerable, was nothing. For providing protection, a nuclear arsenal owned and operated by a Western European nation might stand in relation to the American stock of missiles as a fig leaf to a coat of armor. But in case of a battle, the armor would not, in de Gaulle's view, and might not, in the view of other Europeans, be available. A fig leaf was better than being altogether naked.

At the heart of American opposition to nuclear proliferation within NATO was the fear of entrapment. The Americans did not voice this fear in so many words. To do so would have been undiplomatic, and risky. It would have suggested that the NATO allies might behave recklessly. It could have been construed as implying what the Europeans most feared: that there were wars they would wish to fight that the United States might prefer to avoid. So, American officials referred to the dangers of proliferation in euphemisms: It could lead, they said, to "instability"; it would "complicate" international politics by introducing an unwanted measure of "uncertainty" into national calculations.[27]

There were general reasons why proliferation called up the specter of entrapment for the United States. Small national nuclear arsenals might be tempting targets for preemptive Soviet attacks. In a crisis the Soviet Union might strike at European nuclear arsenals out of confidence of being able to eliminate them; by contrast, if only the far larger, less vulnerable American force were involved the Soviets might behave more cautiously. It was not any particular scenario that troubled the American government in the early 1960s, however, so much as the fact that nuclear weapons were so powerful, national and international experience with them was so limited, and the task of coming to terms with one other major nuclear weapon state had been so trying, that any change in the nuclear status quo was worrisome. The spread of nuclear weapons seemed dangerous because the consequences were not readily predictable. The price of nuclear war was likely to be so high that nothing that might bring it closer was worth risking. In a nuclear environment control seemed all-important, and the diffusion of nuclear capability would make it easier for other nations to act independently and therefore weaken American control. In its most general but also most basic form, American aversion to proliferation came down to a bet like that of Pascal, who reasoned that he had nothing to lose and everything to gain by believing in God: Perhaps no harm would come of an increase in the number of states possessing nuclear weapons; but the harm, if it did come, was potentially so vast that strenuous efforts to keep the number constant were fully justified.[28]

The threat of nuclear proliferation came to be called, in the United States, the "nth country problem." The term suggested that numbers alone made a difference where the national possession of nuclear weapons was concerned. More were worse, no matter which the new nuclear states happened to be. One state in particular, however, especially worried Americans – the Federal Republic of Germany. As the largest nonnuclear NATO member and the one most directly exposed to the Soviet Union, Germany was the logical candidate to follow Britain's and France's nuclear examples. A nuclear-armed Germany was a particularly unhappy prospect. Memories of the Third Reich were still fresh. The Federal Republic had not yet fully established itself as a responsible, sober, peaceful, democratic member of the international community.

A nuclear-armed Germany, especially one torn loose from its NATO moorings, was worrisome to contemplate. Not the least worrisome thing about it was its potential effect on the Soviet Union. Ever since the division of the country, and of Europe, had become a fact of international life, the Soviets had made the denial of nuclear armaments to West Germany a cardinal principle of their foreign policy. Two terrible German invasions in the twentieth century had made the Soviets extraordinarily sensitive to German military power. The United States refused to assist the French nuclear weapons program in no small part out of the fear that the Germans would demand comparable treatment. A German nuclear arsenal in particular, and nuclear proliferation in Europe in general, were as unacceptable to the United States as ways of reinforcing deterrence as flexible response was to the Europeans. So although

both sides agreed on the problem, neither would countenance
the other's preferred solution.

The enduring alliance

Nuclear politics in NATO in the 1960s resembles, in retrospect, a play without a third act. A crisis arose: The development of a Soviet capacity to strike the United States raised
fears of abandonment and called into question the credibility
of deterrence in Europe. Various solutions were brought forward. None, however, was put fully into practice. Neither flexible response nor proliferation won complete acceptance on
both sides of the Atlantic. The Europeans regarded the first as
an invitation to abandonment of a particular kind – decoupling; the Americans worried that the consequence of the second would be entrapment.

The Europeans did in fact accept flexible response in 1967,
but in a way that seemed to undercut the American purpose in
proposing it in the first place. They agreed in principle that
the alliance should adopt the policy, but argued that the existing nonnuclear forces in Europe sufficed to carry it out. Rather
than putting more troops, tanks, and airplanes into the field,
they were content to change the name of the mission of those
that were already there.

The European solution to the problem that Soviet strategic
power created for NATO – national nuclear forces – had a
complicated history, but it, too, was never fully implemented.
The United States proposed a scheme known as the Multilateral Force (MLF) for sharing control of some nuclear
weapons. This received serious attention beginning in 1963.
The idea was for Polaris submarines to be manned by multinational crews. It was, for the Americans, a decidedly second-
best solution to NATO's problems. They were not anxious to
surrender any degree of control over any nuclear weapons.
They feared, however, that the certain consequence of their
refusal to do so would be political upheaval in the alliance
and perhaps an independent German nuclear arsenal.[29] On the
delicate, crucial question of whose finger would actually rest

on the submarines' nuclear triggers, the American designers of the MLF were deliberately vague. Finally, in late 1964, President Johnson effectively rejected the scheme.

The problems that Soviet nuclear power created were not only not clearly solved in the 1960s, they reappeared, in different guise, in the 1970s. Concern arose within the alliance over a perceived Soviet advantage in long-range theater nuclear forces, which consisted of Western European-based nuclear weapons capable of striking targets within the Soviet Union and Soviet weapons aimed at Western Europe, and whose relative capacities came to be known as the "Eurostrategic balance."[30] The Western debate about this issue echoed the controversy about flexible response during the Kennedy years. Although the forces in question differed, the basic issue was the same – the requirements of deterrence. The United States had the same fear that the perceived imbalance in non-nuclear forces had stirred during the previous decade – namely, that the Soviet Union would win an engagement at that level, compelling NATO either to accept defeat or to escalate the conflict to the level of intercontinental nuclear war, which would expose North America to nuclear bombardment. The preferred American response was to deploy long-range theater forces comparable to those of the Soviet Union, and in December 1979, NATO voted to do so.[31]

As with flexible response in the 1960s, however, this called up European fears of decoupling, of the separation this time not of nuclear from nonnuclear weapons but of theater-range from strategic armaments. Like the first, the second suggested the separation of the United States from Europe as a theater of war, and this, the Europeans feared, could weaken deterrence by calling into question the willingness of the United States to put all of its military might into the defense of Europe. The French Foreign Minister put it plainly: "The approach based on the concept of a Eurostrategic balance implies that there can be a separate balance of nuclear capabilities assigned to the European theater, isolated from other elements of deterrence. It leads to a 'decoupling' which is precisely what we are trying to avoid. In other words, it would be tantamount to rec-

ognizing that the United States' central strategic forces do not
cover Western Europe."[32]

The years that followed the demise of the MLF in 1964 were
far from harmonious ones for NATO. Apart from the question
of how to respond to the Soviet nuclear threat to the United
States, disputes over a wide range of issues cropped up. Economics took its place beside security as a source of conflict.
The Atlantic partners quarreled about trade, monetary, and
balance of payments policies. At one juncture the United
States hinted that the continuation of the American nuclear
guarantee of Europe would depend upon economic concessions from the Europeans. Political disputes strained relations
as well. The American war in Vietnam aroused little enthusiasm in Europe. The 1973 Middle East War imposed an even
more serious strain. The alliance partners found themselves,
in effect, on opposite sides. The Europeans, fearing for their
oil supplies from the Arab states of the Persian Gulf, issued
statements sympathetic to the Arabs and largely refused to
help the United States resupply Israel while the fighting was
in progress.

In 1980 the alliance found itself once again divided, this
time over how to respond to the seizure of American diplomatic personnel held as hostages in Iran and to the Soviet invasion of Afghanistan. The United States favored a strong response to both. The Europeans worried about alienating the
governments in Tehran and Moscow. The difference stemmed
in part from a divergence of interests, from which all alliances
suffer. The Europeans' economic stake in Iran, and the political
benefits they drew from the relaxation of tensions with the
Soviet Union, were both greater than the Americans', so they
had more to lose from poor relations with each. The most serious falling-out within the alliance in the years following the
demise of the controversies over the MLF and flexible response occurred not between the United States and the Europeans but between two European members, Greece and Turkey, over the governance of the island of Cyprus. A Cypriot
political crisis in 1974 prompted Turkish occupation of the
island and triggered Greek withdrawal from active participation in NATO affairs.

Still, despite the fact that old problems were not conclusively resolved and new ones arose, NATO remained intact through the 1970s, in more or less its original form, something that had seemed extremely unlikely at the beginning of the 1960s. Then the status quo in the alliance, resting as it did upon the American nuclear guarantee, appeared untenable. Change seemed inevitable. Because Soviet aggression seemed the certain alternative to them, flexible response and national nuclear arsenals seemed essential, to the Americans in the first instance, to the French in the second. They proved to be unnecessary. Why was this so?

It is arguable that, appearances to the contrary notwithstanding, the proposed solutions for the problem that the Soviet capacity to attack the United States posed for NATO were put into practice, perhaps not as fully as the proponents had hoped, but fully enough to keep the Soviet Union at bay. The European agreement in principle to the policy of flexible response was, arguably, more than a semantic maneuver. The nonnuclear forces of NATO and the Warsaw Pact were seen to be more evenly balanced in 1967 than they had been in 1961. This was not because the Americans and the Western Europeans had fielded more troops, however, but because estimates of the number of troops opposing them had become increasingly precise, and the more precise they became the smaller they were. It appeared in retrospect that throughout the 1950s the West had consistently overestimated them. The Europeans' 1967 conclusion that, in effect, NATO had been practicing flexible response all along was not wholly self-serving. It was, at least to some degree, accurate.[33]

As for the preferred European solution to the problem, national nuclear forces, the French could claim to have put it into practice. They did proceed to equip themselves with a nuclear striking force. By 1979 it consisted of four submarines with sixteen missiles each and eighteen intermediate-range missiles. By American and Soviet standards this force was small. The French, however, could argue that, by their standard of deterrence, it was adequate. The French force, despite the protection that submarines provided, might not be absolutely certain of inflicting the level of damage on the Soviet

Union in case of a Soviet attack that the Americans had defined as necessary for deterrence. It was very likely, however,
to do considerable damage if used. If not kill him outright, the
French could plausibly threaten to "tear an arm off the bear"
in retaliation for a Soviet attack.[34]

The Germans got no nuclear weapons, and not even the partial control over part of the American arsenal that the MLF
envisioned, which remained under the command of the American President. They may not, however, have wanted to have a
German finger resting on a nuclear trigger. They may simply
have wished to be certain that they would not be relegated to
the role of spectators in the alliance, with no say at all in its
policies.[35] "Control" in the English sense of the term, one student of NATO politics noted, implies physical possession;
contrôle in the French usage connotes planning and political
direction.[36] The Germans may have wanted the second, not
the first. The alliance's Nuclear Planning Group, which came
into being on the initiative of the United States after the abandonment of the idea of nuclear sharing, provided it.

None of these explanations for the persistence of NATO in
its original form is entirely satisfactory, however, given the
widely shared alarm of the early 1960s. If NATO forces
seemed a better match for those of the Soviet Union and Eastern Europe after the middle of the decade, the American government never felt able to declare them an even match, or better.[37] Nor was there any reason for the Germans to feel
confident that the French nuclear arsenal, however powerful
it was, protected them. If the United States would not risk
New York to save Paris, after all, why would the French risk
Paris to save Hamburg? The logic of the French view of deterrence led to a German national nuclear arsenal.

There is another possible explanation for NATO's durabil-
ity. Political relations between East and West improved.[38] The
leaders of the American and Soviet governments met periodically. The two countries reached modest agreements limiting
nuclear weapons: the Limited Test Ban Treaty of 1963, the
Nonproliferation Treaty of 1968, and the Strategic Arms Limitation treaties of 1972 and 1979. A host of scientific and cul-

tural exchanges began. In Europe the status of Germany was put on a firmer footing by a series of accords signed in 1969 and by the Conference on Security and Cooperation in Europe, which convened in Helsinki in 1975 and produced what amounted to a belated European peace treaty, thirty years after the end of World War II.

A state's security is the result of both its own capabilities and others' intentions, of its military power and its diplomatic achievements. NATO, it might be argued, concentrated on the second rather than the first. This explanation is not entirely satisfactory either, however. It reverses the proper order of things. Detente, the improvement of political relations between NATO and the Warsaw Pact, was less a cause than a consequence of miltiary stability. Because they felt secure, the Germans, the Europeans, and the Americans could seek limited reconciliation with the Communist countries.

Peace may have reigned in Europe because the Soviet Union never intended to disturb it. Soviet intentions during the Cold War cannot be known in the absence of firsthand evidence. It is certainly true that in the immediate postwar years the Soviet government had its hands full with reconstructing its own country and tightening its grip on Eastern Europe. It is also true that, once conquered, Western Europe would have been difficult for the Soviet bloc to digest. Still, without some military disincentive it is hard to imagine that the Soviets would not have found some way to exert influence, if not control, over the European members of NATO. This, after all, is a familiar feature of international politics. It is the way that great powers have ordinarily behaved. It is almost a law of international relations that large countries abhor a vacuum of power.[39] This is not to say that the Soviet Union has ever been seriously inclined to invade, or even to hold in political thrall – to "Finlandize" – Western Europe. It is to say that in the absence of some form of deterrence, such an inclination very likely would have appeared.

A telling reason why the structure of the Atlantic alliance remained intact, despite the conviction that this could not happen, is that alternatives to it loomed as grossly unattrac-

tive. The Europeans refused to support, if not the principle of
flexible response, at least the policy of making substantial ad-
ditions to the alliance's nonnuclear forces; the Americans opposed national nuclear forces. Sharper departures from the
founding alliance arrangements were even less feasible. The
Europeans had no inclination to switch from the American to
the Soviet bloc, and they could not have expected to float between the two and remain free from Soviet influence without
substantial military forces of their own. These they could have
had. A multinational European military force could have
drawn on a larger pool of capital and technology than that of
either the United States or the Soviet Union. Such a force,
however, especially insofar as it was nuclear, would have presented the same problem that the MLF raised, the problem of
deciding whose finger was to rest on the trigger. Eliminating
the United States made this problem no easier to solve. A Europe-wide force would have had to be underpinned, and thus
preceded, by some measure of political unity. Since 1945 European unity has been a perpetual dream and a recurring
hope, but not a reality. The Europeans clung to the United
States, "in good logic and bad, in bad times and good,"[40]
therefore, partly because they had no attractive alternative.

There is an analogy here to the international monetary system. The dollar was as central, and as crucial, to the system
that the Bretton Woods conference of 1944 produced as the
United States nuclear arsenal was to NATO at its inception.
The growth of other national economies and American economic distress eroded the power of the dollar relative to other
currencies, giving rise to a felt need for a substitute bulwark of
the system. All possible substitutes, however – gold, Special
Drawing Rights issued by the International Monetary Fund,
and a joint European currency – proved to have drawbacks
that rendered them unacceptable. So the dollar, in weakened
form, has remained at the center of the system, as the principal
form of international reserve and the most popular medium of
international exchange.

The absence of an attractive alternative, however, once
again is not a wholly satisfactory explanation for NATO's per-

sistence. World War II did not extinguish the will to national independence in Western Europe. Had their safety and political integrity depended on it, the Europeans would have paid the price of a single Europe-wide or several separate national nuclear arsenals, or of building up the alliance's nonnuclear strength. They did not have to pay it. Why did the status quo in Europe *not* change? There is plainly no single answer, but one important reason is that NATO's initial arrangements for the deterrence of the Soviet Union continued to work throughout the 1960s and 1970s.

The Berlin and Cuban crises of 1961 and 1962, respectively, seem in retrospect to bear out NATO's sturdiness. When they occurred they heightened Western Europe's sense of vulnerability. American nuclear power did not prevent a Soviet challenge at the heart of Europe, or ninety miles from the coast of the United States. In both cases, however, the Soviet challenge was turned back. West Berlin remained a free city in the midst of the Soviet sphere of influence; intermediate-range missiles capable of carrying nuclear warheads to targets within the United States were removed from Cuba. In both cases the United States issued an explicit nuclear threat. In both cases the crises were resolved in favor of the status quo, which the United States was trying to preserve. No further crises of comparable magnitude followed.

Even de Gaulle's foreign policy provides support for the proposition that NATO's capacity for deterrence remained robust. In truth, considerations of nuclear deterrence were secondary matters in his foreign policy; what was primary was to assert French independence and to magnify French influence in the world. De Gaulle could afford to regard nuclear politics as secondary because he could be confident that the alliance's nuclear arrangements *would* deter the Soviet Union, despite his professed skepticism as justification for France's nuclear weapons program.[41] He could formally withdraw from the alliance because he knew that he would still enjoy its protection.

Insofar as NATO did keep at bay a Soviet Union able to mount nuclear strikes against the continental United States, both the Europeans and the Americans were proven partly right and partly wrong about the requirements of deterrence. The United States was right that nuclear weapons under exclusively American control sufficed but wrong in insisting that a more diversified defense force was necessary. The Europeans were right that nuclear weapons alone would deter the Soviets but wrong in believing that these had to be in European, as well as American, custody.

This was so, arguably, because the extraordinary power of nuclear weapons stifled any temptation to attack, which uncertainty about an American response might have encouraged. The Europeans could not be certain that the Americans would risk New York to protect Paris, but the Soviets could not be sure that they would *not* do so. The nuclear revolution made uncertainty an argument for restraint. As Raymond Aron put it, "when no one was able to gauge the precise ratio of strength ahead of time, an adventure seemed tempting by virtue of its very unpredictability; now that this unpredictability involves fatalities on the order of tens of millions, even the most adventuresome of leaders might conceivably be inclined to caution."[42] The result has been that, as one student of postwar European politics put it, "successive doctrines may have lacked the rational precision that experts thought necessary, and force levels and capabilities have usually fallen short of those required by doctrine, but the Russians have shown themselves to be most prudent in probing the alliance's self-advertised military deficiencies."[43] Soviet behavior in this sense represented the triumph of common sense over logic.[44] Former British Defense Minister Denis Healey once suggested that one chance in a hundred of a nuclear response to aggression will deter an enemy, although it may not reassure a friend.[45] The observation explains a great deal of the history of the Atlantic alliance.

This leads to a final effect of nuclear weapons on alliances. Because American nuclear weapons did deter the Soviet Union, they made it possible for NATO's original framework to remain in place, and this suppressed normal national impulses for independence. Transatlantic relations would not, in all likelihood, have differed drastically from the shape they

took had there been no nuclear weapons. The United States
and the Soviet Union would still have been far stronger than
any single European state. The Soviets would not have permitted an independent united Germany, and perhaps would not
have been willing to countenance a united Germany of any
political stripe. The United States, for its part, would not have
wanted a Soviet-dominated Germany. The Cold War alignment appears, in retrospect, all but inevitable. With such an
alignment Western Europe would certainly have sought a security connection with the United States, with or without a
nuclear arsenal. The Europeans would have had to rely upon
the United States for protection, especially in the early postwar period. But they would likely not have remained as dependent as has been the case.

The international monetary system again offers a suggestive
analogy. At the end of World War II, the European economies
were in ruins, and not only was the dollar supreme but American economic policy determined that of Western Europe. As
the Europeans recovered, and grew prosperous, they gained a
measure of economic independence. None is the equal of the
United States in economic terms. There is no substitute for the
dollar. The United States remains by far the most powerful
single nation in the politics of international economics. But
the Europeans and the Japanese do have some independent
influence. The balance of influence and initiative between Europe and America in economic matters has shifted markedly
in thirty years; where security is concerned, nuclear weapons
have perpetuated a balance that was as lopsided in 1980 as it
was in 1949.

That it remains lopsided amounts to a curious reversal. The
distribution of nuclear force within NATO was at its founding
a consequence, and is now a cause of European weakness. At
first the Europeans could not, and now they will not, and because of the sturdiness of nuclear deterrence they need not,
assemble a nuclear arsenal themselves. In 1949 the United
States issued a nuclear guarantee because the Europeans were
weak. Now the Europeans are weak because they have, after
all, the American nuclear guarantee.

7

The Nuclear Presidency

History of the nuclear presidency

International politics operates on three levels. The anarchical structure of the international system produces the problem of security that is common to all states. The character of each individual state – its history, its political system, the temperament of its citizens – shapes its response to that problem. Ultimately, however, it is the people of each state who decide how to respond. The basic unit of international politics is the individual.

Each of the three levels is important in Thucydides's account of the Peloponnesian War. He finds the fundamental cause of the conflict to be the structure of the system of independent city–states in fifth-century B.C. Greece. "What made war inevitable," in his view, "was the growth of Athenian power and the fear which this caused in Sparta,"[1] a fear ultimately rooted in the fact that in a system without a supreme authority any powerful member automatically becomes a potential threat to all the others. The contrast between democratic, commercial Athens and autocratic, agrarian Sparta is a major theme in the chronicle. Thucydides depicts the roles of individual Athenians and Spartans as crucial. He stresses particularly the roles played by the leaders on both sides.

If his history has a hero it is the Athenian Pericles, a shrewd, steady, and farsighted statesman who was not only able to divine the proper course for Athens but to persuade his fellow citizens to follow it.[2] Athens's downfall began with the death of Pericles. When he passed from the scene, the leadership of the city–state fell into the hands of men less able, less unselfish, and less dedicated to the public weal than he. They embarked on the ill-fated Sicilian expedition, which ended in calamitous defeat for Athens.[3]

The importance of leadership for international relations since the fifth century B.C. scarcely needs to be documented. Most of the recorded history of war and diplomacy is the history of monarchs, generals, and other political leaders. What impact have nuclear weapons had on this third level of international politics?

The nuclear revolution has given one man, at least, an enormous responsibility. He is the American President. He has the power of command over the American nuclear arsenal. His finger rests on the nuclear trigger. The final decision to squeeze it is his. A military officer carrying a small satchel follows him everywhere. The satchel contains the communications equipment that connects the President with the thousands of nuclear warheads in the American arsenal. Authorization for firing them must come from a coded radio signal. The President has custody of the code.[4]

The President's supreme nuclear authority dates from the beginning of the nuclear age. The President, not the Congress, authorized the Manhattan Project, which developed the first atomic bombs; most congressmen did not become aware of them until the destruction of Hiroshima. President Truman, who was not in the habit of choosing the Air Force's targets during World War II, personally approved the two nuclear raids. After the war, he made certain that atomic energy came under civilian, not military, authority, and he emphasized that civilian authority meant presidential control.[5] In November 1950, when asked at a press conference whether the atomic bomb would be used in Korea, Truman suggested that the matter would be decided by the military. Immediately afterward the White House issued a statement denying this: "By law, only the President can authorize the use of the bomb."[6]

The question of nuclear authority arose again during the 1964 presidential election, when the Republican candidate, Barry Goldwater, proposed that NATO field commanders be able to initiate nuclear strikes in Europe without explicit permission from the White House. The suggestion touched off a public furor that helped to destroy his candidacy and moved President Lyndon Johnson to say that "No president of the United States can divest himself of responsibility for such a decision [to use nuclear weapons]" and Secretary of Defense Robert McNamara to assert that "the man to make that decision is and must continue to be the President of the United States."[7] Since 1964 the authority to order the use of nuclear weapons has remained in the hands of the President.[8] If the President is killed or disabled, "the constitutional succession of command is the legal ... proper authorization route. The command and control system and release procedures are geared to that civilian succession."[9] Whether, amid the chaos and destruction of a nuclear war, the chain of command would be strictly observed cannot be foretold. The order to fire a nuclear shot can *legally* be given, however, only by the President, whoever he happens to be.

The concentration of nuclear authority in the hands of a single person runs counter to the effects of the two previous modern military revolutions, which promoted, on the whole, the diffusion of command responsibility. The eighteenth century marked the last stage of the "Age of the Great Captains," when rulers like Frederick the Great personally led their armies into battle.[10] Napoleon was the last and perhaps the greatest of these, but the Napoleonic revolution and the beginning of the mechanical revolution in warfare ushered in the age of war by committee. The most important committee came to be the general staff, a group of officers charged with planning and managing battles, which became an increasingly familiar feature of European armies in the nineteenth century. Prussia was the pioneer in developing the institution, and Prussian victories in the wars of German unification made it popular.

Each military revolution expanded the scale of war, and this was one reason for the dispersal of authority. The French "nations in arms" put more men than ever before into the army. The railroad, which was part of the mechanical military revolution, made it possible to place huge national armies in the field all at once. Before the Napoleonic revolution, wars un-

folded one battle at a time, and in almost all cases the commander could see the whole battlefield himself. By the twentieth century Franklin Roosevelt was presiding over a war
whose theater stretched all the way around the world.

The first two modern revolutions in warfare made battle
more complicated as well. The machinery became more intricate, and there was more and more of it to be coordinated. The
task far outstripped the powers of a single person.[11]

The centralization of nuclear authority in the United States
is not, however, wholly without precedent. It arises, in part,
from the ever-expanding reach of rapid communication. What
the telegraph was to the messenger in the nineteenth century
the radio, television, and satellites of the present day are to the
telegraph: a quantum leap forward in communication. Lyndon
Johnson was able personally to select targets for the American
Air Force to bomb in North Vietnam because he could convey
his wishes instantly to a commander halfway around the
world.

Centralization of military authority arises, as well, from the
requirement for rapid military action. Nuclear weapons provoked two fears that made the capacity to respond instantly
seem necessary. The first was the fear of a disarming surprise
attack, which would cripple the American nuclear force and
leave the United States defenseless. The second was the fear
on the part of the Europeans that the United States would not
come to their defense. In both cases, in order to keep the Soviet Union at bay, it seemed necessary for the United States to
be visibly prepared to respond instantly to Soviet aggression.
Decentralized arrangements might better produce a rapid response to aggression but would give broad authority to military commanders in the field, as Goldwater suggested, which
would violate the American tradition of civilian control of the
military.

The Soviet arrangements for using nuclear weapons are not
a matter of public record. It may be that, despite the Russian
and Soviet tradition of concentrated political authority, the
nature of the Soviet political system makes for *less* nuclear
authority in the hands of a single person than is the case in the
United States. The American political system is open. Its pro-

visions for using nuclear weapons cannot remain wholly secret. Because the adversary is bound to know something of these arrangements, for the sake of effective deterrence the Americans must promote the impression that the United States is capable of rapid nuclear response, which means reposing the authority to order a response in one person rather than leaving it to a procedure that could be time-consuming. The Soviet system operates in secret. The Soviets do not have to make their arrangements for using nuclear weapons explicit, and so they do not have to assign responsibility to one person. Moreover, the prerogatives of position in the Soviet system are less clearly defined than in the United States. There is less distinction between the man and the office. The boundaries of responsibility in the United States are relatively well fixed by law and custom. In the Soviet Union they are constantly being contested. To bestow nuclear responsibility on one person, therefore, would be to concede what is perpetually at issue in Kremlin politics.

Finally, the Soviets may feel that the capacity to decide upon a nuclear strike instantly is less urgently required than the Americans believe. On the other hand, in practice the two sets of arrangements may in fact be similar. No President would be likely to bring the American nuclear arsenal into action without consulting at least a small circle of advisors; similarly, the circle of Soviet officials in charge of nuclear weapons is not likely to be large.

The presidential monopoly of legitimate authority over the American nuclear arsenal testifies not only to the reach of modern means of communication and the requirements for nuclear deterrence, but also to the special character of the bomb. The decision to use nuclear weapons involves, after all, the choice of a particular explosive. Ordinarily this is a tactical decision, and not an especially important one. The choice of targets, not of weapons, has usually commanded the attention of the highest civil authorities. Nuclear weapons are so different from other kinds of armaments, however, and their use would be so momentous, that the decision to employ them is considered as important as any that can be made.

Presidential control of nuclear weapons fits the letter of the American Constitution. The President is constitutionally the commander in chief of the armed forces, and as such is in charge of conducting wars that must, however, be begun by a congressional declaration. A decision to use nuclear weapons is technically part of the conduct of war. But a nuclear war would likely be "a new war in every sense save the legal one."[12] The presidency has not been vested with such enormous authority because of a constitutional quirk.

There have been opportunities to broaden, if not to shift, the responsibility for triggering the American nuclear arsenal. In the wake of the Vietnam conflict presidential authority in foreign policy was extensively debated. A War Powers Act making more explicit than does the constitutional language the division of authority between Congress and the executive branch over armed conflict was passed in 1973. It left unaltered the nation's arrangements for nuclear weapons; indeed, the debate barely touched on them.[13] Subsequently, the Federation of American Scientists proposed that the President be required to secure congressional approval before initiating a nuclear war. The proposal would have had the Chief Executive share his nuclear authority not with field commanders, as Barry Goldwater had suggested, but with other presumably sober, responsible, democratically elected public officials. The intent was to make nuclear weapons more, not less, difficult to employ, and to help guard against a dangerous act by an irresponsible occupant of the White House – a possibility that Richard Nixon's last days in office had brought to public attention.[14] The proposal was worded to permit the President to order nuclear retaliation against an initial Soviet attack on his own so that the provision for consultation would not "affect the deterrent or tie his hands."[15] Nonetheless, it stirred little interest and was not enacted. The President retains authority over the American nuclear arsenal through the actions – or the failure to act – of the elected representatives of the American people.

Whether or not it places the President "in a radically new relation to the whole of human reality,"[16] this authority makes him an extraordinarily powerful person, so powerful as to hark back to a practice that dates from a much earlier period in the West – long before the first modern military revolution – and to non-Western societies that are historically contemporary but culturally distant: the imputation to the ruler of divine powers.[17] Perhaps the reason for delegating nuclear authority to the President is similar to the role that anthropologists have assigned to divine kingship: a means of coping with forces that seem beyond human powers of understanding and control. Whereas for preliterate, agrarian societies this meant typically the weather, on which their lives depended but which they could not influence, in the modern world it has come to mean the huge nuclear stockpiles of the United States and the Soviet Union.

The imperial presidency

The American President does not have divine powers. He is, however, extremely powerful, and his power extends beyond his monopoly of nuclear authority. The growth of presidential power is in fact one of the widely remarked features of the American political system in the nuclear age.

The Constitution establishes the President as the first among equals. He stands at the head of the executive branch of the federal government, which is counterbalanced by the legislative and judicial branches. This balance was purposely crafted. The Constitution's framers had had dismaying experiences with a powerful executive. They had been the victims, as they saw it, of King George III of England. To spare themselves and their successors a recurrence of arbitrary rule, they deliberately parceled out governmental power among different institutions, putting what came to be known as "checks and balances" in place to keep any one of them, especially the presidency, from dominating the others.

For at least a century their design accomplished its purpose. In 1891 Lord Bryce, the British observer of the American political system, said of the President:

He is George III shorn of a part of his prerogative by the intervention of the Senate in treaties and appointments, of another part by the restriction of his action to Federal affairs, while his dignity and his influence are diminished by holding office for four years instead of for life. His salary is too small to permit him either to maintain a Court or to corrupt the legislature; nor can he seduce the virtue of the citizens by the gift of titled nobility, for such are altogether forbidden.[18]

The restraints on presidential authority that Lord Bryce noted appeared in the 1960s and 1970s to have slackened; his late-nineteenth-century picture of the office seemed to have an archaic ring to it. His late-twentieth-century successors, for the most part, have seen a President closer in style and substance to George III than he did. The literature on the modern presidency generally emphasizes the expansion of its authority. The titles of books on the office published in the 1970s, like *The Imperial Presidency* and *Choosing Our King*, bespeak this theme.[19]

Is there a connection between these two postwar institutions, the imperial presidency and the nuclear presidency? It has been asserted that the second is the cause of the first, that there has arisen "the tendency for whoever was given custody of the new [nuclear] weapons to gather into his hands a dangerous array of other powers."[20] Has the impact of nuclear weapons on leaders and leadership in the United States contributed to the expansion of the prerogatives of the head of the executive branch of the federal government?

Evidence to contradict this proposition comes from the experience of other Western liberal states, where executive authority has grown in the absence of large nuclear arsenals. Britain is an instructive case. As in the United States, there is in Britain a tradition of partitioning power, not among different functional branches of government but within the institution that serves both legislative and executive purposes – Parliament. In the nineteenth century power shifted, in Bagehot's famous observation, from Parliament as a whole to the cabinet. Since 1945, parliamentary power has shifted again, from the cabinet to the Prime Minister.[21] Although the British nuclear arsenal that the Prime Minister controls is small compared to that of the United States, collegial responsibility in the British, as in the American, government has given way to individual prerogative.[22]

The expansion of the executive authority in both cases owes a great deal to the process by which ordinary men and women achieved the right to take part in politics and to influence government, which occurred more or less simultaneously with, but separately from, the industrial revolution.[23] At first, the diffusion of political authority reduced the role of the government in Britain and the United States. Laissez-faire was the reigning doctrine of the nineteenth century. In the twentieth century, however, central governments have acquired more and more responsibility for promoting social welfare. This has tended to become the responsibility of the executive, whose authority has grown accordingly. Moreover, since 1945 especially, governments have assumed responsibility for guiding national economies, and macro-economic policy has also become the preserve of the executive.

Nuclear weapons are not the sole cause of the growth of presidential power. Accounts of the "imperial" character of the modern presidency, however, usually emphasize the President's power in foreign, not domestic, policy. So different are his prerogatives in the two areas that it has been argued that the presidency is really two separate offices: one for domestic, the other for international affairs.[24] The proposition may therefore be modified: The President's nuclear authority has expanded his sway over American foreign policy. This proposition has received support from no less authoritative a source than the Supreme Court: "This power [of the President in the areas of national defense and foreign policy], largely unchecked by the legislative and judicial branches, has been pressed to the very hilt in the nuclear-missile age."[25]

But there is evidence that undercuts it. The post-World War II period is not the first instance of expanded presidential authority over foreign affairs. Jefferson, Lincoln, Wilson, and Franklin Roosevelt all were accused of overstepping the constitutionally defined limits in this area. The boundary between executive and legislative powers over the conduct of American foreign policy has in fact been in dispute since the earliest days of the republic. The debate about presidential power between Pacificus and Helvidius in the *Federalist Pa-*

pers centers on George Washington's unilateral proclamation
of American neutrality between Britain and France at the end
of the eighteenth century.

Presidential power has expanded most dramatically in wartime, when normal procedures are suspended and rules are set
aside in the interest of the highest of all national goals – survival. The inherent advantages of the executive over the legislature, especially the capacity to act decisively, come to the
fore then. "In time of war," a 1946 Supreme Court opinion
says, "the nation simply changes gears."[26]

The pattern is a familiar one. Thucydides records that after
war broke out the Athenians not only elected Pericles general
of their army but "put all their powers into his hands" as well.
The result was that "in what was nominally a democracy
power was really in the hands of the first citizen."[27] It is a
familiar part of the history of political thought as well. Ma-
chiavelli, perhaps a modern but certainly not a contemporary
theorist of politics, believed that in time of danger even the
most emphatically republican state would have to deliver
power to a single authority or face ruin.[28] There is even evidence that the framers of the Constitution were willing to
place enormous power in the hands of the President in wartime, despite their misgivings about executive authority, because they read history as showing that the failure to do so
meant disaster.[29]

The framers certainly expected that such wars as the United
States would fight would be occasional, brief affairs. American history through 1945, as a whole, vindicated this expectation. Then came a great change. The United States became involved in international politics permanently, on a grand scale,
locked in a bitter, dangerous rivalry with the Soviet Union.
There was no retiring from the Cold War, no respite from it,
and virtually no conflict anywhere – on the Korean peninsula,
in Indochina, or in the former Belgian Congo – that did not get
caught up in it. The power of the American presidency has
always swelled in time of emergency, and the Cold War made
emergency a permanent condition. After 1945, as one histo-

rian put it, the President "found himself daily in front of issues such as had arisen before only in wartime."[30]

Nuclear weapons contributed something to this continual atmosphere of emergency. The Cold War has no doubt seemed more urgent because nuclear weapons were bound up with it. It would have been a matter of considerable urgency without them, however. It was, in fact, urgent before nuclear weapons took center stage. In 1950, when President Truman ordered American troops to Korea to help repel the invasion from the north, the Soviet nuclear arsenal was in its infancy. Not the new weapons of mass destruction, or at least not they alone, but the way that Americans came to define their role in the world kindled this pervasive sense of emergency, which in turn has enlarged the power of the American chief executive.

Insofar as the President has taken greater command of American foreign policy since 1945, therefore, this has not been wholly – perhaps not even mainly – due to his nuclear authority. The proposition that the nuclear presidency has fed the imperial presidency has, moreover, another shortcoming. Postwar presidents have not been all-powerful, even where issues of foreign affairs were concerned. The President, it is true, was responsible for initiating and conducting the American wars in Korea and Vietnam. In both cases he proceeded at first without the formal assent of the legislative branch. But although the President waged war without Congress, he did not wage it against the wishes of the House of Representatives or the Senate or over the objections of the American public. In each case he was expressing the national consensus that the United States was obliged to resist the spread of communism by all necessary means, including the use of force, and that fighting in Korea and Indochina were acts of resistance.

President Truman secured no formal congressional authorization for the commitment of American troops to battle in Korea. He believed that he needed none. When congressional leaders were apprised of his plans, however, almost none objected. On the contrary, the announcement that American ground and sea forces were being dispatched to the Korean peninsula met with broad approval.[31] So did Lyndon Johnson's military policies in Vietnam. In the summer of 1964, in response to reports of a North Vietnamese attack on several American patrol boats in the Gulf of Tonkin, the Senate passed a resolution authorizing retaliation. Later, with half a million American troops fighting in Indochina, the Johnson Administration cited this resolution as the functional equivalent of a declaration of war. This post hoc interpretation of the Gulf of Tonkin Resolution did some violence to the context in which it was approved. Nonetheless, President Johnson's orders for a sharp increase in the level of American participation in the war aroused almost no significant political opposition at the time.

Both the Korean and the Vietnam wars became unpopular not because the public abandoned its faith in the principles on which the American role was based but because the Truman and Johnson administrations proved incapable of bringing either to a successful conclusion. There is a remarkable similarity in the patterns of public support for each war over time.[32] In both cases, as American casualties rose, the war's popularity fell. Along with it fell the popularity of the President, to the point at which both Harry Truman and Lyndon Johnson declined to run for reelection. So the President has often been swimming with the tide when he has appeared most powerful, and when he has attempted to swim against it he has sometimes been thwarted.

Presidential frustration has extended even to nuclear weapons. The chief executive has kept control over the "doomsday button," but he has not had unchallenged authority to decide which weapons that button will launch. Congress has had a say in this question. It is a question that is ideally suited to congressional influence, because it is decided over time rather than instantly and because it lends itself to bargaining, trading, and compromise. Here the Congress has often opposed and sometimes overruled the President.[33]

The President has been unable to act unimpeded on another important nuclear issue – negotiations with the Soviet Union. Each President since 1945 has favored discussions with the

Soviets on the abolition, or at least the control, of nuclear weapons. Each has wished to go further in these discussions than the Congress, or the national consensus, has been willing to permit. This is a recurrent theme in the postwar period. Some presidents have succeeded in obtaining nuclear agreements with the Soviets. Some have failed. All have tried. The persistence of their attempts is as significant as their occasional failures. It illustrates an important influence that these armaments have had. Presidential support for arms control is the most conspicuous effect on leadership of the nuclear revolution in warfare.

The arms control presidency

Every American President from Harry Truman to Jimmy Carter has been preoccupied with disarmament, or with the more modest goal of arms control, or with both. Each has vowed to do whatever possible to abolish or control nuclear armaments. This is not surprising. Words are cheap, especially words deploring nuclear armaments. Everybody deplores them. No one wants them to be used. The test of commitment on such issues comes with specific proposals to translate principle into practice. Every American public official, for example, gladly sings the praises of the free enterprise system. Not every one, however, is ready to support measures to implement the principles of free enterprise, such as the removal of subsidies for favored industries, the dismantling of tariff restrictions, or the enforcement of the antitrust laws.

So it is with nuclear negotiations. The test of genuine commitment is the willingness to try to accommodate Soviet objectives with American aims, and to brave the wrath of domestic groups that are less than enthusiastic about trafficking with the Soviets. Every postwar President has passed this test. Every one has been willing to go beyond the safety of general platitudes; each has ventured into the thicket of the particulars of nuclear negotiations. This has been true even when relations between the two great powers have been most bitter. It was true even when the United States was waging war with a

Soviet ally in Southeast Asia. The postwar presidents' shared interest in disarmament and arms control stands in contrast, for some, to their policies and proclamations before entering office. Once installed in the White House, however, every President, whatever his previous views on nuclear weapons, has taken up the cause of nuclear negotiation.

Harry Truman was the first nuclear President. He remains the only President, indeed the only person, to have authorized an atomic explosion for other than experimental purposes. His record in office does not mark him as someone likely to have felt deeply about controlling the new weapon that he inherited with the office. His distrust of the Soviet government was apparent almost from the moment he took office. He was in power at the beginning of the Cold War, when the proper, if not cordial, relations between the United States and the Soviet Union that their common struggle with fascism had created turned to hostility. During the Truman presidency both nuclear arsenals were relatively small. It was still possible to consider them more sophisticated versions of the munitions of the past. Between 1945 and 1949 the United States had a monopoly, and after that a distinct advantage, in nuclear weaponry. Truman had, on the face of it, no strong incentive to search for nuclear accommodation with the Soviets – and some reason to be wary of any dealings with them.

He was, however, one of the moving forces behind the first disarmament proposal, the Baruch Plan. This was a scheme to put every facet of nuclear energy, from the mining of uranium to the manufacture of the bomb itself, under international supervision. It was a presidential initiative. In his 1946 State of the Union Address Truman stressed his desire for effective control of the atomic bomb through the United Nations. In November of that year he issued a joint declaration with the prime ministers of Great Britain and Canada – Clement Attlee and McKenzie King – calling upon the UN to accept responsibility for controlling atomic energy. He appointed a committee chaired by Dean Acheson, then Assistant Secretary of State, and David Lilienthal, head of the Tennessee Valley Authority, to work out the details of such an arrangement, and chose the noted financier, Bernard Baruch, to present a modified version of the committee's recommendations to the United Nations.

The Soviet Union emphatically rejected the Baruch Plan. In retrospect, it is difficult to imagine their consenting to any form of international management of atomic energy.[34] But there is no evidence that Truman expected the Plan to fail. He guided it through the channels of the American government and into an international forum in the face of considerable domestic opposition. His Secretary of State, James Byrnes, wanted the United States to keep its exclusive nuclear franchise.[35] Influential members of Congress warned against giving away the nation's atomic secrets through the creation of an international authority.[36] The military was unenthusiastic.[37] The President pushed ahead, undaunted by the reservations of others.

The failure of the Baruch Plan set a pattern that nuclear negotiations followed for the better part of two decades. Truman's role in authorizing its formation and putting it forward carried over into the presidency of Dwight Eisenhower. Eisenhower came to the White House after a career in the Army, but his background did not keep him from feeling sympathetic to the idea of restraints on nuclear armaments.[38] Eisenhower's Republican Party, however, had accused the Democrats of resisting too feebly the ambitions of the Soviet Union and the spread of communism. Republican leaders in Congress took a dim view of negotiations with the Soviets.[39] Eisenhower's Secretary of State, John Foster Dulles, who is usually regarded as having exerted considerable influence on the conduct of American foreign policy, agreed with them. Dulles was suspicious of bargains of any sort with the Soviets.[40] Moreover, during the Eisenhower years the American government embraced a defense doctrine that emphasized the role of nuclear weapons in defending the nation's interests. Finally, President Eisenhower was a man whose concept of the office did not lend itself to the kind of bold international initiatives that nuclear negotiations seemed to require. Eisenhower did not see the presidency as a pulpit or as the nerve center of the political system. He thought of himself rather as sitting atop an organizational pyramid, with the responsibility for addressing only those matters that could not be resolved successfully at lower levels.[41] So his presidency was not auspicious for energetic presidential efforts on behalf of arms control.

But the persistent attempt to find common ground on nuclear matters with the Soviet Union is a distinct feature of the Eisenhower presidency. Eisenhower seized upon the death of Stalin in 1953 as the occasion for a broad offer of improved relations with the Soviets, which he made in what came to be known as the "Chance for Peace" speech.[42] The same year he made a dramatic proposal to the United Nations for joint participation by the two great powers in an international organization to exploit atomic energy for peaceful purposes. This proposal came to be called the "Atoms for Peace" plan. In 1955, acting, as he had with the two 1953 initiatives, more or less on his own, he put forward a proposal for "Open Skies" that would have given each great power the right to make aerial inspections of the other's territory. In 1958 he ordered a moratorium on the testing of nuclear weapons in the atmosphere. In the two last years of his term, following – perhaps not coincidentally – Dulles's death, he threw himself into a strenuous bout of personal diplomacy in quest of accommodation with the Soviets. In 1959 he entertained Nikita Khrushchev and made a round-the-world trip in search of peace. The next year he arranged a summit meeting, with nuclear issues on the agenda, which had to be canceled after the Soviet Union shot down an American U-2 reconnaissance plane.

John Kennedy intended to be an active President, for Eisenhower, he believed, had not been. At the beginning of his presidency, he did not, however, seem likely to be active on behalf of arms control. He came into office promising to close the "missile gap," the dangerous lead in nuclear-tipped intercontinental ballistic missiles that the Soviet Union was thought to hold over the United States. Kennedy ordered a large increase in the size of the American strategic nuclear force at the beginning of his term. He also presided over the creation of the Arms Control and Disarmament Agency, but he did not invest it with real authority. Kennedy's nuclear emphasis, however, shifted during his term of office. His brush with war over the Soviet missiles in Cuba in October 1962 turned his attention to nuclear negotiation. In the final months of his abbreviated term, he signed the Limited Test Ban Treaty, the first formal nuclear accord. He took some political risk in doing so. The example of Woodrow Wilson's humiliating failure to secure American participation in the League of Nations spurred Kennedy to organize a campaign to persuade the Senate to ratify it. The campaign was successful. Kennedy was preparing, before he died, to use the agreement as a principal theme in his campaign for reelection in 1964.

The man who took his place, Lyndon Johnson, had no history of devotion to the pursuit of arms control. He came from a state and a region where Dulles's attitude toward negotiations of any kind with the Soviet Union predominated. In the Senate he had been interested in fortifying the American nuclear arsenal, not restricting it. He had been part of the chorus of Democrats that had decried the missile gap. He had chaired a special subcommittee on military preparedness, which had roundly criticized the Eisenhower administration for keeping the nation's defenses in bad repair. Johnson was determined to leave his mark on American history, but in domestic, not international, affairs. He bent his energies to shepherding through the Congress the largest volume of social welfare legislation since the New Deal. What time remained was consumed by the war in Vietnam, which gradually moved to the center of his concerns.

It is not easy to hammer out arms control agreements with one hand, while waging war with the other. Still, Johnson presided over the consummation of a Nonproliferation Treaty with the Soviet Union, which was ready for signing in 1968. He went further. He tried to start formal discussions on limiting the strategic arsenals of the two great powers. The efforts of his administration paved the way for the grand negotiations of the Nixon years, and might themselves have been more productive had not the Soviet invasion of Czechoslovakia prevented Johnson from officially inaugurating them, just as the U-2 affair had cut short Eisenhower's quest for nuclear agreements eight years earlier.

Richard Nixon, who followed Johnson, had a reputation as a staunch anticommunist and a man as resolutely hostile to the Soviet Union as any public figure of the postwar period. His term of office shows most vividly the attraction of nuclear negotiations for the President, whoever he is. In the 1968 campaign he tried to repeat the Democratic success with the missile issue in 1960 by floating the charge that the incumbent Democrats had permitted a "security gap" to occur, to the disadvantage of the United States. Nixon was suspicious of the Strategic Arms Limitation Talks that Johnson had tried to set in motion. One of his early acts as President was to postpone them until he and his aides could study the matter thoroughly.[43]

Three years later, however, Nixon signed the most extensive arms control accords ever enacted. The 1972 SALT agreements effectively prohibited strategic defensive systems and froze the offensive arsenals of the United States and the Soviet Union. They served, too, as an unofficial charter for continuing those complicated negotiations. Finally, having entered the White House after opposing Lyndon Johnson's efforts to open arms control talks with the Soviets, and then putting aside the negotiation positions that the Johnson administration had developed, Nixon left it clinging to the nuclear agreements he had helped to design, like a man clutching a life preserver in a stormy sea. His plea for his political life rested on his skill at arms control negotiations. His successor, Gerald Ford, with a similar record of indifference, at best, to arms control before assuming office, agreed in principle to a second SALT accord only a few months after inheriting the presidency. And *his* successor, Jimmy Carter, a southerner and an Annapolis graduate, made a second SALT agreement the centerpiece of his foreign policy.

American presidents in the nuclear age, from Harry Truman to Jimmy Carter, form a diverse group. Their personalities and their policies have varied widely. Besides their nuclear responsibility they have had one thing in common: All have pressed for nuclear negotiations with the Soviet Union. Why has this been so?

The presidential burden

The reason for presidential sponsorship of nuclear negotiations lies in the President's role in government and politics or, more properly, his roles, because he plays more than one. He is the focal point, as Richard Neustadt has noted, of four lines of leadership.[44]

He is a partisan leader. He is the head of his political party and the most important player in the ongoing contest for power that takes place in every political system. The President is a professional politician. He comes to office, and stays there, by winning elections. Electoral calculations are therefore a major source of presidential policies. The President has, as well, an international role. His special preeminence in foreign affairs makes him the American official who represents the United States for foreign governments and upon whom they press their claims. As by far the more important of the two officials chosen by the entire electorate, the President is also a national leader. It falls to him to express the national interest, or to try to strike a balance among many competing interests. Finally, the President has an executive role, the chief of the executive branch of the federal government. He must both assert its prerogatives and mediate its intramural disputes. Here his national and executive roles are similar.

His partisan role occasionally pushes the President in the direction of nuclear negotiations. It has proven politically advantageous to go before the electorate with a newly signed nuclear agreement with the Soviet Union in hand. The 1972 SALT accords certainly assisted Mr. Nixon's reelection. But just as often, a reputation for partiality to arms control has seemed a political liability. President Gerald Ford never brought the 1974 protocol on arms limitation that he and Soviet General Secretary Brezhnev signed to the Congress for ratification because, among other things, he feared that this would damage his political standing, especially within his own party. The best evidence that a favorable attitude toward nuclear negotiations is not an unmixed political blessing is the fact that although the postwar presidents who made their political careers wholly or mainly after 1945 all came to the White House with records of staunch support for military preparedness, none was a notable champion of arms control. Presidents Kennedy, Johnson, Nixon, and Ford had understood that the way to move ahead in American politics was to speak out in favor of more, not fewer, weapons. The national political figures who took up the cause of arms restraint before entering the White House never got there. Henry Wallace in 1948, Adlai Stevenson in 1956, and Hubert Humphrey in 1960 made the need for nuclear accommodation an important theme in their respective presidential campaigns.[45]

The President's international role subjects him to appeals for controls on nuclear weapons and even for full-scale disarmament. These come mainly from nations that do not have nuclear armaments, are proud of their abstinence, and want the great powers to follow their example. These nations use the United Nations, both the General Assembly and various special committees, to make their feelings known. The President has thought the good will of these nuclear teetotalers important enough to listen politely, or to have his representatives do so. But he has rarely taken what they have said seriously enough to adjust American nuclear policy to fit their views.[46] International pressures have pushed presidents away from arms control. When Americans and Soviets have negotiated privately the other members of NATO have worried that they will strike a bargain unfavorable to them. It has fallen to the President to soothe these anxieties.

The President's national role means that all roads lead to the White House. Every grievance, every idea, every special interest finds its way to the President's doorstep. Because so many crowd in on him no single group can reasonably expect to have great influence on presidential policy. One group, however, has been able to claim presidential attention and to use it to encourage the interest of several presidents in nuclear negotiations – scientists. The nuclear age has given them prestige and entree to the highest councils of government, a privilege they never before enjoyed in the United States. Their role in making the bomb weighed on their consciences after 1945; having created nuclear weapons, they felt a special duty to help make sure that they would never be used. Many became partisans of nuclear negotiations, and their expertise made them particularly effective. They began to lobby for nuclear restraints as soon as the atomic bomb appeared feasible. Even before Hiroshima the Danish physicist Neils Bohr sounded an alarm about the perils of atomic energy that reached the highest officials of the American government and set in motion the train of events that culminated in the Baruch Plan.[47] Dwight Eisenhower set up a President's Science Advisory Committee, and its members reinforced his instinct to seek nuclear agreements with the Soviet Union. John Kennedy relied heavily upon the advice of his scientific counselors in wrestling with the problem of nuclear testing.[48]

The President's role as a national leader – in effect the national leader – points him in the direction of nuclear negotiations, as well, by making him the natural target of a particular kind of political appeal – one that revolves around the distinction between narrow, concentrated interests and diffuse, general ones.[49] The first, of which the manufacture of armaments is an example, lend themselves to formal organization. Organized interests, called "pressure groups," lobby for favorable policies, usually in the Congress. The second have no natural ethnic, regional, or economic base upon which to build a politically effective organization. The cause of arms restriction falls into this second category, and its proponents have petitioned the President because he is less susceptible to the demands of pressure groups than are other public officials; he is the natural champion of a cause that brings minor or intangible benefits to all, but substantial, palpable economic advantages to none.

The President is the patron of diffuse, overconcentrated interests; thus his national role blends into his executive duties. For the interests dubious of nuclear agreements with the Soviet Union are represented within the executive branch of government as well as outside it. The armed forces often throw their political weight against nuclear proposals that presidents find attractive, and more than one chief executive has certainly felt what Secretary of State Kissinger was moved to say in 1974: "Both sides must convince their military establishments of the benefits of restraint."[50]

Because presidents have found sections of the executive branch inhospitable to their designs for nuclear accommodation, they have often tried to bypass their own governments on nuclear issues and deal directly, personally, with the Soviets. John Kennedy, for example, was at pains to keep the July 1963 negotiations for a test ban treaty under close personal supervision. He sent a small hand-picked party to Moscow to work out its details and kept in direct touch with its members throughout their stay. Richard Nixon devised a formal system for making and carrying out foreign policy, with the National Security Council at its center, that was explicitly designed to circumvent the Congress and the executive bureaucracy. The system worked smoothly during the first round of SALT negotiations, and the 1972 accords stand as its proudest achievement.[51]

His national and executive roles make the President the most powerful potential lobbyist for arms control within the American government. This explains why supporters of arms control, like scientists, have pinned their hopes on him. But they do not monopolize his attention. They cannot compel him to promote their views. It is not always in his political interest – and political interest is the north star of every practicing politician – to heed and act on their advice. So the question remains, why has every postwar President done so?

Each postwar President's enthusiasm for arms control has arisen, in part, from a conflation of his partisan and national roles. If politics is, as Disraeli put it, a scramble "up the greasy pole," then the President sits at the top. Others strive to go higher than they are, to assume positions of greater prestige and acquire more power. He has arrived. He contemplates a different problem: what to do wtih the power that he has.

One thing he invariably does is tend to his long-term reputation. Their standing with posterity, whether it is called honor, glory, or fame, has always mattered to political leaders. To an American President this means the verdict of history. "For most American Presidents, even the less visionary among them," an observer of the office has written, "there have been few concerns more nagging than the distant judgment by history."[52]

In the past the favored avenue to fame was war. Princes strove to impress posterity by heroic deeds on the field of battle. The most celebrated American leaders have, on the whole, been war presidents: Washington, Lincoln, Franklin Roosevelt. Nuclear weapons have changed this. A President now reckons that a contribution to nuclear peace gives him a purchase on the good opinion of the future.

Dwight Eisenhower reflected this change in the approach he planned to make to Khrushchev in their meeting in 1959. He decided to invoke the Soviet leader's "priceless opportunity to go down in history as one of the truly great statesmen of all time, my thesis being that if he would use the power of his position in the furtherance of disarmament, relaxation of tensions, and support of peace, he could capture the respect and admiration of the world for years to come. My proposal was by no means merely a sop to the man's ego. It was a chance which I sincerely believed he had before him."[53] Had the two men been able to make a sweeping settlement of the nuclear issues that they confronted, they would have earned shining places in the annals of diplomacy.

During the Cuban missile crisis, John Kennedy thought of the future generations of Americans – and Russians – whose fates hung in the balance as the two great powers moved toward a collision. In the last painful hours of his presidency, Richard Nixon apparently consoled himself at the prospect of leaving office in disgrace with the thought that the negotiations he had conducted with the Soviet Union would earn for him the honorable reputation of a "peacemaker."[54] Presidents are not more humane than other people. But their political role gives them a particular incentive, in the nuclear age, for putting their humane instincts at the center of their public policies.

It is his executive role that pushes the President most forcefully toward nuclear accommodation. He is the nation's only military *and* civilian official. The intimate acquaintance with the realities of nuclear technology that he shares with the professional military is tempered by a broader perspective. In fact, the President's role as commander in chief of the armed forces gives him not just a different perspective from the military's but an entirely different responsibility. The job of the soldier is to win wars. The task of the President is to decide which wars to fight, and whether victory, if it can be achieved, will be worth the lives and resources that it will cost. The military's responsibility is to receive and carry out orders, including the order to use the nation's nuclear weapons. The President gives the orders; it is he who must decide whether the moment of truth has arrived.

This special nuclear responsibility is embodied – literally – in the man with the satchel who follows the President everywhere. It is this responsibility that has produced the enthusiasm for nuclear negotiations that is a consistent feature of the postwar presidency. Every postwar President has considered nuclear negotiatons with the Soviet Union a way of keeping the nuclear peace, for which he has had a special personal responsibility. This has been so even when the connection between the terms of the proposal in question and the possible outbreak of war has been tenuous. Eisenhower's "Atoms for Peace" program was designed to encourage the peaceful uses of nuclear energy, in particular the generation of electric power, but it did nothing directly to help prevent war.[55] Kennedy's test ban treaty stopped some, but not all, weapon tests and made no provision for the weapons that were already tested and deployed. Even the Strategic Arms Limitation agreements, which have placed a ceiling on the totals of some categories of nuclear armaments, have left both sides with thousands of deadly warheads. The 1972 treaty restricting antiballistic missiles is an exception to this pattern. By ratifying the assured destruction capacity of both the United States and the Soviet Union, the treaty reduced any temptation that either might feel to launch a preemptive attack and so removed, or at least reduced, one possible cause of war. But the temptation to launch a disarming attack is only one cause, and perhaps not the likeliest one, of nuclear war, and perhaps too one that would not have been particularly dangerous even without the treaty.

Presidents have prized nuclear agreements with the Soviet Union not only, perhaps not even mainly, for the instrumental purposes these have served, but for their symbolic value. They stand as symbols of the joint Soviet – American capacity to cooperate, despite their rivalry. If the two great powers can cooperate to reach arms control agreements, by this logic, they can cooperate to avoid war.

Symbolic reassurances are not, perhaps, the firmest imaginable guarantees of peace. But they are the firmest guarantees that the United States and the Soviet Union have been able to give each other. For peace is negative. It is the absence of war. Achieving peace involves refraining from fighting. Judicious diplomacy is the best guarantor of international harmony. But the United States and the Soviet Union have not been able to settle, finally, the issues that divide them that could ignite war. Nor have they been able to abolish nuclear weapons. The horrifying possibility of nuclear war that persists has, not surprisingly, given rise to the desire for some more tangible evidence that such a war will not occur than faith in the discretion and prudence of national leaders. Arms control agreements provide such evidence. They are concrete indicators of peaceful intentions in an era in which, because of the enormous costs and terrors of war, peace is more important than ever before.

Presidents have said as much. Underlying his speech announcing the "Atoms for Peace" plan, according to Eisenhower, was the "clear conviction that the world [was] courting disaster in the armaments race, that something must be done to put a brake on the momentum." He hoped that the plan would serve as a base from which cooperation with the Soviet Union could expand.[56] Kennedy regarded the Test Ban Treaty

202 The nuclear presidency

as a first small step in the long and difficult process of reaching nuclear accommodation with the Soviets. Johnson summed up the connection between arms control measures of all kinds and the need for nuclear peace in his comments on a joint agreement with the Soviet Union to produce less fissionable material, an agreement whose importance was almost entirely symbolic: "We must remember that peace will not come suddenly. It will not emerge dramatically from a single agreement or a single meeting. It will be advanced by concrete and limited accommodations, by the gradual growth of common interests, by the increased awareness of shifting dangers and alignments, and by the development of trust in good faith based on a reasoned view of the world."[57]

Soviet leaders may well have behaved in similar fashion. Although the lines of nuclear authority in the Soviet Union are not publicly known, it is plausible to assume that the First Secretary of the Communist Party, who has invariably emerged as the most powerful member of the Politburo, has considerable nuclear responsibility.

The First Secretaries after Stalin, Nikita Khrushchev and Leonid Brezhnev, seem, like the American presidents, to have championed the cause of nuclear accommodation. After the Cuban missile crisis a struggle apparently took place within the upper echelons of the Soviet leadership over the proper course of relations with the United States. Khrushchev fought for a policy of limited cooperation, against a faction wholly distrustful of the Americans. His preference won out, and the result was the Limited Test Ban Treaty of 1963. Brezhnev, again on the basis of what little evidence is available, seems to have gone through a similar battle in 1972. President Richard Nixon was to visit Moscow in May. In April the United States responded to a North Vietnamese attack on the south with a dramatically escalated campaign of bombing against the north and by mining the harbors of the North Vietnamese cities of Haiphong and Hanoi, thereby blockading them. This could only be interpreted as a concerted affront to the Soviet Union, North Vietnam's principal ally, and so it threatened the Nixon visit and the improvement in Soviet–American relations that the visit was designed to signal. A debate apparently took place within the highest councils of the Soviet Union about whether to cancel the trip. Brezhnev evidently insisted upon proceeding on schedule. His chief critic, Pyotr Shelest, lost the argument, fell from political grace, and was dropped from the Politburo. Nixon arrived and concluded, with Brezhnev, the first Strategic Arms Limitation agreements.[58]

The General Secretary of the Soviet Community Party does not have the same institutional incentives for nuclear negotiation as the President of the United States. The two preside over radically different institutions. But they have a common personal motive for accommodation. Each has the power, or shares the power, to give the order to send a huge nuclear arsenal, or parts of it, hurtling toward the territory of the other. So terrible are the potential consequences of such an order that each wishes to do whatever he can to avoid giving it. One thing each leader can do is to work out nuclear agreements with his counterpart.

The impulse to enact nuclear accords has transcended the partisan differences among the postwar American presidents. It transcends the ideological gulf that separates the American from the Soviet political system. It appeals to a more fundamental emotion than partisanship or ideology.

It is no longer possible to speak with assurance of a single concept of human nature. Social scientists have broken it down into a hundred categories and given human behavior a thousand different interpretations. But the horror of nuclear destruction surely touches something that is shared widely among the different cultural varieties of *Homo sapiens*. The prospect of doomsday, or armageddon, is bound, to put it gently, to be unsettling, especially to the person who has the power to bring it about. Anybody, whatever his political commitments, will want to do whatever is in his power to forestall it. "The sitting President lives daily with the knowledge that at any time he, personally, may have to make a human judgment – or may fail to control someone else's judgment – which puts half the world in jeopardy and cannot be called back. You and I will recognize his burden intellectually; he actually ex-

periences it emotionally. It cannot help but set him – and his
needs – sharply apart from all the rest of us."⁵⁹

The President can devastate a city, an entire nation, even
half a continent with a single command. To the extent that the
supreme leader of the Soviet Union has this sort of power, he,
too, will feel the same responsibility. During the missile crisis
Khrushchev wrote to Kennedy: " I see, Mr. President, that you
too are not devoid of a sense of anxiety for the fate of the
world, of understanding and a proper evaluation of the character of contemporary war and of what war entails."⁶⁰ In similar fashion, although in less urgent circumstances, Leonid
Brezhnev said, "There is no more important task in present
conditions, one touching the destiny of every person on earth,
than to ensure progress toward reducing and eventually re-
moving the threat of a thermonuclear disaster."⁶¹

If this nuclear burden is not unbearable it cannot be easy to
bear. Every American President since 1945 has felt it weighing
on him, personally. So every man who has held the office has
sought agreements with the Soviet Union in order to lighten
it.

When Harry Truman saw aerial photographs of the damage
that the atomic bomb had done to Hiroshima, he was moved to
say that a "terrible responsibility" had fallen upon him and
his associates, a responsibility, he later wrote, "without precedent in history."⁶² Eisenhower once shouted in a discussion of
nuclear strategy, "There's just no point in talking about 'winning' a nuclear war. You might just as well talk about going
out and swimming the ocean." On a similar occasion he remarked, "You know, it is difficult. You come up to face these
terrible issues, and you know that what is in almost everyone's
heart is a wish for peace, and you want so much to do something. And then you wonder . . . if there really is anything you
can do."⁶³ In his memoirs Eisenhower wrote: "Of the various
presidential tasks to which I early determined to devote my
energies, none transcended in importance that of trying to
devise practical and acceptable means to lighten the burdens
of armaments and to lessen the likelihood of war."⁶⁴ "Most
people who talk about nuclear weapons have no conception of

what it all means," John Kennedy remarked after he had borne the presidential responsibility for two and one-half years, "but the fact is that the weapons are there and it is important that we develop a means for settling disputes peacefully instead of, as we have done through history, resorting to the use of arms."[65] Lyndon Johnson, in his account of his years in power, recalled that when he heard his successor pronounce the oath of office two thoughts went through his mind: "First, that I would not have to face the decision any more of taking any step in the Middle East or elsewhere, that might lead to world conflagration – the nightmare of my having to be the man who pressed the button to start World War III was passing; and second, that I had fervently sought peace through every available channel and at every opportunity and could have done no more."[66]

The public statements have a self-serving ring, especially because they are addressed to the audience – history – upon whom presidents have wanted to impress their devotion to peace. But the private words are revealing. And there is no reason to doubt that their nuclear responsibility has weighed heavily on these men. How could it have failed to do so? It would be difficult to believe that this had not obsessed them, that it had not haunted them, that it had not taken up permanent and menacing residence in a corner of each of their minds. It is not necessary to subscribe to any particular theory of the human personality to doubt that it is humanly possible to rest easily with such a responsibility. Harry Truman seemed to rest more easily than any of his successors. He never publicly regretted dropping the bomb and he dismissed others' doubts about the morality of the raids on Hiroshima and Nagasaki. But one section of his library in Independence, Missouri, was reserved for books on the bomb. At the end of one of the volumes was Horatio's speech in the last scene of *Hamlet*. Truman had underlined part of it:

Let me speak to the yet unknowing world
How these things came about: So shall you hear
Of carnal, bloody and unnatural acts,
Of accidental judgements, casual slaughters,

Of deaths put on by cunning and forced cause,
And, in this upshot, purposes mistook
Fall'n on the inventors' heads . . .
But let this same be presently perform'ed,
Even while men's minds are wild; lest more mischance,
On plots and errors happen.[67]

Leaders since Thucydides's day have had to worry about "mischance" and its consequences. The penalties in the nuclear age, however, exceed the darkest imaginings of the past. The responsibility for avoiding them has weighed on the American President. The nuclear age has brought with it a personal nightmare for each man who has held the office since 1945. The drive for arms control has been, for each of them, a way of trying to awaken from it.

The Bomb, Dread, and Eternity

Nuclear annihilation

After the first battles of the Peloponnesian War, as Thucydides tells it, the Athenians assembled to honor their dead. Pericles was chosen to address the public funeral. His speech was a tribute to Athens, praising the city's political institutions and the spirit of its people. The greatness of Athens, he argued, was both the reason and the justification for the deaths of those who fell in its defense. "This, then, is the kind of city for which these men, who could not bear the thought of losing her, nobly fought and nobly died. It is only natural that every one of us who survives them should be willing to undergo hardships in her service."[1]

Death, and the threat of death, are the central experiences of war. All societies have formal ways of recognizing and coming to terms with it. Some way, after all, is needed to persuade men to risk their lives in battle; Pericles plainly had this in mind.[2] It is not, however, simply death in war that societies recognize. Ceremonies and doctrines that provide some cultural context for death are universal features of organized social existence. Their purpose is to emphasize what continues even as an individual life ends; they connect death to life.

The need for "symbolic immortality" seems to be basic to human beings.[3] It can be achieved in biological terms, through a family; it can be achieved in cultural terms, through individual works like books, buildings, or businesses; it can be achieved in social terms, through membership in a group. In each case the person contributes to something of value that survives him.[4] Although he perishes, parts of his life continue. Death is not the end.

The expansion of military force since the French Revolution has exposed ever-larger numbers of people to death in war. Battles have left increasing numbers of men dead and wounded and, especially with the advent of aerial bombardment, more and more people have become potential targets of the weapons that technology has furnished.[5] The three modern military revolutions, the Napoleonic, the mechanical, and the nuclear, each made warfare much more deadly than it had been before. Moreover, the last two, at least, placed far greater strain upon the methods by which societies confer symbolic immortality upon their members than there had ever been before. "We cannot maintain our former attitude toward death," Freud wrote in the midst of World War I, "and have not yet discovered a new one."[6]

Art is the reflection of culture. The art, especially the literature, of the post-Napoleonic period reflected the traumatic impact not so much of the wars as of the revolution, which was more menacing to the literate, cultured classes of Europe. After 1918, however, the war itself had a shattering effect on every form of European art. The new nonrepresentational painting, the atonal music of the postwar period, and the writings of Joyce, Pound, and Eliot had in common the subversion of traditional forms that became the hallmark of modernism. Much of the writing about the war itself after 1918 had a characteristic tone – irony. Irony is the idiom of disproportion, of double meanings, of dashed hopes. Irony is apposite to all wars in the sense that all wars turn out to be worse than expected. World War I was much worse. Insofar as the writing about the war represents a watershed in Western literature – insofar, that is, as it may be said, as one critic put it, "that there seems to be one dominating form of modern understanding; that it is essentially ironic; and that it originates largely in the application of mind and memory to the events of the Great War"[7] – the industrial revolution in warfare may have created a permanent tension between Western society's technical capacity for killing and its cultural capacity for coming to terms with death.

As for the reflection in art of the third modern military revolution, strictly speaking there is, of course, no literature of World War III. The offstage presence of nuclear weapons, however, seems to extend the tone of some of the books about World War II beyond the irony of World War I, just as the nuclear revolution represents a further expansion of the destructive force that the mechanical military revolution had made available. These are not the novels published just after the war, like Norman Mailer's *The Naked and the Dead* and James Jones's *From Here to Eternity*, but rather novels that appeared fifteen, twenty, and twenty-five years after 1945: Joseph Heller's *Catch-22*, Kurt Vonnegut's *Slaughterhouse-Five*, and Thomas Pynchon's *Gravity's Rainbow*. (In this company, as well, belongs *Doctor Strangelove*, a film rather than a book, whose subject is not the second but a third, nuclear, world war.) Aerial bombardment is a major theme in each. And the tone of each is one of black humor, a kind of irony taken to the extreme. If the mechanical revolution in warfare seemed to strain the means by which society offered its members symbolic immortality, the tone of these works suggested that the nuclear revolution had made them utterly absurd.

As reflected in literature, therefore, the nuclear revolution in warfare is the extension of the previous modern military revolution. In each case an increased capacity for destruction imposed a strain on the cultural apparatus for making the prospect of death psychologically tolerable. In another sense, however, the nuclear revolution represents a sharp break with the past. The mechanical revolution in warfare and the *prospect* of nuclear destruction strained the cultural vehicles for symbolic immortality. The *fact* of nuclear war would obliterate them. The Napoleonic and the mechanical revolutions in warfare produced sweeping changes in the societies that they touched. A nuclear war that killed millions of people and laid waste to the cities and towns in which they had lived would likely destroy the ways of life they had followed, just as primitive cultures have died out upon contact with technologically more advanced ones. Although most scientific opinion holds it unlikely, it is even possible that by fracturing the earth's atmosphere, disrupting the ecology of the planet, and sowing deadly radioactivity everywhere, nuclear war could destroy the species *Homo sapiens.*

Nuclear war does not fit into the moral categories that are ordinarily applied to wars.[8] It undercuts familiar political ways of thinking by escaping the bounds of the very definition of war.[9] Similarly, it threatens to shatter the cultural mechanisms for coping with death by destroying everything that makes symbolic immortality possible. The difference between the wars in which the two previous modern military revolutions appeared and a full-scale nuclear war is the difference between destruction and annihilation. It is the difference between the end of an era and the end of a culture. Nuclear weapons, unlike all other weapons known to man, have "the power to make everything into nothing."[10]

How has this prospect affected those who face it? In theory, every human being alive today lives under the threat of nuclear annihilation. In fact, Americans, Russians, and to a lesser extent Europeans have borne the heaviest psychological burdens. At issue here are the effects on Americans, who have much more information about nuclear weapons than do the citizens of the Soviet Union and about whose reactions much more information is available. The question raises another one: where to look for evidence.

The prospect of nuclear annihilation is so daunting that it might be expected to saturate everyday life, and indeed, some observers believe that this has happened. "Impending disaster has become an everyday concern, so commonplace and familiar that nobody any longer gives much thought to how disaster might be averted."[11] "The image of total destruction . . . enters into every relationship involving parents, children, grandparents."[12] In his speech of acceptance for the Nobel Prize for Literature in 1950, William Faulkner said, "There are no longer questions of the spirit. There is only the question: When will I be blown up?"[13]

Tracing the influence of the prospect of everything turning into nothing is therefore an ecumenical (as well as a highly speculative) exercise. Every precinct of human existence is susceptible. This influence may be sought in the inner life of human beings, the psychiatrist's and psychologist's field of study; in social behavior, the realm of the sociologist and historian; and in the popular doctrines, creeds, and myths that offer the most explicit evidence of the impact of the bomb on everyday life. How, then, has the nuclear revolution affected people's thoughts, words, and deeds?

Nuclear images

It is possible that the structure of the human mind has not changed since the beginnings of civilization.[14] If a record of the mental life of all of human history were available, it could be studied for signs of change in 1945. It is not available. The activities of the mind have been subject to systematic study only in the twentieth century, and the record for the recent past is fragmentary at best. With a few specialized exceptions, access to the mind must be indirect, relying on a person's account of his own thoughts and feelings. These are subject to distorted perceptions and selective reporting. Not everybody has volunteered such an account. Still, with all these qualifications, there are at least two groups upon whom it is plausible to assume some nuclear psychological influence.

The first group includes those who are afflicted with severe mental disturbances – psychotics, especially schizophrenics. They tend to feel more acutely and express more dramatically than others the strains in society. They are, in a sense, the billboards of the unconscious. In them the culture's underground streams of mental activity come to the surface. Moreover, schizophrenics often have special anxieties about destruction and annihilation. One way of describing schizophrenia is as the fear of psychic annihilation, of disconnection from the stream of human experience.[15]

Technology looms large in schizophrenic fantasies, which over the years seem to have evolved in conjunction with technological change. Once radios and refrigerators exercised sinister powers of control; now it is televisions and computers that schizophrenics believe are manipulating them.[16] There is not yet, however, a history of psychotic ideation that could demonstrate whether or not nuclear weapons assumed a prominent place in schizophrenic fantasies after 1945. What little evidence there is suggests that these armaments have not been especially prominent.

The second group consists of all of those born between 1940 and 1950. Arguably, they comprise a "nuclear-haunted" generation. There is scattered, although far from conclusive, evidence that nuclear annihilation has been a more prominent theme in their dreams, fantasies, and thoughts than in those of people born before and afterward.[17] They grew up with the nuclear age. Between the ages of three and five the child first has conscious fantasies involving anxiety, first becomes aware of the world outside his direct experience, and first forms his ideas of death.[18] Everyone born between 1940 and 1950 passed through all or part of this period with the bomb very much at the forefront of public consciousness. The year 1945 saw the first two atomic explosions, 1949 the announcement of the first Soviet atomic test, and 1951 the explosion of the first fusion, or hydrogen, bomb.

The danger of nuclear destruction was imprinted on the minds of this generation by photographs of mushroom-shaped clouds that newspapers and magazines frequently printed, by constant fear of war, and perhaps most vividly by air raid drills at school in which students were required to crouch under the desks, which they knew were unlikely to provide any protection from an attack if the stories of the bomb's power were remotely true.[19] In September 1979, Charles R. Hansen, a thirty-two-year-old computer programmer, released to several newspapers details of the design of the hydrogen bomb. He had gleaned the information from public sources, but the government had tried to suppress it. In explaining his fascination with nuclear weapons he "recalled the 'shapeless fears' that his mind held from the day in grade school when air raid drills were held at school."[20]

Not every member of the nuclear generation was so strongly affected by the bomb's dangers. But the prominence of nuclear-induced anxieties when their images of death were being formed may have produced a generationwide psychological pattern: an initial obsession with the bomb, followed by a strenuous effort to push below the level of conscious awareness the fears that it aroused because there was no satisfactory way to come to terms with what it portended, fears that nonetheless did not disappear completely.[21]

Inner states may often be inferred from their outward manifestations. Thoughts, it is assumed, produce deeds, and psychological meaning is ordinarily read into behavior, which is much more readily observed and thus interpreted and even measured. Anxiety of the sort that the threat of nuclear annihilation produced in the generation born between 1940 and 1950 usually issues in behavior of some sort, and the behavior of this generation lends further support to the idea of special nuclear imprinting.

Nuclear behavior

The behavior of the nuclear generation has been distinctive, and in ways that suggest roots in nuclear-induced fears. The generation came to maturity in the 1960s; everybody born between 1940 and 1950 turned twenty sometime during that decade. It was a time full of political turmoil and social change, and especially of patterns of behavior unusual and unexpected enough to require explanation. Three in particular seem connected to the peril of nuclear annihilation.

It was a rebellious decade. The nuclear generation mounted challenges to authority of all kinds. Universities, where many members of this generation spent a sizable part of the 1960s, were frequent targets of displays of displeasure that ranged from marches and rallies all the way to outright assault; occasionally bombs exploded on campus. The students protested features of higher education that they found intolerable, the government's foreign policy, and the treatment of the nation's black citizens as well.

There was unexpected behavior of quite a different sort. Some members of the nuclear generation shunned the attitudes that they were expected to adopt, the roles that they were supposed to play, and the institutions that shaped their parents' lives. A life devoted to the accumulation of material possessions, the propagation of a conventional family, and the occupation of a niche in the world of white-collar jobs was not for them. "Alienation" was the name sometimes given to their disenchantment with the world they were to inherit; their response was to "drop out" of it.

A third striking pattern of behavior in the 1960s was the falling away of restraints on social and especially sexual conduct. The change in sexual mores was so dramatic, particularly among members of the nuclear generation, as to constitute a revolution.

Each of the three patterns has a plausible connection with nuclear dread, for each is, in a sense, a logical reaction to it. Student protest may be interpreted as a protest against the specter of nuclear annihilation by "a generation that is by no means sure that it has a future."[22] Anger at having to live with the knowledge that the end may be just around the corner may have provided part of the impetus for the student activism of the 1960s. As one student put it at the end of the decade, "There is the ever present feeling that I have been cheated of a certain amount of self-determination in my future. My generation is the first that is subject to the very real threat of an arbitrary end to everything. I feel a resentment at times that this specter was thrust on me."[23]

Apathy and retreat are also plausible responses to the nuclear peril. To quote another student, "I think, in general . . . the nuclear threat has made me very cynical. The feeling that mankind is very stupid and very suicidal was for me the only possible explanation."[24] The dropout may have been sapped of the energy to swim in the sea of social activity by nuclear-induced fatalism.

Hedonism, as well, is a plausible reaction to the threat of the end, the *carpe diem* response. The nuclear generation had about it a sense of urgency in the 1960s, both to produce social and political change and to cram all the personal experience possible into what might be a short lifetime. The threat of the bomb may have encouraged the philosophy to which the condemned man subscribes in ordering his last meal. Another member of the nuclear generation reflected, "I do not drink, take drugs, sleep around, live chaotically, believe in revolutionary politics, gamble, and avoid planning solely because of the existence of that threat, but I certainly would be willing to wager it has something to do with it, since its images are nearly inescapable in daily life."[25]

There is another reason for connecting the turmoil of the 1960s with nuclear threat: The nuclear generation was not the first to be obstreperous, cynical, or hedonistic.[26] Their conduct recalls extreme social behavior associated with great disasters or anticipations of disaster in the past. The end, or the fear of it, evoked similar reactions before 1945.

In early modern Europe "millenarian" movements, fired by the certainty that the end of the world was approaching, challenged the existing social order and defied the political authorities. They even established the equivalents of the "liberated areas" students of the 1960s proclaimed the university buildings they seized to be, islands of purity and fervor in the midst of a corrupt world.[27]

The experience of catastrophe left in its wake emotional paralysis and demoralization like the "alienation" of the 1960s. The bubonic plague, which killed perhaps one-third of all Europeans in the fourteenth century, had this effect. "Emotional response, dulled by horrors, underwent a kind of atrophy epitomized by the chronicler who wrote, 'and in these days was burying without sorrowe and wedding without friendshippe.'"[28] The response to the plague is not the only example of the emotional deadening effects of imminent catastrophe. "It is perfectly clear," according to one student of the psychology of the past, "that disaster and death threatening the entire community will bring on a mass emotional disturbance, based on a feeling of helpless exposure, disorientation, and common guilt."[29]

The third syndrome of the 1960s also has historical precedents. Both in millenarian movements and in the aftermath of the plague, customary social restraints, especially on sexual conduct, collapsed. The latter part of the fourteenth century is said to have been "a period of unusual immorality and shockingly loose living, which we must take as the continuation of the devil-may-care attitude of one part of the population."[30] There is even a parallel in fifth-century B.C. Greece. In 430 B.C., Thucydides records, the plague struck Athens. As a result, "people now began openly to venture on acts of self-indulgence which before then they used to keep dark. Thus they resolved to spend their money quickly and spend it on pleasure, since money and life alike seemed equally ephemeral."[31]

Still, the connection between the looming menace of the bomb and the unexpected and unorthodox social trends of the 1960s is a matter of conjecture, not established fact. The parallel between that decade in the United States and the episodes of vast social disruption in postmedieval Europe is far from exact. Both upset the social order. But if the social equivalent of a seismic scale could be designed, the remote upheavals would likely register much more forcefully than those of the recent past. The marches, the strikes, even the violence of the students of the 1960s were a far cry from the hysteria of millenarian movements in the fifteenth and sixteenth centuries, in which people scourged themselves in bloody frenzies and fought pitched battles with the ecclesiastical authorities that sometimes ended in mass slaughter. Student unhappiness in the 1960s with the world they were to inherit falls well short of the torpor that enveloped Europe after the devastation of the Black Death. And although the nuclear generation's disregard for conventional social and secular morality agitated their elders, it represented a considerably less dramatic departure from established custom than the outbreaks of licentiousness witnessed by earlier periods of history.

Moreover, there are plausible reasons other than the threat of nuclear destruction for students' behavior during the 1960s. The sexual revolution was in part the result of advances in the technology of birth control. Alienation may have been a response to the continual intrusion of violence of *all* kinds rather than (or in addition to) the threat of nuclear violence. People born between 1940 and 1950 grew up against the background of World War II and the Holocaust, they heard the continual clatter of guns firing on movie and television screens, they followed the Vietnam War in their homes on television, and they lived through the assassinations of three leaders familiar to all and beloved by many.[32]

Student protest itself is a recurrent feature of social history. European students were active in the 1960s, and the rebellions on both sides of the Atlantic may simply have been part of an age-old struggle, for which no specific cataclysm, actual or impending, is necessary, between parents and children. Students tend to come from the more affluent parts of society, and the activism of American students, like that of those before them in other countries, has been interpreted as springing from guilt at the privileges they enjoyed.[33]

The very size of the nuclear generation may have influenced its behavior. Just as biologists have found that animals become restless when crowded together in too small a space, so the competition to succeed in the "meritocratic" educational system of the United States, which was fierce among the members of the nuclear generation because they were so numerous, may have set off a backlash of resentment in the 1960s.[34] Or student activism and alienation may both have stemmed from a sense of powerlessness and uselessness that living in the large, complicated postindustrial society of the United States after World War II produced.[35]

Finally, even where they influence political events psychological conflicts do not enter the public arena directly. There is an intermediate series of concerns through which they are filtered – politics. The students said, and believed, that they were protesting against the war in Vietnam and the racial inequities of American society. The war, in particular, loomed not only as morally repugnant but as personally threatening. A student could be drafted into the Army, shipped to Vietnam to fight, and killed there. This was reason enough to try to bring the war to an end. Manifest motives can also be the actual ones.

There is a final drawback to attributing the three novel and disruptive social patterns of the 1960s to the psychological impact of nuclear weapons. University students behaved in these ways. But students made up less than half of the nuclear generation, the majority of which did not go to college; and only a minority of college students, generally at the most prestigious institutions, protested, dropped out, or flouted their parents' social and sexual mores.[36] Perhaps fears of the bomb spurred those who did so. How did the rest of American society respond to the nuclear threat?

It is possible that rather than (or in addition to) the bomb affecting *only* members of a certain age group throughout their lives, it affected *everybody*, but only for a specific period. There was a time when the danger of nuclear war was much on the public mind – the late 1950s and early 1960s. The boundaries of a "nuclear epoch" can be fixed with some precision. The logical beginning is the launching of the Soviet Sputnik in 1957; the ending comes with the Cuban missile crisis of 1962 and the signing of the Limited Test Ban Treaty in 1963.

During this half-decade the symbols of nuclear danger seem, in retrospect, more dramatic than before or since.[37] Sputnik marked the first step by man into outer space. The Soviet Union took it, and suddenly the entire heavens seemed a potential launching pad for a surprise nuclear rocket attack on the United States. Four years later, in 1961, President Kennedy stirred fears of war by advising Americans to provide themselves with protection against the radioactive fallout that would linger after a Soviet nuclear assault. Every family was urged to build in its basement what became, in effect, a symbol of nuclear warfare, the bomb shelter. Throughout this period, although there was no war, Americans (and others) were exposed to radioactivity, which came from the open-air tests of nuclear explosives that the United States and the Soviet Union carried out. Scientists discovered that one of the fallout's poisonous ingredients, strontium 90, a potent source of cancer, seeped into the grass on which cows grazed and thence into the milk that people drank. In addition, the two most serious confrontations of the nuclear age between the United States and the Soviet Union took place in those years, over Berlin in 1961 and in the Caribbean in 1962.

American society between Sputnik and the missile crisis resembles one of Freud's classic case studies of neurosis. Sputnik was a trauma that made a danger suddenly vivid, and subsequent events reinforced the sense of peril it created. The result was something like neurotic behavior. There was a preoccupation with nuclear weapons, as well as with competition with the Soviet Union. This was the era when the slogan "better dead than red" became popular, when Khrushchev's remark "we will bury you" was much discussed, and when the American performance in comparison with its Soviet counterpart of everything from the output of the economy to the reading skills of first graders came under intense scrutiny. This "thermonuclear fever"[38] reached its zenith with the rush to build fallout shelters, which in turn touched off debates about whether neighbors who had neglected to construct their own should be admitted in time of nuclear war.

The fever was dissipated by the missile crisis and the Test Ban Treaty. The first brought the fears of war to the surface of public consciousness because it brought the United States and the Soviet Union to the brink of war. It helped to ease these fears because it was resolved short of war, and because out of its resolution came the mutual acknowledgment of the horrors of nuclear conflict and a limited reconciliation between the two powers, which came to be known as "detente." The Test Ban Treaty, because it was the first formal agreement between the two great powers on nuclear weapons, gave the reconciliation an official imprimatur, and removed the nuclear poisons from the air as well. These two events corresponded to the moment in Freud's cases when the patient's unconscious delivers up the childhood trauma that was at the root of his neurosis, enabling him to relive or reenact it symbolically and so rid himself of its burden.[39]

The designation of a "nuclear epoch" as the effect of armaments on the everyday lives of Americans also has shortcomings, however. Analogies, after all, are not explanations. There are large differences between Freud's tours de force of psychological sleuthing and the collective mental history of American society. Freud was a physician, not a social historian. His thought has served (and was intended to serve) mainly as the basis for individual therapy, not sociological research.[40]

Moreover, the fears that Freud treated were lodged in the imaginations of his patients. He distinguished between a "real" danger, "which threatens a person from an external object," and an object of neurotic anxiety, "which threatens him from an instinctual demand."[41] Nuclear weapons are all too real. Measured by the number of them available for warfare, in fact, the danger that they pose has grown considerably since 1963.

If the American thermonuclear fever has nonetheless abated since then, it is perhaps because nuclear armaments have receded from the forefront of public consciousness. No international crises of comparable gravity have taken place since the confrontation in the Caribbean in the fall of 1962. Nuclear anxieties may have submerged psychologically even as the weapons themselves were disappearing from view. In the 1960s the mainstay of the American nuclear arsenal ceased to be the B-52 bomber airplane, the "superfortress" that looked like a huge bird of prey and so made a striking symbol of nuclear danger, and became instead the Minuteman missile, which is buried in a concrete silo underground, and the Polaris submarine, which is similarly hidden from view.[42] This may explain why those born after 1950, and especially after 1960, have seemed less marked by nuclear anxieties.

Still, the nuclear threat persists. A nuclear end remains all too possible. In the past, fears of the end have been associated with particular doctrines, which have been prominent in moments of strain and uncertainty and present virtually everywhere, called "eschatologies." These are accounts of the last times, which connect personal fears with social turmoil and which anticipate and explain the end. What influence has the prospect of nuclear annihilation had on these?

Nuclear apocalyptics

All societies have some idea of the end. All cultures provide some story of how and why the last days will come. The need for an explanation and a justification of the end (as well as the beginning) of everything seems to be as fundamental to human life as the need for symbolic immortality.

The sacred text of the Western religious tradition, the Bible, concerns itself with last things. In particular, the book of Daniel and the book of Revelation foretell dramatic endings. They inspired a body of writing in postbiblical times that foresaw cataclysmic and spectacular conclusions to world history. In these "apocalyptic" writings (the term comes from the Greek word for revelation), signs intelligible only to the elect foreshadow the end, which comes after a time of troubles – often the reign of a tyrannical ruler – culminating in a thunderous final battle, the greatest that the world has ever seen. The compatibility of the apocalyptic schema with nuclear weapons is clear.

Apocalyptic doctrines inspired the social movements that arose periodically from the Middle Ages through the first decades of the Reformation, of which the disruptions of the 1960s were reminiscent.[43] The term "millenarian" that is used to denote them comes from the passage in Revelation that anticipates a thousand-year reign of the Savior between the Second Coming and the Last Judgment.

In the modern age the Bible has lost some of its authority. Not everybody takes Daniel or Revelation literally. This, however, has always been true. Although the relevant passages have always been part of both Jewish and Christian traditions, they have historically received two radically different kinds of interpretations.

The first has taken these passages literally, regarding them as accurate renderings of what is to happen, predictions of the future for which preparations must be made in the present. Apocalyptic literalists have characteristically scanned the events of the day for signs of the approaching end foretold in Scripture. Millenarian movements have drawn their inspiration from this school of interpretation. It has, however, invariably been the minority view.[44]

The second approach to Daniel, Revelation, and similar sections of the Bible has interpreted them in figurative, allegorical fashion. They herald, according to this school, not the material transformation of the world but a spiritual change within each person.

The appeal of each interpretation has, historically, depended on social location. The literal version has been the property of the outcast, the marginal, and the desperate. It has served as a protest against things as they are.[45] It has been a social protest, by those who feel that they have been denied their rightful place in the social order, and a political protest, by a conquered people against their conquerors.[46] Sometimes it has been both. Sabbatai Sevi, the Jewish self-proclaimed Messiah of the seventeenth century, attracted followers of every social station. All Jews, even wealthy ones, had reason to feel socially marginal and physically vulnerable in the Europe of that period.[47]

One account of the origin of apocalyptic doctrine regards it as the prophetic tradition of the earlier parts of the Bible, which foretold the restoration of the proper moral and political order, exaggerated and transformed by the growing hopelessness of the prospect for that restoration. As the prospect of overthrowing the Romans and reestablishing the Jewish kingdom grew fainter, the optimism of the early predictions "yielded to the pessimism of apocalyptic eschatology, held by people clinging to the prophetic promises of restoration, but failing to see how the order of this world could accommodate those promises, prompting them to leave the vision of restoration on the cosmic level of myth."[48] The first interpretation is thus, in a sense, a counsel of desperation. The second, by contrast, has been the doctrine of those who are anything but desperate. It has been the creed of the establishment. This is logical. For those who are doing well in this world, the apocalypse looks unpromising by comparison.

The first interpretation is sometimes applied to the early Christians, even to Jesus himself.[49] The second stems from the period of the established Church, in whose hands temporal power largely rested from the end of the Roman Empire through the Middle Ages, and which therefore would bear some responsibility for imperfections in the temporal world and stand to lose its authority in the millennium.[50]

The foremost Christian proponent of the second interpretation was Saint Augustine, who held that the promise of salvation applied not to the body politic, which was already under Christian dominion, but to the individual soul. Redemption

meant "inner" not "outer" transformation.[51] Augustine's Jewish counterpart was Maimonides, the great Talmudic scholar,
who argued that the coming of the end of days would not in-
validate the body of rabbinic law that had come into being to
govern life in the Diaspora, which would still apply.

A comparable social division is relevant to American attitudes toward the prospect of nuclear annihilation. Such apocalyptic fervor as exists in the United States resides on the
fringes rather than at the core of American society. Fundamentalist Protestants tend to place more emphasis on the nuclear
fulfillment of apocalyptic prophecies than other religious
groups.[52] According to Billy Graham, whose theology, at least,
tends to be fundamentalist, "When the prophets speak of fire
in the world's judgement, or when Peter mentions fire at the
end of the age, it is not likely that they refer to the fire of com-
bustion. It could be the fire of fission, the release of nuclear
power by the splitting of the atom."[53]

Those most committed to literal interpretations of the literature of the apocalypse tend to belong to cults, which lie far
from the mainstream of American society. The leader of the
People's Temple, whose members committed mass suicide in
Guyana in 1978, predicted imminent nuclear destruction and
claimed that following him offered the only hope of salvation.[54] This group bore a striking resemblance to one of the
most prominent European millenarian movements, the radical
Anabaptists who appeared in Münster, in south Germany, in
the sixteenth century. In both cases a charismatic, messianic
leader demanded total obedience from his followers. Both
groups were separated from the rest of society, first in the
sense that their beliefs differed radically from the reigning orthodoxy, and then physically, as they gathered themselves together in isolated bastions. Both felt persecuted – in the case
of the Anabaptists, legitimately so. Their behavior grew ever
more irrational and dangerous, ending, in both cases, in self-
destruction.[55]

The "established" nuclear doctrine of the United States, by
contrast, is the nuclear weapons policy of the American government, the policy of deterrence. This policy is predicated on

the hope – which has hardened over time into an assumption – that nuclear war will not take place. Indeed, it is an important, although far from unanimously accepted, principle of the received doctrine that believing that a nuclear war might be fought, and preparing to fight (and to survive) it, can be positively dangerous, because it makes such a war more likely to occur than it would be otherwise. Civil defense is the exception to this pattern, a form of serious preparation for nuclear war in which participation was probably directly correlated with social standing, rather than inversely related, as has historically been the case with anticipations of the end. The rich were more likely than the poor to build fallout shelters in their basements. Still, these shelters represented attempts to preserve the world as it is, to prevent the transformation that millenarian movements traditionally have welcomed.

The incorporation of the threat of nuclear annihilation into an apocalyptic schema drawn from the Bible has captured the imagination of only a minority of Americans. How have most Americans come to terms with the prospect of the end that the nuclear revolution has raised? Some may regard it in terms that are not conventionally religious. Although still enormously important, Judaism and Christianity are now two doctrines among many. Others have apocalyptic overtones, and notable among them are political ideologies.

The affinities of ideologies with religious creeds have often been noted. The political doctrines of the nineteenth and twentieth centuries typically claim to be authoritative, as do religious doctrines. Ideologies often foresee upheaval leading to a new, different, and better world, just as Jewish and Christian apocalyptic forecasts did. Marxism certainly has these features. It fits the apocalyptic pattern neatly: a period of oppression – of the proletariat by the bourgeoisie – leading to a fierce struggle that ends with the revolutionary victory of the worker and a new day of brotherhood and liberty. Marx never fully described the postrevolutionary society, but neither have the details of life in the millennium always been made altogether clear.

Other forms of literature, especially fiction, show a clearer nuclear imprint. There are novels whose subject is nuclear war, like Nevil Shute's On the Beach. There are, as well, novels with distinctly apocalyptic motifs. Doris Lessing's The Memoirs of a Survivor is a fable that takes place in a time of disruption and chaos and suggests, at the end, apocalyptic redemption: "Both walked quickly behind that One who went ahead showing them the way out of this collapsed little world into another order of world altogether."[56] Lessing's Shikasta[57] is set far in the future and refers to a storm of nuclear destruction leading to a new, fresh, social order.

There is, as well, science fiction, a genre of writing that is filled with cosmic forces, climactic battles, and visions of the future, in which the special importance of technology is evident from its name. The science-fiction writing of the postwar period is not a literature of nuclear apocalypse in the sense that it does not have the prophetic role of similar writing before 1945. Then, fiction was frequently a more accurate harbinger of war in the future than official reports, plans, and scenarios. Now, as one student of this literature put it, "the brutal facts of the new military technologies describe the disaster of nuclear warfare in terms that fiction cannot better."[58] In fact, much of contemporary science fiction seems to offer "a means of escape from perplexed and troubled time, since many tales of interplanetary adventure establish a fantastic world of the future in which the cold war, Communist China, and other problems of the world have been forgotten."[59] Moreover, contemporary literature with apocalyptic traces, both fiction and nonfiction, has inspired no social movements or even social agitation. Almost no one appears particularly upset about the bomb. Americans seem to have abdicated responsibility for nuclear war and peace to their leaders, especially to the President, and to regard the nuclear threat as something to be passively endured, not actively resisted. This is not to say that there is no agitation outside the world of religious cults, however. There is, but the threat of destruction that has inspired it does not come from nuclear weapons.

An anxiety with less literal, dramatic apocalyptic features does affect those close to the core of American society. It is the set of dangers ranged under the heading "ecology:" the exhaustion of the planet's natural resources, overpopulation, and environmental pollution. Together they threaten a stifling, a suffocation, a winding down of human society. The ecological literature warns that "the ecosphere is being driven towards collapse," that "the present course of environmental degradation, at least in industrialized societies, represents a challenge to essential ecological systems that is so serious that, if continued, it will destroy the capability of the environment to support a reasonably civilized human society," that "the present course of human civilization is suicidal."[60] There is an ecological movement – composed of organizations that carry on research, engage in political lobbying, participate in electoral campaigns, and even conduct marches and demonstrations of protest against activities that seem especially harmful.

In a sense, the threat that the degradation of the environment poses and the danger of nuclear annihilation spring from a common source – runaway technology. In both cases science threatens to transform itself from the servant to the executioner of mankind.[61] On the whole, however, they are distinct. Why has the first galvanized greater popular activity among Americans than the second?

There is one difference that may be significant. Apocalyptic literature has a particular form. It has a dramatic structure. Scenarios of ecological doom fit this structure; nuclear forebodings do not. Jewish and Christian apocalypses assign responsibility for the cataclysm; they impute disaster to human sinfulness. Millenarian movements customarily threw themselves into frenzies of piety to atone for the corruption rampant in the world in order to stave off the apocalypse, or, failing that, to qualify for a comfortable destiny in the new world that would arise from the ashes of the old. Similarly, the ecological crisis springs from familiar human flaws: the greed of a consumer society, "the selfish maneuvering of those in power, and their willingness to use, often unwittingly, and sometimes cynically, even environmental deterioration as a step toward more political power,"[62] and the hubris that underlies the assumption that man can control the environment and flout the designs of nature. Nuclear war, by contrast, seems more likely to be the result of a mechanical accident than of moral turpitude. In the popular imagination it is misperception, uncontrolled escalation, the push of the wrong button that triggers annihilation.

The traditional apocalyptic story has a measured, logical plot, like a play.[63] So it is with ecological prophecies. The signs of deterioration and decay are everywhere. The particles of noxious matter in the air and the drinking water can be precisely measured. The forecast of doom is the extrapolation of present trends.[64] Nuclear destruction, by contrast, seems likely to come suddenly, perhaps even without any warning at all, and certainly without the element of individual responsibility. An exchange of intercontinental ballistic missiles could kill millions of people in half an hour.

Perhaps most important of all, apocalyptic tales in the biblical tradition are invariably stories with happy endings. On the far side of the gauntlet of oppression and destruction through which the world must pass lies salvation. After catastrophe comes redemption. Out of chaos rises a better world. The end, and this is the crucial point, is always also a beginning.[65]

Ecological apocalyptics promise a new beginning. The environmental crisis, according to one of its Jeremiahs, has "begun to act upon the central institutions of our society with a force that is profoundly subversive, but which carries within it the promise of cultural renewal."[66] "The needed productive reforms can be carried out without seriously reducing the present level of *useful* goods available to the individual; and, at the same time, by controlling pollution the quality of life can be improved significantly."[67] Disaster, that is, can be prevented if only people will change their habits to be more modest, frugal, and respectful of their natural surroundings. And if they do not reform, the cataclysm will lead to changes in the way people live, through measures that range from turning off lights in order to conserve energy to relocating in rural communal farms in order to lead wholly self-sufficient lives. From the standpoint of human happiness, these changes will represent an improvement over the pollution, noise, and tension of life in urban industrial society.

Nuclear war, however, does not promise a happy ending. It would poison, not purify, the earth. Such survivors as there were would not inherit a new Eden. No renewal or rebirth seems likely to follow. There would be a storm of fiery destruction, and then – nothing.

Apocalyptic literature, both sacred and secular, always ends on a hopeful note.[68] The eternal recurrence of hope is no doubt related to the need for symbolic immortality. Stories or doctrines in which everything turns into nothing cannot provide it. Still, it is not strictly true that, as a book about the theme of death in modern literature put it, "the human imagination has no way of contending with the anxiety of nuclear-induced extinction."[69] It is the Western imagination that cannot encompass nuclear annihilation because of the Western concept of time.

That concept is linear. History is progressive. One stage follows another; one thing causes another. This framework of understanding lends itself to the idea of the end as the transition to paradise, an idea that dominates apocalyptic thinking. It is not, however, compatible with the idea of the end as simply the end, as seems likely in the event of nuclear war.

A non-Western idea is more compatible. This is the idea of time as cyclical, as an endless repetition of archetypes rather than a chain of sequential development. Cataclysm and cosmic transformation recur seasonally. History, in this understanding, goes around and around, not forward.[70]

The cyclical view of history predominated in the West for most of recorded history. The Greeks subscribed to it.[71] As late as the sixteenth century it had wide currency in Europe.[72] In the seventeenth century, however, the linear image of time supplanted it and has held pride of place ever since. This progressive view of history was, arguably, rooted in the apocalyptic schema that had been part of the Western tradition for fifteen centuries.[73]

Perhaps a momentous shift in the opposite direction is taking place. Perhaps, in Mircea Eliade's words, "at a moment when history could do what neither the cosmos, nor man, nor change have yet succeeded in doing – that is, wipe out the human race in its entirety . . . we are witnessing a desperate attempt to prohibit the 'events of history' through a reintegration of human societies within the horizon of archetypes and their repetition." The time may be coming "when humanity, to ensure its survival, will find itself reduced to desisting from any further 'making' of history [and] will confine itself to repeating prescribed archetypal gestures."[74] Unless and until such a time arrives, however, there will exist a tension between the physical properties of nuclear weapons and the cultural apparatus for coming to terms with the end.

There is an irony in that tension, for the two are related. The idea of progress, which Europe embraced in the seventeenth century, led to the fact of material progress, the shaping of the natural world to human design. The zenith of material progress has come with the industrial revolution, and one of its offshoots has been the nuclear revolution. The idea of progress, that is, led, through many intermediate stages, to nuclear weapons. So the end of the world can be achieved, but not imagined, ultimately for the same reason. Insofar as the linear view of time makes it impossible to integrate nuclear annihilation into the Western cultural forms for coping with the end, it may be said that what makes nuclear war possible also makes it unthinkable.

Notes

Chapter 1. The nuclear revolution

1 Sydnor Walker, editor, *The First Hundred Days of the Atomic Age, August 6–November 15, 1945*, (New York, The Woodrow Wilson Foundation, 1946), p. 12.

2 *Ibid.*, p. 66.

3 From Marx's Preface to *A Contribution to the Critique of Political Economy*, reported in Lewis S. Feuer, editor, *Marx and Engels: Basic Writings on Politics and Philosophy* (New York: Doubleday Anchor Books, 1959), pp. 43–4.

4 See Bernard Brodie, *War and Politics* (New York: Macmillan, 1973), p. 382.

5 Quoted in Norman Moss, *Men Who Play God* (New York: Harper & Row, 1968), p. 5.

6 At the end of the war, it should be noted, Japanese defenses against air attack were feeble.

7 Thomas C. Schelling, *Arms and Influence* (New Haven: Yale University Press, 1966, paperback), p. 9.

8 See Michael Walzer, *Just and Unjust Wars: A Moral Argument with Historical Illustrations* (New York: Basic Books, 1977), Chapter 17.

9 This idea is developed in Chapter 8.

10 See Hans J. Morgenthau, "Fighting the Last War," *The New Republic*, October 20, 1979, p. 15, and Michael Mandelbaum, *The Nuclear Question: The United States and Nuclear Weapons, 1946–1976* (Cambridge University Press, 1979), p. 124–8.

11 An extended discussion of the parallel between the Peloponnesian War and the Cold War is P. J. Fliess, *Thucydides and the Politics of Bipolarity* (Baton Rouge, La: Louisiana State University Press, 1966). For a critical commentary on Fliess, see M. I. Finley, "The Classical Cold War," *New York Review of Books*, March 23, 1967, pp. 25–7. Donald Kagan's *The Outbreak of the Peloponnesian War* (Ithaca, N.Y.: Cornell University Press, 1967) gives an account of the origins of the conflict that incorporates the contemporary scholarship on the period and draws comparisons with the outbreak of World War I. These are compatible with the parallel between the Athenian–Spartan rivalry and the Cold War because all three take place in an anarchical system in which there were two principal groups of states.

12 The correspondence is not perfect. The Greek city–states were, on the whole, more fearful of Athens than Sparta, whereas the coalition that the Soviet Union dominates is held together more by coercion than is the alliance between the United States and Western Europe.

13 Kenneth N. Waltz, *Theory of International Politics* (Reading, Mass.: Addison-Wesley, 1979), p. 113.

14 Thucydides, *The Peloponnesian War*, translated by Rex Warner (Baltimore: Penguin Books, 1972, paperback), pp. 53–7.

15 For an argument to this effect, see Telford Taylor, *Munich* (New York: Doubleday, 1979).

16 For an elaboration of this argument see Waltz, *op cit.*, pp. 164ff.

17 Lyndon Johnson, for example, said in 1964, "There is no real comparison between the attitudes of most of the world's governments today and twenty-five years ago on the role of warfare as an instrument of national policy. War is obsolete, obsolete because there can be no winner." Quoted in Robert Osgood, "The Evolution of Force," in Robert E. Osgood and Robert W. Tucker, *Force, Order and Justice* (Baltimore: John Hopkins University Press, 1967), p. 15.

18 The most dramatic example of the influence of nuclear weapons during crises is the Cuban missile crisis. See, for example, Robert F. Kennedy's account, *Thirteen Days* (New York: Norton, 1969). The nuclear influence on the missile crisis is also discussed in Mandelbaum, *op. cit.*, Chapter 6.

19 See Mandelbaum, *op. cit.*, pp. 218–19.

20 The analogy comes from Waltz, *op. cit.*, p. 114.

21 See John Keegan, *The Face of Battle: A Study of Agincourt, Waterloo, and the Somme* (New York: Vintage Books, 1977), Chapter 1.

22 This three-part division of the levels of analysis in international politics corresponds to that of Kenneth N. Waltz in *Man, the State and War* (New York: Columbia University Press, 1959).

23 Osgood, *op. cit.*, pp. 70–1. F. H. Hinsley, however, regards the relative equality of military strength of the major European powers as the main reason for the comparatively limited character of the conflicts among them. See *Power and the Pursuit of Peace. Theory and Practice in the History of Relations between States* (Cambridge University Press, 1967, paperback), pp. 176–82.

24 Eric Robson, "The Armed Forces and the Art of War," *The New Cambridge Modern History. Volume VII: The Old Regime 1713–63* (Cambridge University Press, 1957), p. 164.

25 Clausewitz, *On War* (Princeton, N.J.: Princeton University Press, 1976), Book VIII, Chapter 6B, pp. 894–6.

26 Theodore Ropp, *War in the Modern World* (Durham, N.C.: Duke University Press, 1958), p. 111.

27 Gunther E. Rothenberg, *The Art of Warfare in the Age of Napoleon* (Bloomington, Ind., and London: Indiana University Press, 1978), p. 123.

28 *Ibid.*, p. 100.

29 Ropp, *op cit.*, p. 101.

30 *Ibid.*, p. 110, and Rothenberg, *op. cit.*, p. 130. Plunder had its drawbacks. It provoked resentment, and resistance, where it was common. It was one of the causes of the fierce guerrilla war that Napoleon's army met in the Peninsular Campaign in Spain and Portugal, which was among the most taxing and damaging that it waged.

31 From Saxe's *Reveries de Guerre* (1732), quoted in Michael Howard, *War in European History* (Oxford, England: Oxford University Press, 1976), p. 71.

32 Rothenberg, *op. cit.*, p. 61.

33 Ropp, *op. cit.*, p. 161.

34 *Ibid.*, p. 255.

35 Several books warning of the terrible costs of a major war appeared, including a remarkably prescient six-volume treatise entitled *The Future of War in Its Technical, Economic and Political Relations*, by a Warsaw banker named Ivan S. Bloch. (Sixth volume translated by R. C. Long, Boston, Ginn, 1902) See Brian Bond, "The First World War," in *The New Cambridge Modern History. Volume XII*, second edition, *The Shifting Balance of World Forces, 1898–1945* (Cambridge University Press, 1968), p. 171.

36 The phrase is Raymond Aron's. *The Century of Total War* (Boston: Beacon Press, 1955), Chapter 2.

37 One reason why the Napoleonic revolution favored the offense and the mechanical revolution the defense is that only one side incorporated the revolutionary techniques during most of the wars of the French Revolution, whereas both did so in World War I. But both sides were equipped for mechanical warfare during World War II, which was nonetheless a war of movement in both the European and the Pacific theaters.

38 Osgood, *op. cit.*, pp. 95–6.

Chapter 2. Nuclear weapons and chemical and biological weapons

1 On the Athenians' reaction, see Thucydides, *The Peloponnesian War*, translated by Rex Warner (Baltimore: Penguin Books, 1972, paperback), pp. 88ff. The Baruch Plan, according to Nikita Khrushchev, was a way for the United States "to prevent the development of the atomic industry in other countries, leaving the monopoly of nuclear arms to the United States." He added, "We, of course, could not agree to this." Quoted in Chalmers Roberts, *The Nuclear Years* (New York: Praeger, 1971), p. 17.

2 See Michael Mandelbaum, *The Nuclear Question: The United States and Nuclear Weapons, 1946–1976* (Cambridge University Press, 1979), pp. 27–40, 196.

3 Before then such plans had aimed at unifying Christian Europe for greater success in resisting barbarians. See F. H. Hinsley, *Power and the Pursuit of Peace: Theory and Practice in the History of Relations between States* (Cambridge University Press, 1967, paperback), pp. 14–15, 20.

4 See Hinsley, *op. cit.*, pp. 209–10, and Harold Nicolson, *The Congress of Vienna: A Study in Allied Unity: 1812–1822* (New York: Viking, 1961, paperback), pp. 254–5.

5 Hinsley, *op. cit.*, p. 123. Merze Tate, *The Disarmament Illusion: The Movement for a Limitation of Armaments to 1907* (New York: Macmillan, 1942), pp. 9–10.

6 "The improvement of chemicals since World War I is moderately stated a thousandfold in effectiveness, whether you are talking about lethality or talking about casualty production as distinguished from lethality." *Department of Defense Appropriations for 1959: Department of the Army.* Hearings before a subcommittee of the Committee on Appropriations, U.S. House of Representatives, 85th Congress, 2nd Session (Washington, D.C.: U.S. Government Printing Office, 1958), p. 30.

7   Stockholm International Peace Research Institute, *The Problem of Chemical and Biological Warfare: A Study of the Historical, Technical, Military, Legal and Political Aspects of CBW, and Possible Disarmament Measures.* Volume IV, *CB Disarmament Negotiations, 1920–1970* (Stockholm: Almqvist and Wicksell; New York: Humanities Press, 1971), pp. 26–7, 84ff.

8   *CB Disarmament Negotiations, 1920–1970*, p. 30; Matthew Meselson and Julian Perry Robinson, "Chemical Warfare and Chemical Disarmament," *Scientific American*, April 1980, pp. 38, 47.

9   Biological weapons, which cause death or disease in man, plants, or animals following multiplication within the target organism, and which are often classed with chemical weapons, fall closest to the disarmament end of the scale. The United States has renounced not only the use but the fabrication of biological weapons, and has done so unilaterally and unconditionally. On this scale non-lethal chemical weapons, including herbicides, which destroy plants, and gases that incapacitate but do not kill humans, like CS or tear gas, arguably stand further from disarmament than the lethal varieties. American policy has differed for these two categories of weapons in the recent past. See pp. 30, 32–3.

10   Meselson and Robinson, *op. cit.*, pp. 38, 40. American supplies of chemical munitions in Germany are reportedly adequate for only two days of fighting.

11   Stockholm International Peace Research Institute, Volume I, *The Rise of CB Weapons* (Stockholm: Almqvist and Wicksell; New York: Humanities Press, 1971), p. 153.

12   Thucydides, *op. cit.*, p. 402.

13   For a discussion of both episodes see Michael Walzer, *Just and Unjust Wars: A Moral Argument with Historical Illustrations* (New York: Basic Books, 1977), pp. 4–13.

14   See Michael Howard, *War in European History* (Oxford, England, Oxford University Press, 1975), pp. 6–7.

15   The traditional distinction is between *jus ad bellum*, the justice of a particular war, and *jus in bello*, the just conduct of war. Walzer, *op. cit.*, p. 21. For a historical account of the development of the two, see James Turner Johnson, *Ideology, Reason and the Limitation of War* (Princeton, N.J.: Princeton University Press, 1975).

16   Stockholm International Peace Research Institute, Volume II, *CB Weapons Today* (Stockholm: Almqvist and Wicksell; New York, Humanities Press, 1973), pp. 119, 188.

17 "CBW: 1962–67; 1968–68; 1969–72." Based on a case by For-
rest R. Frank, *Commission on the Organization of the Government
for the Conduct of Foreign Policy* (Murphy Commission). *Appendix
K: Adequacy of Current Organization: Defense and Arms Control*,
Volume IV (Washington, D.C., United States Government Printing
Office, 1975), p. 313.

18 *Ibid.*, p. 322.

19 *Ibid.*, pp. 306, 308.

20 For contrasting views of the likelihood that the Soviet Union
employed chemical weapons in Afghanistan, see the testimony before the Senate Foreign Relations Committee of Matthew Meselson
and Matthew Nimetz, April 24, 1980.

21 For the German attitude toward chemical weapons see "Study
Advises US Advance in Chemical Weapons," *Arms Control Today*,
January 1979, p. 3. The Federal Republic's distaste for chemical armaments is further reflected in its refusal to train its troops for combat involving their use.

22 The American government has declared that it will not begin a
war with the Soviet Union but that in a nonnuclear conflict that
NATO is losing, escalation to a nuclear defense of Europe is not
ruled out. This policy is designed to prevent the Soviets from pressing their presumed advantage in nonnuclear weaponry on the central front.

23 *Nuclear Test Ban Treaty*, Hearings Before the Committee on
Foreign Relations, U.S. Senate, 88th Congress, 1st Session (Washington, D.C.: U.S. Government Printing Office, 1963), pp. 43, 294,
296.

24 Stockholm International Peace Research Institute, Volume III,
CBW and the Law of War (Stockholm: Almqvist and Wiksell; New
York: Humanities Press, 1973), p. 103.

25 Walzer, *op. cit.*, p. 41.

26 *Ibid.*, pp. 129–37, 151–9. As he describes it, the war convention
is partly empirical – how men at war have behaved (or have been
instructed to behave) – and partly normative – how they ought to
behave.

27 There is "a continuous line of development from Gentilis via
Grotius to the Hague Conventions of 1899 and to the Geneva Protocol." *CBW and the Law of War*, p. 23.

28 See Frank, *op. cit.*, p. 307.

29 See Walzer, *op. cit.*, p. 275.

30 *Ibid.*, pp. 278–83.

31 *Ibid.*, p. 42.

32 Robert Divine, *Blowing in the Wind: The Nuclear Test Ban Debate, 1954–1960* (New York: Oxford University Press, 1978), p. 267.

33 The enhanced radiation warhead was criticized, as well, on the grounds that by making nuclear weapons seem less damaging and more readily usable it lowered the threshold, and thus raised the likelihood, of nuclear war. But other types of "tactical" nuclear weapons were open to, and received, the same criticism without touching off a comparable public uproar.

34 During the controversy over the neutron bomb one scientist who opposed it wrote, "On a personal note, as a professional radiation protection scientist, I look upon the whole idea of 'proper selection of radiation casualty criteria' to 'optimize' the results on the battlefield [the mission of the neutron bomb] – with considerable revulsion. This is exceeded only by chemical weapons and the results produced by them, which, to my thinking, represent the epitome when it comes to the wrong use of science." By implication, radiation and chemical weapons are more repulsive than garden-variety nuclear weapons, which are also, after all, produced by scientists. Jorma K. Miettinen, "Enhanced Radiation Warfare," *The Bulletin of the Atomic Scientists* 33:7 (September 1977): 35.

35 On the nuclear power controversy see, for example, William Sweet, "Opposition to Nuclear Power in Europe," *The Bulletin of the Atomic Scientists* 33:10 (December 1977): and Dorothy S. Zinberg, "The Public and Nuclear Waste Management," *The Bulletin of the Atomic Scientists* 35:1 (January 1979): 34–9.

36 S. A. Goudsmit, "An Irrelevant Debate," *The Bulletin of the Atomic Scientists* 33:3 (March 1977): 67. Similarly, another scientist wrote that he felt "virtually certain that the probability of an uncontrolled nuclear catastrophe arising from the accidental misuse of some of the many thousands of nuclear weapons in national arsenals is far greater than it is from a few hundred meticulously monitored reactors. Bombs are designed to produce catastrophe. The ultimate safeguards for bombs are increasingly dependent on human behavior, not upon the sequential cluster of well-considered technical devices incorporated in a reactor." Cyril Stanley Smith, "Weapons are the real problem." *Ibid.* The point is not just that a bomb going off would cause more damage than a power plant accident, but that the average person has a greater chance of suffering from the first than from the second. In 1957, during the test ban controversy, a group of scientists issued a similar statement asserting that the possibility of nuclear war was a greater danger than the fact of radioactive fallout. Divine, *op. cit.*, p. 161.

37 This is not to say that nuclear reactors are not hazardous at all and that opposition to nuclear power is wholly unfounded.

38 Stockholm International Peace Research Institute, Volume V, *The Prevention of CBW* (Stockholm: Almqvist and Wiksell; New York, Humanities Press, 1971), Appendix I, "The Claims that CB weapons are less inhumane than other weapons," pp. 124–9, and J. B. S. Haldane, *Callinicus: A Defence of Chemical Warfare* (London: Kegan, Paul, Trench, Trubner, 1925). "Callinicus" means "he who conquers in a noble or beautiful manner." See p. viii.

39 Frederic J. Brown, *Chemical Warfare: A Study in Restraints* (Princeton, N.J.: Princeton University Press, 1968), p. 236. This was not the only reason why Germany did not use chemical weapons in World War II. See *ibid.*, pp. 230–45.

40 James William Morley, "Realism in the Military Defense of Japan," in Franklin Weinstein, editor, *US–Japan Relations and the Security of East Asia: The Next Decade* (Boulder, Colo.: Westview Press, 1978), p. 57. The government was forced by the opposition to enshrine these principles in a formal resolution of the Diet. Takuya Kubo, "Meaning of the U.S. Nuclear Umbrella for Japan," in *ibid.*, pp. 109–10.

41 Kubo, *op. cit.*, p. 111.

42 Included in a list of characteristics common to all known cultures compiled by the anthropologist George P. Murdock are cleanliness training, ethnobotany, food taboos, and hygiene. Cited in Edward O. Wilson, *On Human Nature* (Cambridge, Mass.: Harvard University Press, 1978), p. 22.

43 *CB Weapons Today*, p. 118.

44 This general argument is drawn from Mary Douglas, *Purity and Danger: An Analysis of Concepts of Pollution and Taboo* (New York: Praeger, 1966). "I believe that ideas about separating, purifying, demarcating and punishing transgressions have as their main function to impose system on an inherently untidy experience" (p. 4).

45 A good statement of the case is to be found in Wilson, *op. cit.*

46 *Ibid.*, p. 88.

47 *Ibid.*, p. 68. Wilson continues, "In early human history phobias might have provided the extra margin needed to insure survival: better to crawl away from a cliff, nauseated by fear, than to walk to its edge absent-mindedly. The same could be true of phobias about poisonous substances."

48 Frank, *op. cit.*, p. 318.

49 Howard, *op. cit.*, p. 12.

50 Noel Perrin, *Giving Up the Gun: Japan's Reversion to the Sword, 1543 – 1879* (Boston: Godine, 1979). On the role of the chivalric code in the Hundred Years War see John Barrie, *War in Medieval Society: Social Values and the Hundred Years War, 1337– 99* (London: Weidenfeld & Nicholson, 1979), Chapter 3.

51 Bernard and Fawn M. Brodie, *From Crossbow to H-Bomb* (Bloomington, Ind.: Indiana University Press, 1973, paperback), pp. 10–11.

52 Bern Dibner, "Leonardo: Prophet of Automation," in Latislo Reti and Bern Dibner, editors, *Leonardo Da Vinci Technologist* (Norwalk, Conn: Burndy Library, 1969), p. 45.

53 Howard, *op. cit.*, pp. 4–5.

54 Herbert F. York, *The Advisors: Oppenheimer, Teller and the Superbomb* (San Francisco: W. H. Freeman, 1976), p. 52.

55 *The Prevention of CBW*, p. 24.

56 On this general subject, see M. D. Feld, "The Military Self-Image in a Technological Environment," in Morris Janowitz, editor, *The New Military* (New York: Russell Sage Foundation, 1964), pp. 159ff. The role of the institutional self-interest of the military in the nuclear age is also discussed below; see pp. 100–1, 131.

57 Frank, *op. cit.*, pp. 317–18.

58 Wyndham D. Miles, "The Idea of Chemical Warfare in Modern Times," *Journal of the History of Ideas* 21:2 (April–June 1970):298. Cultural restraints operated as well. The Admiralty pointed out that the use of gas would violate the rules of war.

59 *CB Weapons Today*, pp. 132ff; *The Rise of CB Weapons*, p. 306.

60 This problem is even more pronounced for biological weapons. Germs act so slowly and unpredictably that no attacking force using them could be sure of shielding itself from their effects. This is undoubtedly one reason for the unilateral, unconditional American renunciation of biological weapons. *CB Weapons Today*, p. 125.

61 "Binary" gases are designed to avoid this hazard. They consist of two chemicals that are innocuous singly but deadly when combined, which can be transported separately to the battlefield and there mixed together when the moment for using them arrives.

62 Miles, *op. cit.*

63 *The Rise of CB Weapons*, pp. 90–5; *CB Weapons Today*, pp. 95–8; Meselson and Robinson, *op. cit.*, pp. 40–4.

64 Although neither has concentrated on developing specially designed delivery vehicles for chemical payloads, each has so many airplanes, artillery shells, rockets, and missiles for other purposes that finding delivery systems for chemical attacks would not be difficult.

65 *CB Weapons Today*, p. 163. The precise character of the Soviet chemical weapons program is the subject of disagreement. Chemical weapons cannot be monitored as closely by standard surveillance techniques as can nuclear weapons.

66 Meselson and Robinson, *op. cit.*, p. 38.

67 There might be expected to be more chemical than nuclear proliferation. Each requires both access to the relevant materials and mastery of the techniques of fabrication. If the second is equally difficult for both kinds of armament, the first can be more readily achieved for chemical than for nuclear weapons. That there is not more chemical proliferation, or more states employing gases that are simpler to manufacture than the most lethal varieties, may well be due, therefore, to the special cultural restraints that attach to chemical munitions.

68 *CB Today*, p. 189.

69 Matthew Meselson, editor, *Chemical Weapons and Chemical Arms control: Papers and Discussions from a Conference at the American Academy of Arts and Sciences*, Boston, January 21–22, 1977 (Washington, D.C.: Carnegie Endowment for International Peace, 1978), p. 22. *The Rise of CB Weapons*, p. 102; Brown, *op. cit.*, p. 11.

70 Mandelbaum, *op. cit.*, Chapters 3 and 4.

71 See Meselson, editor, *op. cit.*, pp. 3, 6, 97, 99 and *The Prevention of CBW*, p. 31.

72 "If the Manhattan Project (and its Soviet equivalent) had failed, what would have been the character of post-war international politics? One may suggest that ... the new geography of power, with the intercontinental distances dividing the principal adversaries, would have ensured the development and procurement of long-range successors to the B-29 (e.g. the B-36 and so on) – the exponentially rising unit costs of which would have spurred the development of 'unconventional' weapons (e.g. nerve gas)." Colin Gray, "Across the Nuclear Divide," *International Security* 2:1 (Summer 1977): 28.

73 *The Prevention of CBW*, pp. 97–8.

Chapter 3. The balance of power in the nuclear age

1   This is the sense in which, according to Kenneth N. Waltz, balance of power is the theory of international politics. By theory he means the explanation of a law or regularity. The regularity here is the tendency toward the preservation of the independence of the constituent units of the international system. The theory, or explanation for this, is the tendency of these units to try to strengthen themselves, which, mediated through the structure of the international system, yields a pattern of equilibrium. Kenneth N. Waltz, *Theory of International Politics* (Reading, Mass.: Addison-Wesley, 1979), especially pp. 116–23.

2   Thucydides, *The Peloponnesian War*, translated by Rex Warner (Baltimore: Penguin Books, paperback, 1972), p. 103, 129.

3   *Ibid.*, pp. 299, 300.

4   *Ibid.*, p. 300.

5   See Herbert Butterfield, "The Balance of Power," in Herbert Butterfield and Martin Wright, editors, *Diplomatic Investigations* (Cambridge, Mass.: Harvard University Press, 1968), p. 139.

6   Quoted in Inis L. Claude, *Power and International Relations* (New York: Random House, 1962), pp. 43–4.

7   See Waltz, *op. cit.*, pp. 89–91.

8   Claude, *op. cit.*, p. 74. "Many scholars who ascribe good results to the system in past centuries maintain that it cannot repeat its successful operations in our time." *Ibid.* "The classical balance-of-power system, based on mechanical premises, cosmopolitanism, and the existence of a limited framework, was dated as soon as the great new forces of the nineteenth century gained their feet." Edward Vose Gulick, *Europe's Classical Balance of Power* (New York: Norton, paperback, 1967), p. 307.

9   See Waltz, *op. cit.*, pp. 118, 163.

10   Robert Osgood makes a similar distinction, between a "comprehensive" balance, which "requires continual maintenance of a fairly stable balance of power" and a "limited" one, which "requires only combined opposition to periodic drives for hegemony or preponderance." He does not, however, associate the first with the nineteenth and twentieth centuries and the second with the eighteenth. Robert Osgood, "The Evolution of Force," in Robert Osgood and Robert W. Tucker, *Force, Order and Justice* (Baltimore: Johns Hopkins University Press, 1967), p. 97. For another similar although not identical

distinction, see F. H. Hinsley, *Power and the Pursuit of Peace: Theory and Practice in the History of Relations between States* (Cambridge University Press, 1967, first published 1963), pp. 195–6.

11   The parallel goes further. The managed economy and the "managed" balance of power of the nineteenth and twentieth centuries represent modifications, not fundamental transformations, of the original systems. There are two basic ways of organizing economic activity: the market, on the one hand, and the command economy, where a central authority sets input quotas and output targets, on the other. See Charles E. Lindblom, *Politics and Markets* (New York: Basic Books, 1978). The market is a decentralized, anarchical system; the command system is hierarchical. Despite the impact of Keynes's thought and the ever-greater government involvement in the workings of the modern economy, "the great principles of self-interest and competition, however watered down or hedged about, still provide basic rules of behavior which no contemporary economic participant can afford to disregard entirely. It is not the neat world of Adam Smith in which we live, but the laws of the market can still be discerned if we look beneath its surface." Robert Heilbroner, *The Worldly Philosophers*, fourth edition (New York: Simon & Schuster, 1972), p. 57. Similarly, the international systems of both the nineteenth and twentieth centuries were and are far more anarchical than hierarchical; national self-interest and interstate competition continued to be the touchstones of every major state's foreign policy, but in each case leavened by international cooperation as well. Both laissez-faire systems, economic and international, it has been argued, were historically particular exceptions. The nineteenth century enjoyed prosperity without central management because "the normal weakness of the inducement to invest was offset by special factors: rapid population growth, new inventions, the opening up of new continents, the state of confidence, frequent wars, etc." Robert Skidelsky, "Keynes and the Reconstruction of Liberalism," *Encounter*, (April 1979), p. 31. The eighteenth-century international system similarly achieved equilibrium without conscious direction or self-restraint because the major European powers chanced to be more or less equal in strength, in contrast to the preceding century when France towered over the others. Hinsley, *op. cit.*, pp. 180ff. There is, it should be noted, a significant difference between the two systems. Government intervention in the economy brings some economic activity under hierarchical control. The economic system becomes

partly anarchical and partly hierarchical. The international system remains *entirely* anarchical even when there is cooperation among the great powers. That cooperation remains voluntary. Compliance with government edicts in a mixed economic system is not.

12 Thucydides, *op. cit.*, p. 242.

13 Osgood, *op. cit.*, p. 108.

14 Claude, *op. cit.*, Chapter 4, and Osgood, *op. cit.*, pp. 97–8.

15 Gulick, *op. cit.*, p. 144.

16 *Ibid.*, pp. 154–5.

17 *Ibid.*, p. 280.

18 In 1920 the same objection played a role in keeping the United States out of the League of Nations.

19 Harold Nicolson, *The Congress of Vienna. A Study in Allied Unity, 1818 – 1822* (New York: Viking Press, 1961, paperback).

20 Henry Kissinger, *A World Restored* (New York: Grosset & Dunlap, 1964, paperback), pp. 221–31.

21 *Ibid.*, p. 30.

22 See Hinsley, *op. cit.*, p. 205. Hinsley argues that Castlereagh's opposition to the conception of the Holy Alliance arose, as well, from "his sense of the limits of the practicable in international collaboration." He knew, that is, that it would not work (p. 206).

23 The term was Palmerston's. Hajo Holborn, *The Political Collapse of Europe* (New York: Knopf, 1957), p. 34.

24 See Hinsley, *op. cit.*, pp. 211–12.

25 To make the two terms parallel, either the nineteenth-century balance of power ought to be called the "Napoleonic" system, after the military revolution that underpinned it, or the twentieth-century system should be called the "Geneva" or "summit" system, for the meetings at which the United States and the Soviet Union have discussed issues relevant to international equilibrium.

26 There is an episode similar to the aftermath of World War I in Thucydides's account, an attempted collective security arrangement that ended not in a managed balance of power system but in war. This was the peace of 422–1 B.C. Athens and Sparta divided Greece into separate spheres of influence. They pledged joint action against any enemy invasion of either's territory. Each promised, as well, to intervene in case of an internal rebellion against the other. "In case of a rising of the slaves," one provision of their accord read, "the Athenians are to come to the aid of Sparta with all their strength, according to their resources." Thucydides, *op. cit.*, p. 362. Although "for six years and ten months they refrained from invading each other's territory," according to Thucydides, "abroad ... the truce was never properly in force, and each side did the other a great deal of harm, until finally they were forced to break the treaty made after the ten years, and once more declare war openly on each other." *Ibid.*, p. 363.

27 Russia was not able to take full military advantage of its population.

28 There is controversy about the sincerity of Metternich's offer to keep Napoleon on the throne of a France that would be restored to its prewar borders. See, for example, Kissinger, *op. cit.*, p. 101.

29 Holborn, *op. cit.*, p. 23.

30 Gulick, *op. cit.*, pp. 236, 248ff.

31 "From the point of view of a weak state sacrificed to it, the balance of power must appear a brutal principle. But its function in the preservation of international order is not for this reason less central." Hedley Bull, *The Anarchical Society* (New York: Columbia University Press, 1976), p. 108.

32 See Hinsley, *op. cit.*, pp. 214–15.

33 On the difference between rules and patterns, see Waltz, *op. cit.*, pp. 120–1.

34 For more on the fortuitous origins of international tranquility in the nineteenth century see Osgood, *op. cit.*, p. 104.

35 Hinsley, *op. cit.*, p. 249.

36 *Ibid.*, p. 250.

37 See Michael Mandelbaum, "International Order and Nuclear Stability: The First Nuclear Regime," in David C. Gompert, editor, *Nuclear Weapons and World Politics* (New York: McGraw-Hill, 1977), pp. 17–19.

38 "Text of Basic Principles," May 29, 1972. Reprinted in John H. Barton and Lawerence D. Weiler, editors, *International Arms Control* (Stanford, Calif.: Stanford University Press, 1976), pp. 383–4.

39 Waltz, *op. cit.*, p. 163.

40 The point is controversial. For a fuller discussion, see Chapter 5.

41 Waltz, *op. cit.*, p. 172.

42 "Turkey formed part of the European dominated international system from the time of its emergence in the sixteenth century, taking part in wars and alliances as a member of the system. Yet in the first three centuries of this relationship it was specifically denied on both sides that the European powers and Turkey possessed any common interests or values; it was held on both sides that agreements entered into with each other were not binding, and there were no common institutions, such as united the European powers, in whose working they cooperated. Turkey was not accepted by the European states as a member of international society until the Treaty of Paris in 1856." Bull, *op. cit.*, p. 14.

43 See Martin Wight, "The Balance of Power," in Butterfield and Wight, editors, *op. cit.*, pp. 167–8.

44 Gulick, *op. cit.*, p. 67; Claude, *op. cit.*, pp. 90ff.

45 Butterfield, *op. cit.*, p. 142; Holborn, *op. cit.*, p. 16.

46 This is one of the major themes of Kissinger, *op. cit.* See, for instance, p. 297.

47 Holborn, *op. cit.*, p. 72.

48 See Michael Mandelbaum, *The Nuclear Question: The United States and Nuclear Weapons, 1946–1976* (Cambridge University Press, 1979), Chapter 4.

49 For another discussion of this question, see Miles Kahler, "Rumors of War: The 1914 Analogy," *Foreign Affairs* 58:2 (Winter 1979): 374–96.

50 This is not to say that the controversy about responsibility for the outbreak of war in 1914 has completely died away. The two books by Fritz Fischer, *Germany's Aims in the First World War* (New York: Norton, 1967, published in Germany in 1961) and *The War of Illusions* (London: Chatto and Windus, 1975, published in Germany in 1967), caused a considerable stir in Germany and some excitement in professional historical circles in the English-speaking world. F. H. Hinsley has argued that the distinction between long-range impersonal causes of the war, on the one hand, and the events of the July crisis, for which responsibility may be assigned, on the other, is a false one. By July 1914, in his view, events had slipped out of anybody's control. In the years leading up to the war, by contrast, Germany bears a greater share of the blame for provoking international tensions than any of the other major powers. Hinsley, *op. cit.*, Chapter 13.

51 Hinsley, *op. cit.*, pp. 228–30.

52 F. S. Northedge and M. J. Grieve, *A Hundred Years of International Relations* (London: Praeger, 1971), p. 117.

53 Hinsley, *op. cit.*, pp. 260ff.

54 See Stanley Hoffmann, "The Elusiveness of Modern Power," *The International Journal* 30:2 (Spring 1975):183–206.

55 See Stanley Hoffmann, *Primacy or World Order: American Foreign Policy Since the Cold War* (New York: McGraw-Hill, 1978), pp.

115ff. For the view that the nature of power has not fundamentally altered, see Waltz, op. cit., pp. 184–92.

56 See A. J. P. Taylor, The Struggle for Mastery in Europe, 1848– 1918 (Oxford University Press, 1971, paperback) pp. xxix ff.

57 Some argued in the second half of the 1970s that the United States was lagging behind – but in nuclear terms. See Chapter 5.

58 Hinsley, op. cit., p. 301; David Calleo, The German Problem Reconsidered: Germany and the World Order, 1870 to the Present (Cambridge University Press, 1978), pp. 37–8, 49–52.

59 Hoffmann, Primacy or World Order, p. 115. The logic of interdependence applies, as well, to the military relationship between the United States and the Soviet Union.

60 Waltz, op. cit., pp. 170ff; Osgood, op. cit., p. 176.

61 Waltz, op. cit., p. 181.

62 See Albert Wohlstetter et al., Swords from Plowshares, The Military Potential of Civilian Nuclear Energy (University of Chicago Press, 1979), Chapter 5.

63 Northedge and Grieve, op. cit., p. 72.

64 Mandelbaum, The Nuclear Question, Chapter 5.

65 See, for example, Herman Kahn, On Escalation: Metaphors and Scenarios (New York: Praeger, 1965).

66 For a brief summary of the argument, see Kahler, op. cit., pp. 390–2.

67 Julien Benda, quoted in Herman Wouk, "Foreword," The Winds of War (Boston: Little, Brown, 1971).

Chapter 4. Arms competition: the nuclear arms race and the Anglo–German naval rivalry

1 Thucydides, The Peloponnesian War, translated by Rex Warner (Baltimore: Penguin Books, paperback 1972), pp. 105, 128.

2 See Chapters 2 and 3.

3 For a list see Samuel P. Huntington, "Arms Races: Prerequisites and Results," in Carl J. Friederich and Seymour E. Harris, editors, Public Policy: A Yearbook of the Graduate School of Public Administration Volume IX (Cambridge, Mass., Harvard Graduate School of Public Administration), p. 43. This list does not include the regional, nonnuclear races that have taken place since 1945 – between Israel and the Arab states, for example, and between India and Pakistan.

4 See Carlo M. Cipolla, "Introduction," in Carlo M. Cipolla, editor, *The Fontana Economic History of Europe: The Industrial Revolution* (London: Fontana Books, 1973), p. 7.

5 David Landes, *The Unbound Prometheus: Technological Change and Industrial Development in Western Europe from 1750 to the Present* (Cambridge University Press, 1972, paperback), p. 1.

6 Bernard Brodie, "On the Objectives of Arms Control," *International Security* 1:1 (Summer 1976): 30. Brodie calls it "the stereotype of the modern arms race."

7 The Royal Navy was built first according to the "two-power" standard and then to the requirement that it exceed the number of German capital ships by 60 percent. See Huntington, *op. cit.*, p. 42, n. 3. The Germans built first according to the risk theory and then, after 1905, aimed at parity with the British. See below, p. 97. The United States has proclaimed assured destruction as the standard its strategic nuclear arsenal must meet. The Soviet Union is the exception; no publicly enunciated standard of adequacy exists. See below, pp. 140–1, 144–5.

8 See Bernard Brodie and Fawn M. Brodie, *From Crossbow to H-bomb* (Bloomington, Ind.: Indiana University Press, 1973, paperback), Chapters 1 and 5.

9 The categories are from Michael Howard, "The Forgotten Dimensions of Strategy," *Foreign Affairs* 57:5 (Summer 1979): 978.

10 Quoted in Elting E. Morison, *Men, Machines and Modern Times* (Cambridge, Mass.: MIT Press, 1966), p. 12.

11 On the emphasis that the shift from sail to steam placed upon superiority in numbers see Bernard Brodie, *Sea Power in the Machine Age* (Princeton, N. J.: Princeton University Press, 1941), pp. 93ff. The significance of numerical superiority in nuclear armaments beyond the point at which the capacity for assured destruction is secured is discussed in Chapter 5.

12 Arthur Marder, *The Anatomy of British Sea Power* (Hamden, Conn.: Archon Books, 1964), p. 25.

13 They were not free of all logistical restraints; steamships required periodic refueling at overseas coaling stations.

14 Brodie, *Sea Power in the Machine Age*, p. 57.

15 Arthur Marder, *From the Dreadnought to Scapa Flow*, Volume I, *The Road to War, 1904–1914* (London: Oxford University Press, 1961), pp. 56–70; Marder, *The Anatomy of British Sea Power*, pp. 536–8.

16 Hajo Holborn, *The Political Collapse of Europe* (New York: Knopf, 1963), p. 76.

17 *Ibid.*

18 Secretary of Defense Robert McNamara was one such official. "Interview with Robert McNamara," *U.S. News and World Report*, April 12, 1965, p. 52. Cited in Albert Wohlstetter, "Is There a Strategic Arms Race?" *Foreign Policy* 15 (Summer 1974): 18.

19 See Volker Berghahn, *Germany and the Approach of War in 1914* (New York: St. Martin's Press, 1972), pp. 66-70, 106.

20 It has been argued that because nuclear weapons are so powerful, even a small nuclear arsenal can deter a nation with a large one. The argument has come not from the Soviet Union, whose nuclear arsenal cannot be described as small, but from France, whose arsenal cannot be described as anything but small. See Chapter 6, pp. 163-4, 169-70.

21 When each side reciprocally overestimates and overbuilds, the result is to ratchet the level of armaments continuously upward. This has been called the "action-reaction cycle" or the "spiral model." See George Rathjens, "The Dynamics of the Arms Race," in *Arms Control: Readings from Scientific American* (San Francisco: W. H. Freeman, 1973), pp. 177-87, and Robert Jervis, *Perception and Misperception in International Politics* (Princeton, N.J.: Princeton University Press, 1976), pp. 62-7.

22 See Kenneth L. Moll, "Politics, Power and Panic: Britain's 1909 Dreadnought 'Gap,'" in Robert Art and Kenneth Waltz, editors, *The Use of Force* (Boston: Little, Brown, 1971). Moll argues that the spurt in naval construction that the overestimation of German building in 1909 encouraged provided the British fleet with a margin of superiority that proved useful in World War I. The British proposed an exchange of information on building programs, including inspection, to prevent overestimation. The Germans did not agree. A. J. P. Taylor, *The Struggle for Mastery in Europe, 1848-1918* (Oxford, England: Oxford University Press, 1971, paperback), p. 459.

23 The Kennedy administration knew that there was no missile gap *before* making the final decision to deploy a thousand Minuteman missiles. Domestic political pressures pushed the total higher than strictly strategic calculations seemed to require. See Desmond J. Ball, *The Strategic Missile Programme of the Kennedy Administration*, unpublished manuscript, Australian National University, 1976. If the United States had deployed fewer missiles in the 1960s, the Soviet Union might have deployed fewer in the 1970s. Then again, the Soviets might have done precisely what they did do – steadily increase the size of their strategic arsenal. If so, the United States would probably have followed suit, and the result of the arms race by the end of the 1970s would have been the same, although the rhythm would have been different. On the question of how accurate American estimates of Soviet strategic plans have been and the extent to which American nuclear weapons programs have been geared to these estimates, see the articles by Albert Wohlstetter and his critics in *Foreign Policy*, numbers 15, 16, 19, and 20.

24 For the case that public opinion influences the government of the Soviet Union, see "The Soviet Experience and the Measurement of Power," in Jerry Hough, *The Soviet Union and Social Science Theory* (Cambridge, Mass.: Harvard University Press, 1972).

25 On the general restraints that the democratic revolution has imposed see F. H. Hinsley, *Power and the Pursuit of Peace, Theory and Practice in the History of International Relations* (Cambridge University Press, paperback, 1967), p. 284.

26 See C. J. Lowe and M. L. Dockrill, *The Mirage of Power* (London: Routledge and Kegan Paul, 1972), p. 32.

27 The term is from Morison, *op. cit.*, pp. 41–2.

28 See Graham T. Allison and Frederic A. Morris, "Armaments and Arms Control: Exploring the Determinants of Military Weapons," in *Arms, Defense Policy and Arms Control, Daedalus* 104:3 (Summer 1975): pp. 99–129. The tendency for different parts of the government to pursue their own interests is sometimes called "bureaucratic politics." For general discussions of the subject, see Graham T. Allison, *Essence of Decision: Explaining the Cuban Missile Crisis* (Boston: Little, Brown, 1971), and Morton Halperin, *Bureaucratic Politics and Foreign Policy* (Washington, D.C.: The Brookings Institution, 1975).

29 See James Kurth, "Why We Buy the Weapons We Do," *Foreign Policy* 11 (Summer 1973): 33–56.

30 The phrase probably comes originally from the sociologist C. Wright Mills in *The Power Elite* (Oxford University Press, 1956).

31 The fullest description of the British military-industrial complex is in Marder, *The Anatomy of British Sea Power*, Chapter 3. See also James R. Kurth, "The Political Consequences of the Product Cycle: Industrial History and Political Outcomes," *International Organization* 33:4 (Winter 1979): 17–18, 20.

32 See Marder, *The Anatomy of British Sea Power*, p. 36.

33 Eckart Kehr, *Battleship Building and Party Politics in Germany, 1894–1901*, edited, translated, and with an introduction by Pauline R. Anderson and Eugene N. Anderson (Chicago: University of Chicago Press, 1975, first published in Germany, 1930), pp. 365–75, 399.

34 Tirpitz's "ideas were to determine the German Navy's course, outlook and fate far beyond his own tenure of its secretaryship (1897–1916)." He was "a brilliant tactician and organizer, a born leader of men; a past master of intrigue; resourceful, indefatigable in the pursuit of his aims; utterly unscrupulous in his methods." Herbert Rosinski, "Strategy and Propaganda in German Naval Thought," in H. G. Thursfield, editor, *Brassey's Naval Annual, 1945* (New York: Macmillan, 1945), p. 126.

35 See Berghahn, *op. cit.*, pp. 32ff, 79ff, and 100ff, and Jonathan Steinberg, *Yesterday's Deterrent: Tirpitz and the Birth of the German Battle Fleet* (London: MacDonald, 1965), Chapters 4 and 5 and pp. 23–5.

36 Berghahn, *op. cit.*, pp. 27–8, 92; Kehr, *op. cit.*, pp. 175, 184, 239.

37 See Roman Kolkowicz, "The Military," in H. Gordon Skilling and Franklyn Griffiths, editors, *Interest Groups in Soviet Politics* (Princeton, N.J.: Princeton University Press, 1973, paperback), p. 131.

38 See Skilling and Griffiths, *op. cit.*, especially Skilling, "Interest Groups and Communist Politics: An Introduction" and "Groups in Soviet Politics: Some Hypotheses."

39 Timothy J. Colton, *Commissars, Commanders, and Civilian Authority: The Structure of Soviet Military Politics* (Cambridge, Mass.: Harvard University Press, 1979), p. 244.

40 "While conditions for the development of an inner cohesion and institutional self-awareness were inauspicious during the oppressive Stalin era, the years since, having witnessed a progressive ideological disillusionment, a new stress on functional and professional excellence, the disappearance of the terror machine, and acceptance of the principle of collective leadership, have greatly favored the military's role as an articulate interest group." Kolkowicz, *op. cit.*, p. 138.

41 In his memoirs, Khrushchev says that he told Eisenhower: "Some people from our military department come and say 'Comrade Khrushchev, look at this! The Americans are developing such and such a system. We could develop the same system but it would cost such and such.' I tell them there's no money; it's all been allotted already. So they say, 'If we don't get the money we need and if there's a war, then the enemy will have superiority over us.' So we talk about it some more; I mull over their request and finally come to the conclusion that the military should be supported with whatever funds they need." *Khrushchev Remembers: The Last Testament*, translated and edited by Strobe Talbott (Boston: Little, Brown, 1974), p. 412.

42 Kolkowicz, *op. cit.*, pp. 141–2; Colton, *op. cit.*, pp. 201, 203, 246–7.

43 Ball, *op. cit.*

44 Winston Churchill, *The World Crisis* (New York: Scribner's, 1923), p. 33. See also E. L. Woodward, *Great Britain and the German Navy* (Oxford, England: Clarendon Press, 1935), p. 228.

45 "He was not only the technical architect of the ill-fated German navy but also the first nationalistic manipulator of mass opinion in Germany. His ability to organize mass support had something of the Hitlerian touch, although the admiral addressed a higher social class than did Corporal Hitler." Holborn, *op. cit.*, p. 81.

46 Kehr, *op. cit.*, pp. 177–81.

47 *Ibid.*, p. 55, and Steinberg, *op. cit.*, p. 142.

48 This argument is in keeping with the revisionist interpretation of Wilhelmine foreign policy, which assigns a major share of the responsibility for World War I to Germany and that interprets German international behavior in the years leading up to World War I in part as an effort to cope with domestic tensions arising from the contradictory political system and ultimately from deep divisions in the society. The process of revision was set in motion by Fritz Fischer's two books, *Germany's Aims in the First World War* (New York: Norton, 1967) and *The War of Illusions* (London: Chatto and Windus, 1975). On the domestic political purposes of naval policy see Berghahn, *op. cit.*, pp. 3, 30, 212, and Anderson and Anderson, "Introduction" to Kehr, *op. cit.*, p. xx. Although Kehr's book received little notice when it first appeared in 1930, during the 1960s and 1970s historians have revived interest in it.

49 Fischer, *Germany's Aims*, pp. 27–8.

50 Between the two world wars the British were much more receptive to Hitler's hints that their empire would remain untroubled if they allowed the Germans to carry out their designs on the continent unimpeded. See Klaus Hildebrand, *The Foreign Policy of the Third*

Reich (Berkeley, Calif.: University of California Press, 1973, paperback), pp. 51–9. So, the British refusal to contemplate such an arrangement before 1914 may have had something to do with their perception of the balance of strength in European politics and of the likelihood, and likely costs, of war. Still, in the end, the British did not accept this arrangement with Hitler either.

51 On this general point, see Joseph J. Kruzel, *Parchment and Swords* (New York: Free Press, forthcoming).

52 See Michael Mandelbaum, *The Nuclear Question: The United States and Nuclear Weapons, 1946–1976* (New York: Cambridge University Press, 1979), pp. 186–9.

53 For a fuller discussion of this motive for the United States, and especially for American presidents, see pp. 201–2.

54 For a further discussion of this issue, see p. 162.

55 See Mandelbaum, *op. cit.*, pp. 129–57.

56 Holborn, *op. cit.*, pp. 75–8. "Counterfactual" history must always be a matter of speculation. But Germany went to war out of a combination of ambition and desperation. A differently arranged Europe might have been better placed to accommodate German ambition – the British might have been more sympathetic to it – and less conducive to desperation – the Germans might not have felt encircled.

57 See John Ellis, *The Social History of the Machine Gun* (New York: Pantheon, 1976).

58 On the influence of Mahan, see Margaret Tuttle Sprout, "Mahan: Evangelist of Sea Power," in Edward Mead Earle, editor, *Makers of Modern Strategy* (Princeton, N.J.: Princeton University Press, 1943), p. 415; Marder, *The Anatomy of British Sea Power*, p. 461; Berghahn, *op. cit.*, p. 35. On Mahan's influence in Britain, see Marder, *From the Dreadnought . . .* , p. 4.

59 Brodie, *Sea Power in the Machine Age*, p. 92.

60 Holborn, *op. cit.*, p. 76; Steinberg, *op. cit.*, p. 201; Rosinski, *op. cit.*, p. 130.

61 The point is controversial. It assumes that both sides accept some version of assured destruction and that new weapons contribute to rather than undercut it. See Chapter 5.

62 Technical change may, of course, make the weapon that is the subject of the competition obsolete. If the underlying political rivalry persists, however, the result will be a competition in weapons using the new technology and another quantitative arms race.

Chapter 5. Arms competition: the nuclear arms race and tariff competitions

1   James R. Schlesinger, *Annual Defense Department Report, FY 1975* (Washington, D.C.: U.S. Government Printing Office, March 4, 1974), p. 34.

2   The history of the standard of assured destruction suggests that American officials in fact believed that the wherewithal to destroy considerably smaller fractions of the population and the industry of the Soviet Union would deter Soviet mischief, but because the levels of destructive capacity finally decided on were readily available there was no reason not to set the standard accordingly. Schlesinger's explanation of the origins of assured destruction a decade later refers to the possible shortcomings, for the purpose of deterrence, of levels of destruction "substantially below" – not *marginally* below – those upon which the American government ultimately decided.

3   The American submarine fleet is probably less vulnerable than that of the Soviet Union because its vessels have greater range, and its techniques for evading sonar detection are more sophisticated.

4   In fact, the treaty restricted each side to two systems. Later the number was reduced to one. The United States has chosen to deploy none.

5   Quoted in Lawrence Freedman, *U.S. Intelligence and the Soviet Strategic Threat* (London: Macmillan, 1977), p. 198. See also Alain Enthoven and K. Wayne Smith, *How Much Is Enough? Shaping the Defense Program, 1961–69* (New York: Harper Torchbooks, 1971), p. 103.

6   Quoted in Raymond Garthoff, "Mutual Deterrence in Soviet Policy," *International Security* 3:1 (Summer 1978): 142.

7   Arming itself in nonnuclear terms may make a state worse off than before, if this sows suspicion and hostility among other states where none existed previously. Or more weapons may yield more security. The point is that increments of nuclear force above what is necessary for assured destructive have, according to this view, *neither* effect.

8   Neither of these statements is wholly correct, of course, but both are accurate enough to serve a heuristic purpose. See Richard Caves and Victor Jones, *World Trade and Payments: An Introduction* (Boston: Little, Brown, 1973), p. 3.

9   Strictly speaking, in market economies the purpose of economic activity is profit; the result is welfare.

10   The definitions of security and welfare here are simplified. They are useful, however, for analytical purposes.

11   The parallel is inexact here. The imposition of a tariff lowers welfare; the acquisition of weaponry beyond the level of assured destruction, by a strict construction of the optimizing doctrine, does not diminish security; it simply wastes money.

12   The other four countries that have detonated nuclear explosions – Britain, France, the People's Republic of China, and India – do not have arsenals large enough to qualify unambiguously as having the capacity for assured destruction. India, as of 1980, did not have a nuclear arsenal, properly so-called, at all.

13   Enthoven and Smith, op. cit., p. 177.

14   Jacob Viner, "Power versus Plenty in the Seventeenth and Eighteenth Centuries," in The Long View and the Short (Glencoe, Ill.: Free Press, 1958), pp. 285, 286.

15   See Michael Mandelbaum, The Nuclear Question: The United States and Nuclear Weapons, 1946–1976 (Cambridge University Press, 1979), pp. 3–4, 124–7.

16   For those who believe that it can be achieved, "victory" in a nuclear war between the United States and the Soviet Union may depend less on the hardware at the disposal of each than on the tactics employed in using them. Such Soviet writings on strategic war as exist seem to emphasize preemption. A strategic mercantilist of this persuasion could give credence to the idea of victory, therefore, without necessarily believing that this requires a larger nuclear arsenal than that of the other side.

17   James R. Schlesinger, Annual Defense Department Report, FY 1976 and 197T (Washington, D.C.: U.S. Government Printing Office, February 5, 1975), p. II-7.

18   Ibid., p. I-13. For an elaboration and critical discussion of this position, see Patrick M. Morgan, Deterrence (Beverly Hills, Calif.: Sage Publications, 1977), pp. 130ff.

19   Schlesinger, Annual Defense Department Report, FY 1975, p. 38.

20   Schlesinger, Annual Defense Department Report, FY 1976 and FY 197T, p. II-9.

21   Schlesinger, Annual Defense Department Report, FY 1976 and 197T. The list of articles registering alarm at an actual or impending "counterforce gap" is a long one. See, for example, Paul Nitze, "Assuring Strategic Stability in an Era of Detente," *Foreign Affairs* 54:2 (January 1976): 207–32.

22 See Robert Jervis, "Why Nuclear Superiority Doesn't Matter" *Political Science Quarterly* 94:4 (Winter 1979–80), 612–33; Thomas C. Schelling, *Arms and Influence* (New Haven, Conn.: Yale University Press, 1966), Chapter 1; Glenn H. Snyder, *Deterrence and Defense, Toward a Theory of National Security* (Princeton, N.J.: Princeton University Press, 1961), Chapter 1.

23 In this sense the missile crisis is a more useful precedent for relations between the Soviet Union and the People's Republic of China.

24 Mandelbaum, *op. cit.*, pp. 144–54.

25 Paul Samuelson, *Economics: An Introductory Analysis*, sixth edition (New York: McGraw-Hill, 1964), p. 660.

26 See, For example, Richard Pipes, "Why the Soviet Union Thinks It Could Win a Nuclear War," *Commentary* (July 1977) 21–34; Fritz Ermarth, "Contrasts in American and Soviet Strategic Thought, *International Security* 3:2 (Fall 1978) 138–55; and Benjamin S. Lambeth, "The Political Potential of Soviet Equivalence" (Santa Monica, Calif.: The Rand Corporation, 1977).

27 "In the Soviet perception, the United States has continued, notwithstanding SALT and detente, to seek military superiority . . . powerful forces are believed to continue to seek advantage and superiority in order to compel Soviet acquiescence in American policy preferences." Garthoff, *op. cit.*, p. 135.

28 Economists ordinarily regard tariffs as second-best means to these ends, in that they can be achieved at lower cost in overall welfare by different economic measures. Caves and Jones, *op. cit.*, p. 253.

29 In the theory of comparative advantage, when foreign competition drives a firm out of business its workers simply transfer to industries in which the country enjoys a comparative advantage in the international economy and that therefore are booming. In practice, matters are not so simple. Workers often cannot readily move to areas where the thriving industries are located or easily master the skills necessary for a new job.

30 The parallel goes further. The description of each has a similar history. First came the discovery and development of the optimizing doctrine. The equivalents for security of Ricardo and the exponents of comparative advantage who followed him were the nuclear strategists of the 1950s and 1960s, who worked out the conditions for survival in a world of two formidable nuclear states. After descriptions and explanations of the doctrine in each case came accounts of the gap between theory and practice. One of the most influential books about American politics in the twentieth century was a study of the way tariffs are set. E. E. Schattschneider's account of the Smoot-Hawley tariff of 1928, *Politics, Pressure, and the Tariff* (New York: Prentice-Hall, 1935), portrays rapacious special interests using a panoply of lobbying techniques to impose tariffs that enrich the industries they represent at the expense of unrepresented consumers. The bureaucratic politics literature on the development of the American nuclear arsenal has a similar air of piercing the veil of doctrine to reveal the political reality that lies behind it. "A careful review of the literature of arms control and strategy finds no important issue less studied than the question of what determines the number and character of the weapons in American and Soviet force postures." Graham T. Allison and Frederic A. Morris, "Exploring the Determinants of Military Weapons," in F. A. Long, editor, *Arms, Defense Policy, and Arms Control, Daedalus* (Summer 1975): 101. This school of analysis arises from the obvious disparity between "rational models of decision-making," with their grounding in doctrine, and "the donnybrook world of service rivalries, bureaucratic jostling, and the clash of parochial interests of pressure groups that determine the way that nations behave in practice." Marshall D. Shulman, "Arms Control in International Context," in Long, editor, *op. cit.,* p. 53. The bureaucratic politics school of analysis differs from earlier writing on the American military–industrial complex, particularly the work of sociologist C. Wright Mills, who seems to have coined the phrase in *The Power Elite* (Oxford University Press, 1956). In explaining the American side of the arms race the first school emphasizes the impulse for organizational self-perpetuation, the second the motive of financial gain. They have, moreover, quite different perspectives on the Cold War. Mills suggested that groups standing to gain from it artificially provoked, or at least worked to inflame, the rivalry between the United States and the Soviet Union. Bureaucratic politics analysts tend to concede a legitimate role for American nuclear weapons and to concentrate on weapons in excess of what assured destruction requires.

31 Caves and Jones, *op. cit.,* p. 236.
32 *Ibid.,* p. 241.

33 *Ibid.*, p. 291.

34 For a similar but more detailed and nuanced scheme of possible preferences in an arms competition see Thomas C. Schelling "A Framework for the Evaluation of Arms Control Proposals," in Long, editor, *op. cit.* pp. 187–200. The conditional optimizer's logic is relevant to arms races involving nonnuclear weapons.

35 Caves and Jones, *op. cit.*, p. 263.

36 See, for example, Jon Woronoff, "The Trade War with Japan," *Worldview* 22:7–8 (July–August 1979): 23–6.

37 The ABM question is not an entirely satisfactory illustration of the point in question in that its critics charged not simply that it was "excessive" by doctrinal standards but that it undercut the doctrine itself. (The charge carried more weight against the initial proposal to defend cities than against the system to protect ballistic missiles upon which the administration ultimately settled. Critics feared, however, that the second kind would lead to the first.) Perhaps a better example of the split between conditional and pure optimizers is the controversy over the MX missile, which gathered momentum in the late 1970s.

38 On armaments see G. W. Rathjens, Abram Chayes, and J. P. Ruina, *Nuclear Arms Control Agreements: Process and Impact* (Washington, D.C.: Carnegie Endowment for International Peace, 1974), pp. 13ff, and Jane M. O. Sharp, "Arms Control and the Alliance," in *The Atlantic Alliance: The First Thirty Years* (Geneva: Annals of International Studies, 1979), pp. 104–6. On tariffs see Rayond Bauer, Ithiel Pool, and Lewis Dexter, *American Business and Public Policy* (New York: Atherton Press, 1965), p. 79.

39 Schattschneider, *op. cit.*, p. 136.

40 The German economist Friedrich List, quoted in Charles Kindleberger, *Economic Response: Comparative Studies in Trade, Finance, and Growth* (Cambridge, Mass.: Harvard University Press, 1978), p. 53.

41 See Mandelbaum, *op. cit.*, pp. 74–87.

42 See Stephen D. Krasner, "United States Commercial and Monetary Policy: Unravelling the Paradox of External Strength and Internal Weakness," in Peter J. Katzenstein, editor, *Between Power and Plenty: Foreign Economic Policies of Advanced Industrial States* (Madison, Wis.: University of Wisconsin Press, 1978). See also below, pp. 197–8.

43 Kindleberger, *op. cit.*, pp. 57, 60.

44 Bauer, Pool, and Dexter, *op. cit.*, p. 29.

45 Michael Mandelbaum and William Schneider, "The New Internationalisms: Public Opinion and American Foreign Policy," in Kenneth A. Oye et al., editors, *Eagle Entangled: U.S. Foreign Policy in a Complex World* (New York: Longman, 1979), p. 38.

46 Viner, *op. cit.*, p. 441.

47 Quoted in Kindleberger, *op. cit.*, p. 52.

48 Les Aspin, "The Defense Budget and Foreign Policy: The Role of Congress," in Long, editor, *op. cit.*, p. 156.

49 On a per capita basis other countries do as well as, or better than, the United States. Overall, the United States does best simply because, of all the industrialized Western countries, it is by far the largest. What is required to be a great power does not vary with the size of the country. Thus it can be true both that the price of being a great power is relatively low for the United States and that, as Kenneth N. Waltz has noted, the price for countries other than the United States (and the Soviet Union) is increasingly high. Waltz points out that limitations of scale work decisively against the "middle powers." Kenneth N. Waltz, *Theory of International Politics* (Reading, Mass.: Addison-Wesley, 1979), p. 183. If Japan were the size of the United States – that is, twice its present population – and if Japan had accumulated a nuclear arsenal over thirty years (and had been as prosperous for all of those thirty years as it has been for the last fifteen), then Japan could have built a nuclear arsenal of the same size as cheaply as the United States.

50 Joseph A. Pechman et al., *Setting National Priorities: The 1979 Budget* (Washington, D.C.: The Brookings Institution, 1977), pp. 17, 258. The percentage of national income devoted to armaments by the major European powers in 1914 was roughly comparable. For Germany it was 4.6 percent, for France 4.8 percent, for Russia 6.3 percent, and for Britain (which had a formidable navy but a small army) 3.4 percent. A. J. P. Taylor, *The Struggle for Mastery in Europe, 1848 –1918* (Oxford University Press, 1971, paperback), p. xxxix.

51 See Albert Wohlstetter, "Rivals, But No 'Race,'" *Foreign Policy* 16 (Fall 1974):62.

52 See John Reilly, "The American Mood: A Foreign Policy of Self-Interest," *Foreign Policy* 34 (Spring 1979):74–86.

53 Stanley Sienkiewicz, "SALT and Soviet Nuclear Doctrine," *International Security* 2:4 (Spring 1976):96–7.

54 See Seweryn Bialer, *Stalin's Successors: The Politics of Change in the Soviet Union* (Cambridge University Press, 1980), p. 18; and

Jerry F. Hough and Merle Feinsod, *How the Soviet Union Is Govern-ed*, an extensively revised and enlarged edition of Merle Feinsod's *How Russia Is Ruled* (Cambridge, Mass.: Harvard University Press. 1979), pp. 551–2.

55 See Thane Gustafson, *Reform in the Soviet Union* (Cambridge University Press, 1981). On the other hand, in the late 1950s and early 1960s, Nikita Khrushchev seems to have tried to bring about a shift away from military spending. The military resisted, and not only did he fail, he was ousted from power. His dismissal probably had several causes, however. He was unpopular in the upper ranks of the party, where his "harebrained schemes" and especially his attempts at reorganization had made enemies. So his fate does not necessarily show that a concerted attempt to shift from guns to butter in the Soviet Union is bound to fail. See Thomas Wolfe, *Soviet Power in Europe* (Baltimore: Johns Hopkins Press, 1970), Chapter 8.

56 Matthew P. Gallagher and Karl F. Spielman, Jr., *Soviet Deci-sion-Making for Defense: A Critique of U.S. Perspectives on the Arms Race* (New York: Praeger, 1972), p. 78.

57 On this point, see Ermarth, *op. cit.*, p. 139; Garthoff, *op. cit.*, p. 117; and Sienkiewicz, *op. cit.*, p. 95.

58 See Garthoff, *op. cit.*, p. 114.

59 Ibid., p. 115.

60 On the evidence for a Soviet debate over arms deployment, see Lawrence T. Caldwell, *Soviet Attitudes to SALT* (London: Adelphi Paper 75, 1971), and Samuel B. Payne, Jr., "The Soviet Debate on Strategic Arms Limitation, 1969–72," *Soviet Studies* 27:1 (January 1975):27–45.

Chapter 6. NATO: the nuclear alliance

1 Thucydides, *The Peloponnesian War*, translated by Rex Warner (Baltimore: Penguin Books, 1972, paperback), p. 128.

2 See above, pp. 100–2 and 131.

3 Thucydides, *op. cit.*, p. 514.

4 In Thucydides's history the ambassadors from Mytilene de-scribe the Athenian alliance system in terms that recall the relations between the Soviet Union and Eastern Europe. Their account is not disinterested, however, because they are trying to break away from Athens. And the fact that they can contemplate breaking away dis-tinguishes the Athenian from the Soviet system.

5 See Robert E. Osgood, "The Evolution of Force," in Robert E. Osgood and Robert W. Tucker, *Force, Order, and Justice* (Baltimore: Johns Hopkins University Press, 1967), pp. 72−5.

6 Another reason is the rising emphasis on national self-determination and territorial integrity. These principles, of course, have often been honored in the breach. But since the French Revolution, as states have come to be regarded less as the property of the sovereign and more as the home of the nation, it has become less acceptable to pass people back and forth between sovereign jurisdictions as in a casual game of Monopoly. Insofar as the transfer of territory has been its purpose, war has thus become, to some extent, less acceptable and therefore, to an even more limited extent, less feasible.

7 NATO has become a more or less permanent alliance because it has been an unusually successful defensive arrangement. Alignments of two or more nations persisted for decades, moreover, well before the nineteenth century. The Franco−Swedish alliance of the seventeenth century is an example. Previous long-lived alliances, however, unlike NATO to date, were tested by war. See George Liska, *Nations in Alliance* (Baltimore: Johns Hopkins University Press, 1962), p. 133.

8 See above, pp. 59−77.

9 See Osgood, *op. cit.*, p. 86.

10 "A sense of malaise and dysfunction can be found in a row of titles that run from Henry Kissinger's *The Troubled Partnership* through Stanley Hoffmann's *Gulliver's Troubles* to the series of studies edited by David Landes under the title of *Western Europe: The Trials of Partnership*." Stephen J. Barrett, "Retreat from a Shared Vision," in Derek Leebaert, editor, *European Security: Prospects for the 1980's* (Lexington, Mass.: Lexington Books, 1979), p. 27.

11 Kenneth N. Waltz, *Theory of International Politics* (Reading, Mass.: Addison-Wesley, 1979), p. 166.

12 Thucydides, *op. cit.*, p. 59. See also Chapter 1.

13 *Ibid.*, pp. 62−3.

14 *Ibid.*, p. 418.

15 Neither World War I nor the Athenian alliance with Corcyra is an unalloyed example of entrapment. Germany was prepared for war in 1914 and encouraged the Austrian ultimatum to Serbia. Similarly, Athenian policy was based on the belief that "whatever happened, war with the Peloponnese was bound to come." *Ibid.*, p. 62.

16 *Ibid.*, p. 77.

17 "Highly technical matters that used to be the exclusive concern of military officers are now the subject of national and international controversy because they are suffused with political import." Osgood, *op. cit.*, p. 27.

18 A third way to reassure the Europeans was to carry out commitments elsewhere, whatever the cost, as a sign of good faith. The need to maintain a reputation for fulfilling pledges was offered more than once as a reason for fighting in Vietnam, even when the initial commitment had come to seem, in retrospect, unwise. Shortly before he joined the Nixon administration Henry Kissinger wrote, ". . . the commitment of five hundred thousand Americans has settled the issue of the importance of Vietnam. For what is involved now is confidence in American promises. However fashionable it is to ridicule the terms 'credibility' or 'prestige,' they are not empty phrases; other nations can gear their actions to ours only if they can count on our steadiness." "The Vietnam Negotiations," reprinted in Henry Kissinger, *American Foreign Policy,* expanded edition (New York: Norton, 1974), p. 112.

19 The comparison comes from Liska, *op. cit.*, p. 7.

20 In 1954 a Rand Corporation paper raised the question of the reliability of the American guarantee in the face of a Soviet intercontinental striking force. See Morton Halperin, "The U.S. Nuclear Umbrella and Japanese Security," in Franklin B. Weinstein, editor, *U.S. – Japan Relations and the Security of East Asia: The Next Decade* (Boulder, Colo.: Westview Press, 1978), p. 93. John Foster Dulles's speech enunciating the doctrine of deterrence through the threat of massive retaliation sparked a debate about the credibility of NATO's deterrent forces.

21 The Kennedy administration proposed two responses to the growth of the Soviet long-range striking force. The other was a standard of strategic adequacy to which it tried to tailor the American strategic nuclear arsenal. This standard was "assured destruction," the capacity to deliver a crushing blow to the Soviet Union after riding out a massive Soviet assault. It meant being proof against a disarming attack (see above, pp. 117–20). The setting of this standard did not comfort the Europeans, however, because their safety depended on the ability to cope with a different challenge, which assured destruction was not desgined to meet – a Soviet nonnuclear attack on Europe. There seemed little doubt that the United States would respond to a nuclear attack on its homeland in nuclear fashion. So the credibility of a threat to reply to a nuclear assault on the United States in nuclear terms depended simply on the American technical capacity to do so. The standard of assured destruction meant simply the ability to retain such a capacity under any circumstances. To threaten to respond to a nonnuclear assault on some other country, however, would not, it was thought, be credible without at least a clear margin of nuclear superiority, which the standard of assured destruction neither mentioned, nor required, nor encouraged. Assured destruction could protect the United States, against which a Soviet attack would almost certainly be nuclear, but not Western Europe, which would likely receive a nonnuclear blow.

22 See Catherine McArdle Kelleher, *Germany and the Politics of Nuclear Weapons* (New York: Columbia University Press, 1975), p. 284.

23 The Kennedy administration's announcement, in 1962, that it was modifying the American strategic nuclear targeting doctrine also aroused European fears of decoupling. The Secretary of Defense, Robert McNamara, said that in the event of nuclear war the United States would not simply hurl all of its nuclear explosives at the Soviet Union at once, in "spasm" fashion. Instead, there would be an attempt to follow the custom of prenuclear wars and concentrate on the enemy's military forces, to the exclusion (to the extent possible) of the civilian population. The Europeans suspected that this "counterforce" or "no cities" doctrine amounted to a subtle kind of decoupling, because if there were a distinction between civilian and military targets there could be one as well between North American and European ones, which could weaken deterrence in Europe.

24 See Robert Osgood, *NATO: The Entangling Alliance* (Chicago: University of Chicago Press, 1961), pp. 227, 268.

25 *Ibid.*, pp. 131–2.

26 *Ibid.*, pp. 38, 238.

27 Occasionally American officials used blunter language. In a widely noted speech in 1962, Secretary of Defense Robert McNamara termed small, independent nuclear forces "dangerous, expensive, prone to obsolescence and lacking in credibility as a deterrent." Speech delivered at Ann Arbor, Michigan, June 16, 1962, reprinted in *Survival* 4:5 (September–October 1962):195.

28 For an exposition of American fears of the consequences of nuclear proliferation within NATO, see Osgood, *NATO: The Entangling Alliance*, pp. 271–3. For specific reference to entrapment see Raymond Aron, *The Great Debate*, translated from the French by

Ernst Pawel (Garden City, N.Y.: Doubleday, 1965), p. 142.

29 John Steinbruner, *The Cybernetic Theory of Decision: New Dimensions of Political Analysis* (Princeton, N.J.: Princeton University Press, 1974), pp. 189, 226, 258–61.

30 See Robert Metzger and Paul Doty, "Arms Control Enters the Gray Area," *International Security* 3:3 (Winter 1978–79):23.

31 For an account of the development of this controversy, see Fred Kaplan, "Worry Over New Missiles for NATO," *New York Times Magazine* (December 9, 1979): 46, 55–7, 84–90.

32 Louis de Guiringaud, quoted in Doty and Metzger, *op. cit.*, 23–4.

33 See Alain Enthoven and K. Wayne Smith, *How Much Is Enough: Shaping the Defense Program, 1961–1969* (New York: Harper & Row, 1972, first published 1971), Chapter 4. For a more recent estimate of the overall balance of nonnuclear forces in Europe see Henry Stanhope, "New Threats – Or Old Fears?" in Leebaert, editor, *op. cit.*, p. 57.

34 In 1974 the United States went some distance toward recognizing the strategic worth of the British and French nuclear arsenals. A NATO declaration referred to "The European members . . . two of whom possess nuclear forces capable of playing a deterrent role of their own contributing to an overall strengthening of the deterrence of the Alliance." *Department of State Bulletin*, July 8, 1974, p. 43.

35 See Kelleher, *op. cit.*, pp. 279–80.

36 Alastair Buchan, "The Reform of NATO," *Foreign Affairs* 40:2 (January 1962):165–82.

37 See, for example, Enthoven and Smith, *op. cit.*, p. 156.

38 See Anton DePorte, *Europe Between the Superpowers* (New Haven, Conn.: Yale University Press, 1979), p. 195.

39 For an exposition of this argument see Robert W. Tucker, *The Radical Left and American Foreign Policy* (Baltimore: Johns Hopkins University Press, 1971).

40 DePorte, *op. cit.*, p. 193.

41 "How deeply he believed [the arguments in favor of French nuclear weapons] – rather than in the more general idea that renouncing an independent nuclear force meant resignation to permanent, barely influenceable dependence on other nations, and submission to small-power status in a world where the negative productivity of nuclear power was enormous – is unclear. . . . It is likely that he deemed America's guarantee still probably sufficient to deter the Russians despite his well-publicized doubts. . . . But it does not follow that he was insincere in wondering whether, if the improbable occurred, and the Russians ran risks they had so far avoided, the guarantee that had failed to deter would also be carried out." Stanley Hoffmann, "De Gaulle's Foreign Policy: The Stage and the Play, the Power and the Glory," in Hoffmann, *Decline or Renewal? France Since the 1930s* (New York: Viking Press, 1974), p. 299.

42 Aron, *op. cit.*, pp. 211–12.

43 DePorte, *op. cit.*, p. 192.

44 The phrase is Robert E. Osgood's.

45 Michael Howard, "The Relevance of Traditional Strategy," *Foreign Affairs* 51:2 (January 1973): 262.

Chapter 7. The nuclear presidency

1 Thucydides, *The Peloponnesian War*, translated by Rex Warner (Baltimore: Penguin Books, 1972, paperback), p. 49.

2 *Ibid.*, pp. 133, 138, 163.

3 *Ibid.*, p. 164.

4 Joel Larus, *Nuclear Weapons, Safety and the Common Defense* (Columbus, Ohio: Ohio State University Press, 1967), pp. 84–6. This is almost certainly an authenticating, not an enabling, code. The weapons could be fired without a presidential order, although not by a single person. In official public discussions of the nuclear chain of command, which are rare, the President is said to have the power to "release" the weapons. The term implies a physical act, but it is also often used in a legal sense, as in signing a release. Making it possible for the President, and the President alone, to arm every one of the thousands of American nuclear weapons would require a formidable feat of engineering. Such an arrangement, moreover, would have a strategic drawback. A Soviet attack that destroyed the President and his entourage and a single fusion warhead could lay waste to the nation's capital might paralyze the American nuclear force, permitting the Soviet Union to win a nuclear war with the United States by "decapitation." See "First Use of Nuclear Weapons: Preserving Responsible Control," *Hearings before the Subcommittee on International Security and Scientific Affairs of the Committee on International Relations, House of Representatives, 94th Congress, 2nd Session, March 16, 18, 23, and 25, 1976*. (Washington, D.C.: U.S. Government Printing Office, 1976). On unauthorized nuclear use see especially pp. 76 and 94. On the purpose of the code, see George H.

Quester, "Presidential Authority and Nuclear Weapons," in *ibid.*, p. 214.

5 Harry S Truman, *Memoirs: Volume Two: Years of Trial and Hope* (Garden City, N.Y.: Doubleday, 1956) and Sydnor Walker, editor, *The First One Hundred Days of the Atomic Age, August 6– November 15, 1945* (New York: The Woodrow Wilson Foundation, 1946), p. 6.

6 "First Use of Nuclear Weapons: Preserving Responsible Control," p. 178.

7 "Authority to Order the Use of Nuclear Weapons. (United States, United Kingdom, France, Soviet Union, People's Republic of China)," prepared for the Subcommittee on International Relations by the Congressional Research Service, Library of Congress (Washington, D.C.: U.S. Government Printing Office, December 1, 1975), p. 2.

8 Hearings on the subject in 1976 revealed one minor exception to this rule. The North American Air Defense Commander was authorized to release nuclear weapons that were "low in yield, purely defensive in nature, and would be used over friendly territory or open seas . . . in response to a threat of 'first use' by the opposition and under actual war conditions." Revocation of this authority was apparently underway at the time of the hearings, however. "First Use of Nuclear Weapons: Preserving Responsible Control," p. 49.

9 *Ibid.*, p. 50.

10 See Theodore Ropp, *War in the Modern World* (Durham, N.C.: Duke University Press, 1959), Part I, especially p. 20.

11 "[The General staff] seems to be the only way by which large armies can be handled in the field, even with methods of communication which were not available in the mid-nineteenth century." *Ibid.*, p. 139.

12 "First use deserves more than one decision-maker. A proposal of the Federation of American Scientists to restrict presidential power to initiate nuclear war," *The Bulletin of the Atomic Scientists* 32:3 (March 1976): 54.

13 *Ibid.*

14 See Quester, *op. cit.*, p. 218.

15 "First use deserves more than one decision-maker," 54.

16 Jonathan Schell, *The Time of Illusion* (New York: Knopf, 1976), p. 386.

17 "A sense of security is somewhat like religious faith in its belief that there is a higher being with the power, knowledge, and pres-

ence to protect people in a threatening world constantly in turmoil. Similarly, the essence of the faith from which a sense of security derives is that there is a supreme being at the apex of the political system who is the fountainhead of that faith. Nuclear power therefore has created the need for a god. This notion should not be surprising. Most civilized societies have gone through periods when kings and emperors assumed some kind of divine form." Franz Schurmann, *The Logic of World Power: An Inquiry into the Origins, Currents, and Contradictions of World Politics* (New York: Pantheon Books, 1974), p. 12.

18 James Bryce, *The American Commonwealth* (London: Macmillan, 1891), pp. 36–7.

19 "By the early 1970s the American President had become on issues of war and peace the most absolute monarch (with the possible exception of Mao Tse-tung) among the great powers of the world." Arthur M. Schlesinger, Jr., *The Imperial Presidency* (Boston: Houghton Mifflin, 1974), p. 11.

20 Schell, *op. cit.*, p. 381. Schell's argument about the connection between the nuclear and the imperial presidency is ingenious if not altogether convincing. The policy of deterrence, he says, depends for its effectiveness upon the credibility of American resolve to act firmly and decisively, and this came after 1945 to mean the credibility of the President. So global peace has hinged on how other countries have perceived him, and he – that is, the men who have successfully held the office – has asserted wider and wider powers to ensure a perception of strength. A similarly elaborate and provocative, if not wholly persuasive, argument is to be found in *The Logic of World Power*. The author, Franz Schurmann, distinguishes between "ideology" and "interests." The first is an articulated vision; the second are narrower and more specialized. The American President in the postwar period, he argues, has been the champion of an ideological foreign policy; business and the Congress have supported foreign policies that advance particular interests. An important source of the President's intramural strength in promoting ideological policies, according to Schurmann, has been his nuclear authority: "Whenever America's nuclear power expanded in absolute and relative terms, so did the power of the chief executive within the bureaucracies of the government" (p. 160).

21 Bagehot differentiated between a "distinguished" or ceremonial purpose, which Parliament as a whole continued to serve, and an "efficient" or effective role, which in his day belonged to the cabinet and which in ours, according to Richard Crossman, has passed to the Prime Minister. See R. H. S. Crossman, "Introduction" to Walter Bagehot, *The English Constitution* (Ithaca, N.Y.: Cornell University Press, 1966), pp. 49ff.

22 In both France and the Federal Republic of Germany, the executive has assumed considerable power in the postwar period. France does not have a formidable nuclear arsenal; Germany, of course, has none at all. Neither country, however, has a long and clearly defined tradition of restrictions on executive authority, as do the United States and the United Kingdom.

23 See above, p. 99.

24 Aaron Wildavsky, "The Two Presidencies," in Aaron Wildavsky, editor, *The Presidency* (Boston: Little, Brown, 1969).

25 Quoted in *The New Yorker*, April 2, 1976, p. 30.

26 Justice Burton dissenting in *Duncan v. Kahanamoku*. Quoted in Ernest R. May, "The President Shall be Commander in Chief," in Ernest R. May, editor, *The Ultimate Decision* (New York: George Braziller, 1960), p. 5.

27 Thucydides, *op. cit.*, pp. 163, 164.

28 *The Discourses*, Book I, Chapter 24. Cited in Schlesinger, *op. cit.*, p. 306.

29 May, *op. cit.*, pp. 12–18.

30 Ernest R. May, "Eisenhower and After," in May, editor, *op. cit.*, p. 215.

31 Dean Acheson, *Present at the Creation* (New York: Norton, 1971), p. 413. Glenn D. Paige, *The Korean Decision* (New York: Free Press, 1968), pp. 189–90, 195–200, 216–21, 262–8.

32 See John E. Mueller, *War, Presidents, and Public Opinion* (New York: Wiley, 1973), pp. 65, 155.

33 See, for example, Morton H. Halperin, *Bureaucratic Politics and Foreign Policy* (Washington, D.C.: The Brookings Institution, 1974), especially Chapter 16.

34 See Michael Mandelbaum, *The Nuclear Question: The United States and Nuclear Weapons, 1946–1976* (Cambridge University Press, 1979), pp. 23–33.

35 Joseph I. Lieberman, *The Scorpion and the Tarantula. The Struggle to Control Atomic Weapons* (Boston: Houghton Mifflin, 1970), p. 136.

36 *Ibid.*, pp. 151, 153, 219.

37 *Ibid.*, p. 287.

38 His background may in fact have contributed to what became his passion for peace. He, after all, had seen war at first hand. He had another reason for wanting to restrain the arms race, which neither his predecessor nor his successor shared. He believed that the level of public spending to which the nuclear competition with the Soviet Union was driving the United States would ruin the American economy.

39 David Capitanchik, *The Eisenhower Presidency and American Foreign Policy* (London: Routledge and Kegan Paul, 1969), p. 56.

40 See Emmett John Hughes, *The Ordeal of Power* (New York: Atheneum, 1963), pp. 104ff.

41 See Arthur Larson, *Eisenhower: The President Nobody Knew* (New York: Scribner's, 1968), Chapter 2.

42 Hughes, *op. cit.*, p. 103.

43 John Newhouse, *Cold Dawn* (New York: Holt, Rinehart and Winston, 1973), p. 133.

44 Richard Neustadt, "The President at Mid-Century," in Wildavsky, *op. cit.*, p. 196.

45 Eugene McCarthy in 1968 and George McGovern in 1972 were also unsuccessful "peace" candidates. But they put greater emphasis upon ending the war in Vietnam than on curbing the competition in nuclear armaments with the Soviet Union.

46 The Limited Test Ban Treaty of 1963 was an exception to this rule. Every country was prey to the radioactivity that nuclear tests spewed into the atmosphere, and almost every one registered a protest against these tests. Nehru of India, who remained deliberately neutral between the two great global competitors, became the leading critic of atmospheric testing. His views carried weight with the United States, which was courting his favor. The leader of America's closest ally, British Prime Minister Harold Macmillan, was also eager to have a test ban. He helped keep the issue alive when the negotiations between the United States and the Soviet Union stalled by prodding President Kennedy to continue them, and he dispatched his own special emissary to Moscow to accompany Kennedy's representative, Averell Harriman, on the successful mission to fix the terms of the treaty in July 1963.

47 Lieberman, *op. cit.*, Chapter 2; Robert Gilpin, *American Scientists and Nuclear Weapons Policy* (Princeton, N.J: Princeton University Press, 1962), Chapter 2.

48 Arthur M. Schlesinger, Jr., *A Thousand Days: John F. Kennedy in the White House* (Boston: Houghton Mifflin, 1965), Chapter 27.

49 See below, pp. 129–30.

50 Kissinger press conference in Moscow, July 3, 1974, in *The Department of State Bulletin*, July 29, 1974, p. 210.
51 In fact, almost every President has designated a special representative for nuclear negotiations. Harry Truman chose Bernard Baruch to present the first American disarmament plan because he hoped that Baruch's enormous prestige would mute congressional objections to putting the bomb under international control. Eisenhower named Harold Stassen his Special Assistant for Disarmament. Stassen was supposed to report directly to the President and to "cooperate closely with the State Department." (Dwight D. Eisenhower, *Waging Peace, 1956–61* (New York: Doubleday, 1965), p. 469. But the State Department did not help him. The task of contending with both the Soviets and Dulles proved too much for Stassen, who finally resigned. Kennedy appointed Arthur Dean and John McCloy, Wall Street lawyers with experience in government, records as reliable opponents of communism, and ties to the Republican party, as his personal disarmament representatives. He plucked Averell Harriman, a distinguished diplomat and former Ambassador to the Soviet Union, out of the State Department to lead the American test ban delegation. Richard Nixon and Gerald Ford relied upon Henry Kissinger's personal discussions with Soviet leaders to move the Strategic Arms Limitation Talks toward agreement. During the first stage of SALT, while the official negotiating parties met in Helsinki and Vienna, Kissinger opened a "back channel" of communication with the Soviet Ambassador in Washington, Anatoly Dobrynin. After 1972 he flew directly to Moscow several times to confer with the members of the Soviet Politburo about nuclear matters.

Lyndon Johnson was the exception that proves the rule. When the issue of restrictions on strategic armaments first arose, he insisted that a consensus position be hammered out at the lower levels of the federal government before proceeding to talks with the Soviets. But the government was so divided – the armed forces were so chary of any negotiations – that no consensus could be reached (Newhouse, *op. cit.*, p. 108). Only Johnson's personal intervention galvanized the American government to the task of working out an approach to the talks. And only presidential power within the American political system has sustained the commitment to arms control that the United States has kept since the dawn of the nuclear age.
52 Hughes, *op. cit.*, p. 84.
53 Eisenhower, *op. cit.*, p. 432.

54 Bob Woodward and Carl Bernstein, *The Final Days* (New York: Simon & Schuster, 1976), pp. 422–3.

55 Ironically, the program may have had the opposite effect by spreading atomic reactors whose fuel and byproducts can be used to make bombs throughout the world.

56 Dwight D. Eisenhower, *Mandate for Change* (Garden City, N.Y.: Doubleday, 1963), p. 254.

57 Lyndon B. Johnson, *The Vantage Point: Perspectives of the Presidency, 1963–1969* (New York: Holt, Rinehart & Winston, 1971), p. 467.

58 See Henry Kissinger, *White House Years* (Boston: Little, Brown, 1979), pp. 1204–5.

59 Neustadt, "Testimony," in Wildavsky, *op. cit.*, p. 515.

60 *The Department of State Bulletin*, November 19, 1973, p. 640.

61 Quoted in Joseph A. Pechman, editor, *Setting National Priorities: The 1979 Budget* (Washington, D.C.: The Brookings Institution, 1978), p. 262.

62 Lieberman, *op. cit.*, p. 120; Truman, *op. cit.*, p. 2.

63 Hughes, *op. cit.*, pp. 203, 105–6.

64 Eisenhower, *Waging Peace*, p. 467.

65 John F. Kennedy, *The Public Papers of the President, 1963* (Washington, D.C.: U.S. Government Printing Office, 1964), p. 612.

66 Johnson, *op. cit.*, p. 566. Jimmy Carter, defending the SALT II treaty with the Soviet Union "seemed emotional about the pact" to a *New York Times* reporter when he said: "I have only one life to live on this earth, as you have. I think the most important single achievement that could possibly take place for our nation during our lifetime is the ratification of the SALT treaty that we have just negotiated with the Soviet Union." Bernard Gwertzman, "Carter Meeting with Brezhnev Set for June 15," *The New York Times*, May 11, 1979, p. 1.

67 Cited in Merle Miller, *Plain Speaking: An Oral Biography of Harry S Truman* (New York: Putnam, 1973), pp. 230–1.

Chapter 8. The bomb, dread, and eternity

1 Thucydides, *The Peloponnesian War*, translated by Rex Warner (Baltimore: Penguin Books, 1972, paperback), p. 148.

2 On the various reasons why men do fight see John Keegan, *The Face of Battle. A Study of Agincourt, Waterloo, and the Somme* (New York: Vintage Press, paperback, 1977).

3 See Robert J. Lifton, *The Broken Connection* (New York: Simon & Schuster, 1979), pp. 5–6, 13.

4 Theodore Lidz, *The Person: His Development Throughout the Life Cycle* (New York: Basic Books, 1968), pp. 500–1.

5 War touched noncombatants long before the twentieth century, however. Thucydides records that the Athenians decided to bring all citizens into the city at the beginning of the war, and that those living outside its boundaries "were far from pleased at having to move with their entire households. . . . It was sadly and reluctantly that they now abandoned their homes and the temples time-honoured from their patriotic past, that they prepared to change their whole way of life, leaving behind them what each man regarded as his own city." Thucydides, *op. cit.*, p. 135.

6 Sigmund Freud, "Reflections on War and Death," in Sigmund Freud, *Character and Culture* (New York: Collier Books, paperback, 1963), p. 124. Freud argued that "civilization" covers man's basic, primitive feelings about death with layers of defense, which war strips away. The source of distress in 1915 was not so much the scale of the killing, in Freud's view, as the thickness of the accumulated cultural defenses that had fallen away. "How far we have moved from this primitive state in our conventionally civilized attitude toward death! . . . [War] strips us of the later accretions of civilization, and lays bare the primal man in each of us." *Ibid.*, p. 132.

7 Paul Fussell, *The Great War and Modern Memory* (New York: Oxford University Press, 1975), p. 35. Of course, prophets and agents of cultural dissolution – Nietzsche, Freud, and Einstein – were present before 1918. But the war brought to the surface cultural currents and speeded trends that had existed previously.

8 See Michael Walzer, *Just and Unjust Wars: A Moral Argument with Historical Illustrations* (New York: Basic Books, 1977), Chapter 17.

9 See Michael Mandelbaum, *The Nuclear Question: The United States and Nuclear Weapons, 1946–1976* (Cambridge University Press, 1979), pp. 124–8.

10 Robert J. Lifton, *Death in Life: The Survivors of Hiroshima* (New York: Random House, 1967), p. 278.

11 Christopher Lasch, *The Culture of Narcissism: American Life in an Age of Diminished Expectations* (New York: Norton, 1978), p. 4.

12 Lifton, *The Broken Connection*, p. 338.

13 Quoted in Rexford G. Tugwell, *A Chronicle of Jeopardy, 1945 – 1955* (Chicago: University of Chicago Press, 1955), p. 1. On the other hand there is the view that "the threat of destruction, though constant, is invisible and unnoticed." Walzer, op. cit., p. 271.

14 Freud believed this. See Frank E. Manuel, "The Use and Abuse of Psychology in History," Daedalus 100:1 (Winter 1971): 198.

15 Robert J. Lifton, "End of the World Imagery Linked with Actual Holocaust Experiences," Seminar, Center for International Studies, Massachusetts Institute of Technology, April 17, 1978.

16 See V. Tausk, "On the Origins of the 'Influencing Machine' in Schizophrenia," translated by Dorian Feigenbaum; Psychoanalytical Quarterly 2 (1933): 519–56.

17 The idea is drawn from Robert Liebert, Radical and Militant Youth: A Psychoanalytic Inquiry (New York: Praeger, 1971), Chapter 11, especially pp. 239ff; Kenneth Keniston, Young Radicals: Notes on Committed Youth (New York: Harcourt Brace and World, 1968), Chapter 7; discussion and correspondence with David Riesman; and discussions with psychiatrists and members of this generation. All this amounts to evidence for the existence of a "nuclear generation" that is suggestive but hardly conclusive.

18 Lidz, op. cit., pp. 195–8, 497.

19 Liebert, op. cit., p. 239.

20 Wallace Turner, "Amateur Expert on Weapons: Charles R. Hansen," New York Times, September 18, 1979, p. C7.

21 See Lifton, The Broken Connection, pp. 363–5. Lifton has explored at length the psychological impact of nuclear weapons. In The Broken Connection he suggests that their influence has been enormous. They have, he says, produced psychic "dislocation," which in turn has led to "totalism" (p. 297) and "victimization" (p. 302). The first refers to totalitarian political systems, the second to the kind of persecution of ascriptively defined groups that reached its apogee in Nazi Germany. The antecedents of both go back to the beginning of recorded history. Each, it is true, reached its zenith in the twentieth century, but before Hiroshima. Since 1945 the worst cases of victimization have, on the whole, taken place in parts of the world little influenced by nuclear weapons.

22 George Wald, A Generation in Search of a Future. A Speech Delivered as Part of the "March 4th Movement" at the Massachusetts Institute of Technology (Stoughton, Mass.: Press of the Nightowl, 1969), p. 16. The full quotation is: "Anybody can do the simple calculation that shows that two percent [chance of nuclear war] per year means that the chance of having that full-scale nuclear war by 1990 is about one in three, and by 2000 it is about fifty-fifty. I think I know what is bothering the students. I think we are up against a generation that is by no means sure that it has a future."

23 Quotation from a student paper written in the 1960s, in Liebert, op. cit., p. 235. See also Lifton, The Broken Connection, pp. 365–6.

24 From a student paper on the effect on personal development of having been born in the nuclear era, quoted in Liebert, op. cit., p. 237.

25 Ibid. "A belief that one would never live to be a grown-up discouraged any patience for the acceptance of the need to grow up. Indeed, like Peter Pan ... the bomb allowed the transformation of the present into a never-never land in which no gratification need be postponed and one could celebrate here what Tom Wolfe aptly called the 'happiness explosion' instead of the unhappy one we once feared." Ron Rosenbaum, "The Subterranean World of the Bomb," Harper's, March 1978, p. 90. See also Lifton, The Broken Connection, p. 342.

26 The last two attitudes go back to ancient Greece, from which the terms themselves come.

27 See Norman Cohn, The Pursuit of the Millennium: Revolutionary Millenarians and Mystical Anarchists of the Middle Ages (London: Paladin, 1970).

28 Barbara W. Tuchman, A Distant Mirror: The Calamitous Fourteenth Century (New York: Knopf, 1978), p. 97. See also Francis Aidan Gasquet, The Black Death of 1348 and 1349 (London: George Bell, 1908), p. 251. The aftermath of the plague has also been compared to the social effects of the mechanical revolution in warf re during World War I. "The Black Death wrought a universal upheaval and transformation of society to which nothing else in history is comparable except the influence of the Great War." James Westfall Thompson, "The Aftermath of the Black Death and the Aftermath of the Great War," The American Journal of Sociology 26:5 (March 1921): 570.

29 William L. Langer, "The Next Assignment," in Bruce Mazlish, editor, Psychoanalysis and History (Englewood Cliffs, N.J.: Prentice-Hall, 1963), p. 97.

30 Ibid., p. 101. See also Gasquet, op. cit., pp. 25, 29.

31 Thucydides, op. cit., p. 155.

32 "To summarize a complex thesis in a few words: the issue of violence is to this generation what the issue of sex was to the Victorian world. ... Inner and outer violence is replacing sex as a prime object of fear, terror, projections, displacement, repression, suppression, acting out, and efforts at control." Keniston, op. cit., pp. 248, 252. For a critique of Keniston and other theories of student behavior in the 1960s, see Stanley Rothman and S. Robert Lichter, "The Case of the Student Left," Social Research 45:3 (Autumn 1978):535–609.

33 This is, in part, the thesis of Lewis Feuer's study of student movements throughout history, The Conflict of Generations. (New York: Basic Books, 1969). See especially pp. 529ff. His general argument can be made compatible with the thesis that the bomb and its implications lay at the root of the campus turmoil in the 1960s if it is assumed that the grievance of the young against the old, the reason for what Feuer calls the "deauthoritarianization of the older generation," (p. 528) was the failure to rid the world of the mortal danger that nuclear weapons pose. See also Erik H. Erikson, Identity: Youth and Crisis (New York: Norton, 1968), p. 243.

34 Gerald Grant and David Riesman, The Perpetual Dream (Chicago: University of Chicago Press, 1978), pp. 191–2; Daniel Patrick Moynihan, "Peace – Some Thoughts on the 1960s and 1970s," The Public Interest 32 (Summer 1973): 3–12.

35 Bruno Bettelheim, "Obsolete Youth," in Bruno Bettelheim, Surviving and Other Essays (New York: Knopf, 1978).

36 R. G. Braungart, "Youth and Social Movements," in Sigmund E. Dragastin and Glen H. Elder, Jr., editors, Adolescence in the Life Cycle: Psychological Change and Social Context (Washington, D.C.: Hemisphere Publishing, 1978), p. 268.

37 During the psychologically formative years of the nuclear generation, the bomb was novel but not as directly menacing to Americans as Sputnik made it seem.

38 Rosenbaum, op. cit., p. 87.

39 Liebert, op. cit., p. 222.

40 Still, Freud was well aware that his ideas might prove useful tools of social explanation as well as medical treatment. He tried his own hand at applying them to society as a whole, especially in his books Totem and Taboo and Moses and Monotheism.

41 Quoted in Richard Wollheim, Sigmund Freud (New York: Viking, 1971), p. 244.

42 See Michael Lesey, "Mixed Images," New York Times Book Review, June 25, 1978, p. 46.

43 These are described in Cohn, op. cit.

44 Paul D. Hanson, The Dawn of Apocalyptic (Philadelphia: Fortress Press, 1975), p. 2.

45 The Interpreter's Dictionary of the Bible, supplementary volume (Nashville, Tenn.: Abingdon, 1976), p. 30.

46 *Ibid.*, pp. 30–1.

47 Gershom Scholem, *Sabbatai Sevi: The Mystical Messiah, 1626–1676* (Princeton, N.J.: Princeton University Press, 1973). Scholem objects to a simplistic class analysis of the Sabbataian movement (p. 4). In fact, it appears to have been both a class and a "national" phenomenon.

48 Hanson, *op. cit.*, p. 26.

49 See Albert Schweitzer, *The Kingdom of God and Primitive Christianity* (New York: Seabury Press, 1968); and Michael Grant, *Jesus: An Historian's Interpretation of the Gospels* (New York: Scribner's, 1977).

50 This was, of course, the indictment made by the Reformation, which touched off several millenarian outbursts.

51 Frank Manuel and Fritzie Manuel, "Sketch for a Natural History of Paradise," *Myth, Symbol, and Culture*, 101:1 (Winter 1972): 83–128. See also Cohn, *op. cit.*, p. 29, and Ernest Lee Tuveson, *Millennium and Utopia: A Study in the Background of the Ideas of Progress* (New York: Harper Torchbooks, 1964, paperback, first published 1949), pp. 16–17.

52 See, for example, a pamphlet entitled "Are We Living in the Last Days?" issued by the Worldwide Church of God, an organization with headquarters in Pasadena, California, which suggests that the crises of the present day correspond to the biblical signs of the imminence of the end.

53 Billy Graham, *World Aflame* (Garden City, N.Y.: Doubleday, 1965), pp. 246–7. His association with the corporate and political leaders of the United States means that Graham cannot be placed on the fringes of American society. There is something of a contradiction between his theology and his social location. See Marshall Frady, *Billy Graham: A Parable of American Righteousness* (New York: Simon & Schuster, 1979).

54 Diane Johnson, "Heart of Darkness," *New York Times Book Review*, April 9, 1979, p. 5.

55 See Cohn, *op. cit.*, pp. 272–329, and William Pfaff, "Reflections on Jonestown," *The New Yorker*, December 18, 1978, pp. 57–63.

56 Doris Lessing, *The Memoirs of a Survivor* (London: Picador, 1974), p. 190.

57 New York, Knopf, 1979. This is the first of a planned multivolume work.

58 I. F. Clarke, *Voices Prophesying War, 1763–1984* (New York: Oxford University Press, 1966), p. 3.

59 *Ibid.*, p. 204; see also pp. 201–3.

60 Barry Commoner, *The Closing Circle: Nature, Man and Technology* (New York: Knopf, 1971), pp. 12, 217–95.
61 See Lifton, *The Broken Connection*, pp. 335–6. The return to a simpler, more rural way of life that some Americans have undertaken may be seen in part as a strategy for surviving a nuclear war.
62 Commoner, *op. cit.*, p. 294.
63 "The whole drama must be seen as it unfolds, and each succeeding event makes the action clearer, exactly as each act in a play." Tuveson, *op. cit.*, p. 4.
64 For a notable example see D. H. Meadows et al., *The Limits to Growth* (New York: Universal Press, 1972).
65 Cohn, *op. cit.*, pp. 20–1; Harold A. T. Reiche, "The Archaic Heritage: Some Myths of Decline and End in Antiquity," Seminar, Center for International Studies, Massachusetts Institute of Technology, March 20, 1978, p. 5.
66 Theodore Roszak, *Person/Planet: The Creative Disintegration of Industrial Society* (Garden City, N.Y.: Anchor Press, 1977), p. xix. Roszak suggests that the resolution of the ecological crisis will produce change in people's personalities as well. "There is a planetary dimension to the spreading personalist sensibility which links the search for an authentic identity to the well-being of the global environment." p. xxx.
67 Commoner, *op. cit.*, p. 295.
68 See Clarke, *op. cit.*, pp. 176, 183, 199.
69 Lawrence L. Langer, *The Age of Atrocity: Death in Modern Literature* (Boston: Beacon Press, 1978), p. 61.
70 Mircea Eliade, *Cosmos and History: The Myth of the Eternal Return* (New York: Harper Torchbooks, 1959), and Hanson, *op. cit.*, p. 407.
71 Eliade, *op. cit.*, pp. 87ff.
72 Tuveson, *op. cit.*, p. 56.
73 *Ibid.*, pp. xi, 75. Eliade, *op. cit.*, p. 145.
74 Eliade, *op. cit.*, pp. 153–4.

Index

277